Missouri's Black Heritage

REVISED EDITION

Missouri's Black Heritage

Lorenzo J. Greene, Gary R. Kremer, Antonio F. Holland

Revised and updated by
Gary R. Kremer and Antonio F. Holland

University of Missouri Press
Columbia and London

First edition copyright © 1980 by Forum Press
Revised edition copyright © 1993 by
The Curators of the University of Missouri
University of Missouri Press, Columbia, Missouri 65201
Printed and bound in the United States of America
All rights reserved
5   4   3   2   1   97   96   95   94   93

Library of Congress Cataloging-in-Publication Data

Greene, Lorenzo Johnston, 1899–
    Missouri's Black heritage, revised edition / Lorenzo J. Greene,
Gary R. Kremer, Antonio F. Holland. — Rev. and updated by Gary R.
Kremer and Antonio F. Holland.
        p.   cm.
    Includes bibliographical references and index.
    ISBN 0–8262–0904–1 (cloth). — ISBN 0–8262–0905–X (paper)
    1. Afro-Americans—Missouri—History.   2. Missouri—Race
relations.   I. Kremer, Gary R.   II. Holland, Antonio Frederick,
1943–   .   III. Title.
E185.93.M7G73   1993   93–20175
977.8′ 00496073—dc20   CIP

∞™ This paper meets the requirements of the American National
Standard for Permanence of Paper for Printed Library Materials, Z39.48, 1984.

Designer: Rhonda Miller
Typesetter: Connell-Zeko Type & Graphics
Printer and Binder: Thomson-Shore, Inc.
Typeface: Galliard

This revised edition
is dedicated to the memory of
Lorenzo J. Greene
Mentor, Colleague, Friend

Contents

Preface to the Revised Edition

More than a decade has passed since *Missouri's Black Heritage* first appeared in print. Surprisingly, it remains the only book available that seeks to describe and explain, albeit in summary fashion, the African-American experience in the Show-Me State. We have been continually surprised at the wide audience this book has reached; letters and phone calls of inquiry and exploration come to us now just as frequently as they did when the book was first published in 1980.

Much has changed in Missouri and the nation over the past decade. Politically, economically, and socially, individual black Missourians have achieved greater success than in any other decade of our state's history. But for the black masses, especially in the inner cities, much has not changed at all; or, if there has been change, it has been for the worse. All indicators suggest that the economic gap between blacks and whites is wider now than a decade ago. Premature death from drugs, disease, and murder is now more of a problem in the black community than ever before.

Nor has there been a noticeable shift in racial attitudes in the past decade, unless the shift has been toward greater intolerance and hostility. Hate groups, particularly the Ku Klux Klan, have enjoyed renewed vitality in the eighties, and there is every reason to believe that their numbers are growing.

Work on this revised edition had begun almost before the first edition went to press. We knew from the beginning that this is a book that would require periodic updating, both to bring the reader up-to-date chronologically and to reflect the latest scholarship. As a consequence, each of the original eleven chapters has been changed and added to. There is a new final chapter as well, which concentrates on the eighties. Even the personal reminiscence offered by Lorenzo J. Greene has been restored; it now includes original material deleted in the first edition because of space limitations.

In spite of the changes, our purpose remains the same: we hope that this book will promote pride and a greater understanding among African-

Americans of Missouri about their past and an appreciation among whites
of their contributions and struggles. No one advocated and worked toward those goals with more vigor or greater intellect than our mentor and
friend, Lorenzo J. Greene. Sadly, Professor Greene passed away on January 21, 1988. It is to his memory that this book is lovingly dedicated.

Acknowledgments

In preparing this revision we have incurred many debts. First and fore-
most, we are indebted to the many scholars whose writings have enriched
the literature on the African-American experience in Missouri over the
past decade. We have found particularly helpful the work of Carl Ekberg,
William E. Foley, Lawrence O. Christensen, and George Lipsitz. We are
also indebted to Patrick J. Huber, whose research assistance and critical
eye both expedited the book's completion and improved its content considerably. Gerald Early and Lawrence O. Christensen read the entire manuscript and enriched it substantially by pointing out omissions and errors.
Sharon Kremer typed and retyped what must have seemed like endless
changes coming from different people who were at times unable to make
up their minds. Librarians and archivists throughout the state have been
as helpful to us with the revisions as they were with the first edition. Two
persons in particular deserve mention: Harriet Robinson of the Inman E.
Page Library at Lincoln University has been tireless in her effort to help
us find material; and Billie Smith, documents librarian at the Missouri
State Archives, was always digging up government publications that more
often than not proved useful. James M. Denny, Anna Price, and Lynn
Morrow also provided material from their own research. A Faculty Development Grant from William Woods College aided in the completion
of this project.

The following persons were especially helpful in our search for photo-
graphs: Ann Morriss of the Western Historical Manuscript Collection at
the University of Missouri–St. Louis; David Boutros of the Western Historical Manuscript Collection at the University of Missouri–Kansas City;
Duane Schnedeger of the Missouri Historical Society; Katherine Lederer
of Southwest Missouri State University; Mark Herndon of the Missouri
State Archives; Janet Bruce Campbell of the Johnson County Museum

(Kansas); Lynn Morrow of the Local Records Program of the Missouri State Archives; and Mrs. Leona Rice of Jefferson City, Missouri.

Finally, Beverly Jarrett of the University of Missouri Press deserves much of the credit for this revised edition. She had the foresight to challenge us to begin it and the patience and forbearance to see it through to completion. Likewise, our editor at the press, Polly Law, has been most helpful. We only hope that our effort to tell the story of the men and women whose names grace these pages lives up to, at least in some measure, the shining examples with which they have provided us.

Preface to the First Edition

Missouri's Black Heritage represents our effort to provide an account of a neglected aspect of the state's past. Missouri, like the nation as a whole, is the product of the efforts of diverse races, nationalities, and creeds. People from all backgrounds have mixed their heritage, blood, brawn, and brains to create a home for themselves and their children. Students living in a multiracial society in which the largest single minority group is Afro-American should understand the obstacles against which blacks have had to fight. They should also understand that despite these obstacles, many black people have achieved success.

For generations, an ignorance of the value and contributions of black Americans bred fear and hatred. Children were taught that blacks deserved second-class citizenship. Such a position for blacks was sanctioned by law at the highest levels of American society. Black and white children alike were led to believe that black people had made little or no contribution to American civilization and that the treatment they had received from white society was justified by alleged black inferiority and depravity. The net result was that white children grew up with an unjustified sense of superiority, while black children nursed a feeling of inferiority. The barbarities of the slave ships were said to be justified because at least the trip to the New World removed the African from the so-called savage influences of the "Dark Continent." Likewise, it was argued that while slavery was a harsh institution, it was justified because it exposed the "heathen" to the possibilities of salvation in the heavenly kingdom of the Christian God, provided that the slave was content and happy in his bondage.

Perhaps one of the most remarkable things about the black experience in America is that black people have survived despite the treatment they have received. Indeed, they have more than survived—they have played a vital role in structuring the American present. It is crucial, therefore, to understand their past.

Acknowledgments

In writing this book, we accept the responsibility for the selection and interpretation of facts as well as any errors that may exist. We are indebted to our students and colleagues at Lincoln University for their interest and assistance. We are particularly grateful to the Ethnic Studies Center for its financial support and to Darryl C. Cook for his research assistance. We wish also to acknowledge the helpful suggestions from the following individuals who reviewed portions of the manuscript prior to publication: George A. Rawick, University of Missouri–St. Louis; William E. Foley, Central Missouri State University; Warren E. Solomon, State Department of Education; Edward Beasley, Penn Valley Community College; J. Christopher Schnell, Southeast Missouri State University; Enid Muskkin of the Black Motivational Center of Kansas City; Barbara Woods, Director of Black Studies, St. Louis University; Dominic Capeci, Southwest Missouri State University; Nancy Fields, Harris-Stowe State College; Carolyn Dorsey, director of Black Studies, University of Missouri–Columbia; Julia Davis, retired St. Louis teacher; Russell Sackreiter, a social studies teacher in the Columbia Public Schools; Ellen Martin, Jefferson City Senior High School, who shared some of our material with her Missouri history classes; and Lorenzo Thomas Greene.

Additionally, Frederick A. Youngs, Jr., of Louisiana State University and Donald Ewalt, Jr., of Lincoln University read the manuscript in its entirety and made many useful comments. The staffs of the following libraries have also been quite helpful: the State Historical Society of Missouri (Columbia), the Missouri Historical Society (St. Louis), and the Inman E. Page Library of Lincoln University. The *St. Louis American* graciously opened its valuable photo files to us, as did the *Kansas City Star*, the *St. Louis Post-Dispatch*, and the *St. Louis Globe-Democrat*. Also, the Reverend James Blair of Kansas City assisted in the search for photos. Lastly, we wish to express our appreciation to the staff of Forum Press for assistance in the publication of this book, especially to Erby M. Young and W. A. Welsh who recognized the need for *Missouri's Black Heritage* and who encouraged and guided us every step of the way.

Missouri's Black Heritage

The Black Experience in Missouri

A Personal Reminiscence

Lorenzo J. Greene

I arrived in Jefferson City for the first time on a hot, sultry evening in September 1933. I had just completed an overnight trip from New York City to accept a position teaching history at Lincoln University. As I lugged my bags off the train, I had one overriding desire: to reach the university as quickly as possible. Fortunately, several taxis were parked near the station. I hailed one. The first white driver ignored me. The next let me have it straight: "We don't haul niggers. Get that 'nigger' cab over there." Stifling my anger, I took my bags to where two taxis, driven by blacks, were parked.

En route to the university, we passed through a slum area that the cab driver called "The Foot." The school stood atop a hill covered with beautiful trees, shrubbery, and flowers. It was a lovely sight. I was met by a French professor who was acting as caretaker while the president was out of town. He took me to Foster Hall, a freshman dorm, and gave me a room. I quickly showered, changed clothes, and sallied forth to my first meal in Jefferson City.

Across the street from the campus stood a small restaurant. As I approached it, my heart sank. A nauseating smell of rancid grease overwhelmed the fragrance of nearby honeysuckles. Worse, even before I crossed the street, the sight and sound of swarms of bugs and flies, covering and striking against the screen door of the restaurant, literally turned my stomach. I put on a bold face, flailed away at the insects, and quickly entered. The room was dingy and dirty. The proprietor, perspiring and swatting at the winged insects that seemed intent on taking over the place, offered me a seat. Knowing that it would be impossible for me to eat there, I ordered something not included on the menu. "Sorry," the waitress said unsmilingly, "but we are out of that." "Is there another restaurant nearby?" I asked. "Yes, there is one in the hotel down the street but it is closed now," the owner answered. I then inquired whether there was a drugstore open. "Four blocks down the street," the man replied.

The drugstore had a lunch counter. It was now nearly ten o'clock and I was hungry. I sat down at the counter. A young man asked me what I wanted. "A hamburger and a vanilla malted milk," I said. "I'm sorry," he replied, "but we don't serve colored here." I felt both angry and embarrassed, particularly since several white customers were intently watching me with smirks on their faces. Ignoring them, I asked the clerk whether he had any vanilla ice cream. He replied that he did. "You can sell a colored person a pint of ice cream, can't you?" I asked sarcastically. "Yes," he answered. "Well, give me a pint of vanilla, and you do have wooden spoons?" Again an affirmative reply. "Then please put two of them in the bag with the ice cream!" He did so. I left the store, carrying my "supper" with me. Lonely and angry, I retraced my steps to the university. It was my first experience with racism in Jefferson City.

As I ate the ice cream in my dorm room, I looked out of the window. I was unaccustomed to the treatment I had just received. My hunger had left me. I was hurt and sad. All I could do was cry. Disillusioned and dejected, I decided that upon receiving my first paycheck, I would return to New York where the National Urban League had a housing job awaiting me, contingent upon a grant from Washington, D.C.

But events of the next few days changed my mind. The president, administrators, faculty members, and students began arriving, and the academic wheels started to turn. The head of my department invited me to stay at his home until I found suitable living quarters. One night I told him of my experience during my first night on campus. He replied that Jefferson City, like Missouri, was southern in orientation and tradition. Negroes could find only menial employment, housing was segregated, and hotels, restaurants, and amusement places were closed to black people. Schools were segregated. There was no public high school for blacks in Missouri's capital city. Lincoln University, through state funds, filled this gap. White persons called Negroes by their first names. Middle-class Negroes countered by using initials, like "J. B." Jones. Negroes could vote and ride on the street cars. Everything else was segregated.

When classes began, I realized that my services were needed here.

Lincoln had an excellent faculty, drawn from such prestigious universities as Harvard, Columbia, Chicago, Boston, New York, Pittsburgh, Cornell, and others. A group of us planned to make Lincoln an academic replica of Amherst. Student enrollment ranged between three hundred and three hundred and fifty. We had the pick of black students from Missouri, Arkansas, Oklahoma, and other nearby states. Others came from as far away as California and Massachusetts. Many had excellent potential but had been victimized by inferior, segregated schools. Soon, under a group of dedicated teachers, Lincoln was turning out students, many of whom enrolled for higher degrees in the best universities in the nation. Others entered the professions, especially as teachers. I had found my life's work and loved it.

I was also determined to help change the economic and social climate of Missouri—to break down segregation and discrimination. Over the years I aligned myself with various groups: the Missouri Association for Social Welfare, the Missouri Council of Churches, the Urban League, the NAACP, the Missouri Council of Labor, the League of Women Voters, and liberal faculty members and students from various colleges and universities—Jews, Gentiles, professional workers, and laymen—all united together in a crusade for social justice.

There were two struggles that have remained especially dear to me. One was the sharecroppers' protest in southeast Missouri. On January 1, 1939, white and black sharecroppers and tenant farmers of Butler, Pemiscot, Dunklin, and New Madrid counties were evicted by their landlords. On January 10, 1939, as a means of bringing their miserable plight before the world, they moved their pitiable belongings onto Highways 60 and 61. There, in rain, sleet, cold, and snow, unable to obtain aid from local, state, or federal authorities, the croppers eked out a precarious existence for months. Starving, freezing, living in makeshift shelters and having to walk a mile or more for water, they became a spectacle for reporters, photographers, and curiosity seekers.

The striking farm workers demanded the abolition of the sharecropping and tenant farm system, the individual ownership of land, the organization of all farm workers, and wages of fifteen cents an hour for a ten-hour day and twenty cents an hour for all overtime. In addition, they wanted landlords to grant them the privilege of raising pigs and chickens; to furnish them with a milk cow, free pasture, a garden plot, and the use of a team to haul firewood; and to give them the right to raise corn and cotton on a fifty-fifty basis. Finally, they demanded teams or trucks to get their produce to market. When the landlords refused these demands, the sharecroppers walked off or were evicted from the plantations.

In April I spoke to students and teachers at the Negro high school in Charleston and spent the weekend among the sharecroppers. What I saw shocked me: little children with their bellies swollen from lack of food; men, women, and children barefoot in the slush and snow; girls and women scantily clothed, wearing anything to keep warm; shelters made of cardboard, tin, pieces of wood, twigs—anything to protect them from the elements; girls and women cooking out-of-doors with snow and sleet falling into their kettles; and a small church providing temporary housing for nearly one hundred people.

On returning to Lincoln, I told my class in American history about the condition of the sharecroppers. I described their suffering, their sickness, their starving children, and their pitiable attempts to maintain their dignity and strength in the face of almost impossible odds. I asked, "How many of you are from southeast Missouri?" About ten of my thirty-five students raised their hands. "How many of you have heard about the sharecroppers' demonstrations?" Fewer hands were raised. Student interest increased and the discussion consumed the entire class period. One student enquired, "Did the sharecroppers ask what we thought of their condition?" I replied, "Nothing, you are too busy preparing for your spring prom."

Unknown to myself, I had dropped a bomb. Following my second class, while sitting in my office, a knock sounded on the door. Opening it, three young women entered. One of them began: "Mr. Greene, we heard what you said about the sharecroppers and we felt ashamed; so, we called an emergency meeting of the AKA sorority, and we want to ask you a question. Would it be OK if we let our prom go and gave the money to the sharecroppers? We have three hundred dollars."

They left, and soon representatives of the Deltas came in offering the same sacrifice. Before I left for lunch, the president of the student council came to tell me that her organization had pledged eighty dollars to aid the sharecroppers. The sororities, particularly the AKAs and Deltas, gave, solicited, bought, and mended clothing. Other students and faculty members did the same. Money intended for proms went for clothing, food, cartons of baby food, sugar, cod-liver oil, cereal, disinfectants, soap, and the like. Shoes, galoshes, and hats added to the collection. About three hundred dollars in cash was left over.

When all was ready we had amassed nearly a truck full of clothing, shoes, food, medicine, and other necessities. Off we went; the president had allowed the three young women who had led the campaign to accompany me to southeast Missouri. The sharecroppers welcomed us with profuse expressions of thanks. The girls washed and fed the babies and children and helped the women with their chores.

We made several more trips to southeast Missouri. I wrote newspaper and magazine articles and letters to individuals, imploring them to aid the sharecroppers and displaced tenant farmers in any way possible. From various parts of the country came contributions of clothing, small donations of money, and letters inquiring in what way they could help these unfortunate people.

In 1940 we bought land for the sharecroppers, built homes, and helped settle some near Poplar Bluff. Finally, the Farm Security Administration came to the rescue and aided in settling the sharecroppers in homes that they could buy on easy payments. When they could not keep up the payments, we established a volunteer corporation, guaranteed their payments, and set up a store at Lilbourn. There the croppers could obtain food, clothing, and other items donated by involved persons for a pittance or even obtain things, if penniless, free of charge. The project is still in operation at Lilbourn.

The second cause that has remained particularly dear to me was the setting up of the State Human Rights Commission. For several years, this had been high on the priorities of the Missouri Association for Social Welfare and its affiliated organizations.

Each year for a decade or more prior to 1955, black legislators introduced civil rights bills demanding an end to segregation and discrimination. Black legislators, like other blacks, were humiliated by being barred from eating places, hotels, and rooming houses. For years when the legislature was in session black representatives, who could not get other accommodations in Jefferson City, stayed in the dormitories and ate in the cafeteria of Lincoln University. Their individual efforts at changing Missouri law and custom had always ended in failure.

Alternatively, the Missouri Association for Social Welfare, labor and church groups, professionals, and laymen decided to utilize a bipartisan, biracial strategy that included the support of members of both House and Senate. A civil rights bill was introduced in both houses simultaneously.

A key factor was the gubernatorial campaign of 1956. James A. Blair, a liberal Democrat, was running for governor as an independent. His support would be crucial to setting up a state commission on human rights. For the statewide support that our groups promised him, he pledged his word to see that we got our wish. Blair won the election. Only after a furious struggle in the legislature, in which Blair personally intervened, was the bill passed. The purpose of the bill was to eliminate segregation and discrimination in Missouri. Blair later signed it into law, and we had our first Human Rights Commission.

How can we assess the results of our efforts over the years? Spurred by the civil rights movement of the late fifties, sixties, and early seventies, places of public accommodation were opened to all persons. Hotels, motels, restaurants, theaters, public schools, and colleges all willingly or unwillingly desegregated. Black and white children studied together. Appeals to state courts and the liberalism of the United States Supreme Court under Chief Justice Earl Warren witnessed the opening of state, municipal, and private employment, and the upgrading of blacks elected or appointed to public offices.

And what of tomorrow? The picture is not as bright as it could be. Black employment, especially among youths, is at an all-time low; the social climate of the sixties and early seventies has given way to a more conservative and even reactionary one; hate groups, like the Ku Klux Klan and neo-Nazis, brazenly attempt to turn the clock back by preaching the outworn gospel of a "white-people's country." Desegregation of schools is giving way to resegregation in the inner cities as whites increasingly flee to the suburbs. Unemployed blacks turn more and more to crime and drugs. Black study courses in colleges and universities find their budgets cut as these institutions seek to accomplish more with less financial backing. Schoolchildren are being shortchanged by insufficient school funding, teachers' strikes, and discipline problems. In short, the struggle for human rights, which held such bright prospects less than a decade ago, is now a fragmented movement, whose consequences for the future are impossible to predict.

What is needed is a return to the unified movement of the sixties when whites and blacks, Jews and Gentiles, student groups, liberal political leaders, and an enlightened judiciary dedicated themselves to peaceful means for achieving equal rights for all people. We have made progress, yes. But we have a long way to go.

1

Roots

Slavery Comes to Missouri

Black Africans first came to the territory we know now as Missouri early in the eighteenth century. Brought against their will by Frenchmen who enslaved them for profit, blacks were seen as the solution to a severe labor shortage encountered by Europeans everywhere in the New World. Frenchmen, primarily fur trappers and traders, had frequented the Mississippi River valley since the Jolliet-Marquette expedition of the 1670s. The first serious forays of Frenchmen into the land on the western bank of the great river, however, did not occur until 1710 through 1720. During that decade, entrepreneurs based in Illinois crossed the river in search of precious minerals.

In 1717 the French crown granted a monopoly on trade in the valley to the Company of the West, headed by the Scotsman John Law. Two years later, Law merged his business with several others to form the Company of the Indies. Employed by the Company of the Indies, Marc Antoine de La Loere Des Ursins, together with a crew of workmen, began digging for lead and silver in the Mine La Motte area in June 1719. Mining operations at the time were both primitive and arduous, and Des Ursins quickly realized that he would have difficulty maintaining an adequate labor force. On July 10, 1719, he wrote to his superiors: "You can imagine that soldiers do not work at the mines, therefore the sooner we shall get negroes the better it will be. The Frenchmen are unfit for this kind of work, and if they want to work, their wages will in proportion be much higher than the profits from the mine will permit."

Des Ursins soon put to work in the mines five black slaves, presumably brought from the French-controlled island of Haiti. In 1720 Phillippe François Renault was sent from France to direct lead-mining oper-

8

ations. He, too, brought with him a few black slaves, but, as historian William E. Foley has noted: "The scarcity and cost of slaves in French Illinois forced miners to rely primarily on white laborers. Some whites may even have been compelled by the authorities to work in the mines."

One solution to the scarcity of labor was to enslave the Native Americans they encountered in the Mississippi River valley. Although the French continued to enslave Indians through much of the eighteenth century, blacks rapidly replaced Native American slaves.

This change occurred for several reasons. First of all, the continued enslavement of Native Americans by whites threatened to destroy peaceful commercial relations between the Europeans and their Indian neighbors. Whites were greatly outnumbered by Indians, but they found security in the fact that tribes often fought with each other; however, slavery threatened to provide the Indians with a common cause to unite against the Europeans. Furthermore, the Native American was at home in the Mississippi and the Missouri River valleys. He could escape his white owner, flee back to his village, and disappear into the tribe unnoticed by the master. Whites who enslaved Indians were taking a risk. Thrifty Frenchmen feared seeing slaves, who had cost them expensive guns, run off before they could realize a return on their investment. Black slaves, on the other hand, were thousands of miles from home. They were not familiar with the terrain, and their black skins were immediately noticeable anywhere in the New World. Black slaves, the Frenchmen reasoned, were the answer to their labor problems.

By the time Ste. Genevieve was founded as the first permanent white settlement in what is now Missouri (about 1750), black slavery had become a widely accepted and crucially important mainstay of the French-American economy. According to the historian of Ste. Genevieve, Carl Ekberg, "Census figures suggest that throughout the colonial period about forty percent of the town's population consisted of black slaves." The total population of the small river town did not reach one thousand until nearly 1800.

The existence of slavery and the relationship between master and slave in French colonial Missouri was defined by the *Code Noir,* or Black Code, first issued by France's King Louis XIV in 1685. The code clearly defined black slaves as property that could be bought and sold, but it also recognized that slaves were human beings with certain rights. The code, for example, required masters to provide adequate care for their slaves and prohibited the breaking up of families through sales. The code even provided slaves with the right to sue their masters if they thought any of their rights were being transgressed. However, the *Code Noir* was a theoretical statement of how slaves should be treated and did not necessarily reflect the reality of the French masters' treatment of their slaves. While it attempted to place limits on masters' authority over their slaves, the code was largely unenforceable due to the lack of French officials' policing power and the sizable number of black slaves in the Louisiana Territory. Ultimately, the masters wielded the real power over how their slaves would be treated.

French masters employed African slaves in various work in colonial Missouri. In Ste. Genevieve, agriculture played an important role in the community's economy, and a large number of black slaves, both men and women, worked as field hands. But work in the fields was seasonal, and slaves performed other tasks during the off-season as well. Fewer slaves worked in the lead mines of nearby Mine La Motte and Castor Mine, and some worked at salt mining on the La Saline. Others worked as domestics or as oarsmen on riverboats.

The *Code Noir* forbade masters to work their slaves on Sundays or holidays. While the French administrators prohibited slaves from purchasing their own freedom, the Spanish overlords, who assumed control of the Louisiana Territory in the 1760s, allowed the practice of self-purchase. Some slaves used Sundays and holidays to work for wages that could be applied toward their self-purchase, although the purchase price for slaves in Upper Louisiana was usually high. In 1788, for example, François Jasmin, a black slave, and his wife, Catherine, purchased their freedom from their master, Charles Valle, for 800 piastres—a sizeable cash sum for slaves to accumulate. The Spanish practice of self-purchase intended to encourage the slaves to be industrious, to adopt European work ethics, and generally to prevent slaves from using their free time to drink, gamble, dance, or create other disturbances.

But the practice of self-purchase also promoted dishonesty and theft among the slaves. To collect their purchase price more quickly, some slaves stole goods and animals from their masters and other whites and sold them on the black market. An advanced contraband market developed as slaves often traded stolen merchandise with unscrupulous white merchants in exchange for money or liquor.

To combat the contraband trade, the *Code Noir* forbade slaves to sell any merchandise at the markets without the written permission of their masters and sentenced any slave convicted of selling stolen goods to be whipped and branded with the fleur-de-lis. Nevertheless, the traffic in stolen merchandise was usually heavy. The slaves' illegal commerce had damaging repercussions for the entire black population. In 1797 Pierre-Charles Delassus de Luzieres, commandant of New Bourbon, wrote to his Spanish superiors:

> The residence that I have made successively for five years in these two places has put me within reach of not only verifying by myself and under my eyes these daily disorders and brigandages in the fields, woods, enclosed gardens, orchards and farmyards, but also of assuring myself that the majority of these thefts were committed by the slaves, it is only too evident that this kind of man is naturally inclined to thefts, brigandages and to disorders.

The image of the slave as a thief reinforced racist European beliefs about Africans, and this stereotype would haunt blacks in America throughout slavery and beyond.

The system of slavery practiced by the French and Spanish in colonial Missouri drew its stability as an institution from repression and violence against the enslaved. Article 27 of the *Code Noir* prescribed the death penalty for any slave who struck his or her master, mistress, or their children, "causing bruises and making the face bleed." In addition, Article 28 called for assaults committed by slaves against other freeborn persons to be "punished severely, even by death if it is fitting." Other punishments for slaves included whippings, branding with the fleur-de-lis, hamstringing their leg tendons, and cutting off their ears. Such punishments affected not only the offending slave who was disciplined but the entire slave community. Public whippings, brandings, and executions served as powerful tools of social control to keep all the enslaved in their subordinate position.

Article 38 of the *Code Noir* prohibited masters from torturing or mutilating their slaves under penalty of confiscation of their property and prosecution, and it also denied masters the right to kill their slaves. But it did allow masters "in extraordinary circumstances . . . when they think their slaves have deserved it" to chain their slaves and beat them "with rods and ropes." Provisions limiting the master's physical abuse of his slaves were sometimes ignored. In 1783, for example, Jean-Baptiste Lacroix, the overseer of a wealthy Ste. Genevieve merchant, killed Tacoua, a black slave, with a pickaxe because he was displeased with the slave's work. Ste. Genevieve's commandant held an inquest into the murder, but evidence suggests that Lacroix escaped punishment for his crime.

One reason for the brutal treatment of slaves was the close day-to-day contact in which masters and slaves worked and lived. Since most Frenchmen owned only a few slaves and did not need an overseer, the master and his slaves usually worked side by side in the fields or mines. Although such close contact gave slaves the opportunity to manipulate their masters to their advantage, this intimacy also placed slaves under constant supervision and at the risk of receiving more capricious, undeserved beatings at the hands of cruel masters.

Article 43 of the *Code Noir* prohibited the separate sale of "the husband, the wife, and the prepubescent children [puberty was assumed at age fourteen]." There is substantial evidence to indicate that French masters generally abided by this article in colonial Missouri. In April 1766 Louis Viriat purchased a black slave family consisting of Baptiste, his wife, Angelique, and their ten-year-old daughter, Elizabeth, from Joseph Niberville dit Josen. In December 1775 Guillaume Ebert dit Le Compte bought a black slave family, Joseph dit Chacachas, aged twenty-five, his wife, Angelique, aged twenty-one, and their two sons, Joachim, aged five, and Paul, aged one, from François Vallé. The French authorities and masters recognized the value of the nuclear slave family as a means to control slaves and to increase their wealth. In their eyes the nuclear slave family tied slaves to their farms: a slave who was attempting to run away might think twice about leaving his or her family. Furthermore, the concept of the slave family encouraged a husband and wife to have children, thereby reproducing the master's labor force and wealth.

Despite the *Code Noir*, unscrupulous masters sometimes divided their slave families and sold the individuals separately. In December 1777 Jean-Baptiste Pratte bought Genevieve, a twelve-year-old mulatto girl, from Antoine Duclos and his wife, Marie-Jeanne Saucier. And Michel Placet purchased a ten-year-old black boy named Pierre from Joseph Gouvreau in August 1796. Dividing up slave families and selling them separately, although illegal, was more profitable for a master and allowed him to sell off only enough slaves to pay his debts during economic hard times.

While the code allowed slaves to marry, they could only do so with the master's consent. There is evidence to suggest that many business-minded masters discouraged their slaves from marrying. According to Carl Ekberg, the Ste. Genevieve parish records document only fourteen marriages between black slaves during the colonial period, with the last one performed in 1783. This is an amazingly small figure considering that black slaves accounted for between 30 to 40 percent of the town's population from approximately 1770 to 1803. By discouraging formal marriages in the Roman Catholic church, masters did not have to contend with the article forbidding the separate sale of a slave family, since the code specifically defined a family as a husband, his wife, and children below the age of puberty.

Despite Article 6 of the *Code Noir,* which prohibited marriage or cohabitation between whites and blacks, miscegenation or interracial sex was fairly widespread in Upper Louisiana. In fact, the French and especially the Spanish were very race and color conscious. Throughout the Americas, the Spanish devised and put into practice an elaborate classification system describing every conceivable intermixture between the races. A "mulatto" was an offspring of a white and black parent. A "sambo" (or "griffe") had one white grandparent and three black grandparents (one-fourth white); a "quadroon" had three white grandparents and one black grandparent (three-quarters white); and an "octoroon" had seven white great-grandparents and one black great-grandparent (seven-eighths white).

An approximate estimation of miscegenation can be found in the Spanish census reports for Upper Louisiana. The 1787 census for Ste. Genevieve listed thirty-nine mulattoes: nine free and thirty slaves. But by 1800 the mulatto population in Ste. Genevieve numbered eighty-eight: three free and eighty-five slaves. In that year, mulattoes accounted for 25 percent of that community's nonwhite population.

The shortage of available white women and the power masters held over their black slaves contributed to the sexual exploitation of slave women. The most common form of miscegenation was the rape of black and mulatto slave women by white men. However, to characterize all miscegenation as rapes would be misleading. Interracial relationships between French men and black women sometimes went beyond forced onetime encounters. In 1783 Pelagie Carpentier divorced her husband, Charles Valle, the son of Ste. Genevieve's wealthiest merchant, because he kept a mulatto mistress. And wealthy St. Louis entrepreneur Jacques Clamorgan fathered at least four children by three different women of color.

Within these liaisons, mutual feelings of love often developed. From the early 1780s until his death in 1798, the bachelor Antoine Aubuchon, a member of a prominent Ste. Genevieve family, had a common law relationship with a free black woman named Elizabeth, which resulted in ten mulatto children. Some of these relationships between white men and black women went as far as marriage. In May 1801 a French lead miner named Pierre Viviat from Mine La Motte married Rodde Christi, a mulatto woman from Virginia whom he had originally purchased as a slave and then freed. Although there is no evidence of sexual relationships between French women and black or mulatto men, such affairs certainly would have existed, but not to the extent of relationships between French men and black women.

French and Spanish masters occasionally manumitted or freed their slaves in colonial Missouri. One type of emancipation was testamentary manumission, or by decree of a master's will at his death. Testamentary manumission ensured the loyal service of a slave up until the master's death, and it required no economic loss to the master himself. Manumission, then, was a powerful motivating and stabilizing influence on the institution of slavery. By holding out the promise of freedom, a master could motivate his slave to dutifully and loyally perform his or her assigned tasks. In addition, this incentive could induce a slave to accept his or her enslaved position.

Other slaves did not have to wait until their master's death for their freedom. Some masters freed their black or mulatto mistresses. In August 1801 John Burk, a German settler of Ste. Genevieve, manumitted and married Rachel Prior, a mulatto slave from Virginia. Burk had purchased Prior nearly five years earlier, and at the time of their wedding the couple had had two children together. Other masters also freed their mulatto children. In 1809 Jacques Clamorgan manumitted three of his surviving mulatto children, Appoline, Cyprian Martial, and Maximin, whom he had fathered by two different slave mothers. Although it was prohibited by the *Code Noir,* some masters freed their elderly slaves because their value decreased when they became too old to work. Thus, masters did not have to bear the economic expense of feeding, housing, and clothing unproductive slaves.

Many manumissions were conditional; for example, Pierre Viviat liberated Baptiste Orange, a ten-year-old mulatto boy in 1806. But Viviat stipulated in the manumission that "in case his treating me in a way not becoming, then his instrument is to be of no effect, and he, the said Orange, is not to obtain his freedom." With such clauses, masters could guarantee a certain behavior and respect from their former slaves. And while the emancipated slaves were free, their masters still wielded a certain degree of power over them, just as they had done when the blacks were enslaved.

The term *free people of color* described any free person of African descent in the Louisiana Territory. Article 54 of the *Code Noir* granted free people of color "the same rights, privileges and immunities" enjoyed by the freeborn French citizens. However, Article 53 stipulated that freedmen and freedwomen "show singular respect" to his or her former master, his widow, or his children. Thus, a free person of color was constantly reminded that he or she had once been a slave. In addition, the *Code Noir* threatened freedmen and freedwomen with reenslavement for committing various offenses including harboring a fugitive slave, theft, and "licentious conduct." Thus, French and Spanish authorities controlled the enslaved black population in part by controlling the free black population.

According to Carl Ekberg, free people of color never constituted a large segment of the population in Upper Louisiana during the colonial period. In 1791 there were thirteen free mulattoes and thirteen free blacks in Ste. Genevieve and twenty-three free mulattoes and fifteen free blacks in St. Louis. In 1800 there were seventy-seven free persons of color in Upper Louisiana, but with 1,191 African slaves these freedmen constituted only 6 percent of the entire black population.

Free people of color engaged in various work to support themselves and their families. In 1791 the freedman François Jasmin, his wife, Catherine, and their family farmed wheat, corn, and tobacco. Another free person of color, Babeta (probably Elizabeth, Antoine Aubuchon's common law wife), and her family mined lead. In the 1797 census of New Bourbon, the post's commandant, Pierre-Charles Delassus de Luzieres, noted only two free people of color in his community: "Two free negro women named Lisette and Rose, the first 45 years old, she resides in the village of New Bourbon, the latter aged around fifty-eight to sixty years old, she resides at the Saline. They conduct themselves well, work at [farming] and raise animals."

In addition to farming and lead mining, other free mulatto and black men worked as rowers in the boat trade on the Mississippi River, and some may have been hunters and trappers. Some freedmen possessed skills or trades, such as Joseph Barboa, a master mason who worked for the Spanish government on the fortifications at St. Louis.

Occasionally, free people of color rose to great wealth and power. One wealthy St. Louis entrepreneur, Jacques Clamorgan, was born in the West Indies and was thought by some to be a mulatto, although he passed for white. A few freedmen, such as François Monplesy, owned slaves themselves, but this was probably quite rare during the colonial period in Missouri. When a dispute arose over Monplesy's rightful ownership of Gregorio, a black slave, the lieutenant governor of Upper Louisiana, Francisco Cruzat, was called in to rule on the case. Since freedmen who owned slaves were so few, Cruzat had to write his Spanish superior in New Orleans, the governor general of Louisiana, Esteban Miro, for advice on how to rule in this matter of "one person of color owning another." Although most free people of color in Upper Louisiana never owned slaves or accumulated great fortunes, their descendants, the free colored aristocracy, would rise to great wealth and prominence in antebellum Missouri a half-century later.

In Upper Louisiana, black slaves who ran away from their masters were called marrons. In fact, according to Carl Ekberg, the first black person known to have lived permanently in what is now Missouri was a marron named Lusignan, who had escaped across the Mississippi River from his master in Kaskaski in the early 1750s and joined a band of Indians.

However, runaway slaves were often not accustomed to the wilderness and found it difficult to survive in the woods. Some marrons, however, stole provisions from isolated settlements or received food and supplies from friends or relatives still in captivity. In addition to the unfamiliar terrain, runaway slaves had to contend with Native Americans. In colonial Missouri, black slaves and American Indians were not united by a common sense of exploitation at the hands of the white man and were usually not allies. The French, and later the Spanish, civil authorities prevented any alliance between the two groups by offering substantial bounties to local Indian tribes for the capture and return of any runaway slaves. In May 1785, for example, five slaves plundered a storehouse in Ste. Genevieve and escaped into the nearby woods. In August, however, a band of local Cherokees captured the marrons and returned them to the Spanish authorities.

Although the French initially controlled the development of the Upper Louisiana Territory during the eighteenth century, things were destined to change as a result of developments in Europe. During the seventeenth and eighteenth centuries, Spain and France each fought England with the colonies becoming both pawns in the struggle and prizes for the victors. The end of the French and Indian War, or Seven Years War (1756–1763), revealed just how high the stakes were. France went down to defeat at the hands of the English. Spain had entered the war in 1762 with the French to prevent an English victory, but the allies were defeated by the British on land and sea. To pay Spain for her losses, France transferred all of the Louisiana Territory to the Spanish.

One of the first changes that resulted from the Spanish acquisition was the abolishment of Native American slavery, an action that resulted in making blacks the forced laborers of choice. On December 6, 1769, Governor General Alejandra O'Reilly ordered the immediate cessation of Indian slavery. As historian William E. Foley has written, "While O'Reilly intended his 1769 proclamation to improve relations with the region's numerous Indian tribes, it aroused a storm of protests from owners of enslaved Indians."

The Spanish government backed off to the extent that it allowed current slaveowners to retain their Indian slaves but prohibited them from transferring their ownership to another party. One interesting byproduct of this development was a controversy that emerged about the legal status of mixed bloods of Indian and black ancestry. One Afro-Indian woman, Marie Scypion, sued for her freedom in 1799, based upon her Indian lineage; however, it was not until 1834 that a Missouri court sided with Marie, who had already died, and granted freedom to her ancestors.

Slaves were used somewhat differently under Spanish rule. The Spanish employed fewer blacks in the mining industry than the French and used slaves mainly to supply the mother country with agricultural goods. In 1777 Governor Bernardo de Galvez ordered Lieutenant Governor Cruzat to encourage the production of hemp and flax in Upper Louisiana. Cruzat replied that this was impossible without black slaves, and since most of the settlers were poor, the slaves would have to be sold on credit. Galvez assured Cruzat there would be no problem, since the king of France had already contracted to supply the settlers with slaves.

Meanwhile, momentous changes were taking place east of the Mississippi River. England had long controlled the thirteen colonies along the Atlantic Coast, but victory in the French and Indian War had added to her possessions Canada and all the territory in America between the Allegheny Mountains and the Mississippi River. The tremendous expanse of new territory caused Britain to revise her colonial policies by taxing her colonies to help pay her war debts. Americans resorted to open and armed rebellion in 1775, claiming freedom from England in 1776 in the Declaration of Independence. The thirteen fragmented colonies became the United States of America.

Slavery was an important source of disagreement in the vast new American nation, which stretched from the Atlantic to the Mississippi. In fact it nearly wrecked the 1787 constitutional convention, which met in Philadelphia to draw up a stronger instrument of government for the United States. Southern states wanted the slaves counted as residents of the states in which they lived for purposes of political representation, but they did not want the slaves to be counted when it came to levying taxes. Northerners took the opposite position. They wanted slaves counted for taxation, but not representation. Both sections finally agreed to the famous "three-fifths compromise." Slaves would be counted as three-fifths of a person both for purposes of representation and taxation. In addition, slavery would be forbidden in the territory north of the Ohio River (the present states of Wisconsin, Illinois, Michigan, Ohio, and Indiana). One of the immediate effects of this Northwest Ordinance, as it was known, was that many American slaveowners living east of the Mississippi River and north of the Ohio River crossed into Spanish-controlled Missouri Territory to avoid losing their slaves.

The Mississippi River was more than a barrier separating America from the Spanish colonial possessions. It was the major means by which

American farmers in the Mississippi valley could float their produce downstream to the ocean port of New Orleans. From New Orleans the goods could be shipped to markets in England and Europe. The problem was that Spain controlled New Orleans; so the United States had to negotiate with Spain for permission to deposit goods at New Orleans until they could be loaded on ships carrying them across the ocean. That arrangement was written into the Treaty of San Lorenzo in 1795.

In 1789 a violent revolution broke out in France, in part inspired by the example of the American revolution. As the French people struggled with the difficult task of shaping a new government and claiming personal liberties in their Declaration of the Rights of Man, all of Europe became involved—and with Europe, all its colonies in America. After Napoleon took control of the French government in 1799, he quickly invaded and conquered Spain in 1800. He demanded that Spain give him all of the Louisiana Territory. Napoleon hoped to make the French West Indian island of Haiti his base for building an empire in the Americas. Napoleon's army was to take control of New Orleans in 1803.

The American president, Thomas Jefferson, was well aware of the danger posed by a French-controlled New Orleans. France was the world's strongest military power at the time. Holding New Orleans, it could prevent American farmers from shipping their produce down the Ohio and Mississippi rivers to European markets. President Jefferson decided to ally America with England to ensure American farmers the right of deposit at the port of New Orleans.

But the blacks in Haiti had been inspired by the Declaration of Independence and the French Declaration of the Rights of Man, and they wanted the same freedom promised the French. Haiti in 1798 had a black population of five hundred thousand slaves. All were cruelly exploited by a few thousand whites, who were mostly French planters and government officials. The slaves rebelled against their white masters in 1791 and for more than a decade they defeated French, Spanish, and British armies sent to subdue them. They were led by three great black generals: Toussaint L'Ouverture, Jean Jacques Dessalines, and Henri Christophe. Napoleon lost forty thousand of his best troops to the slaves, who declared their independence in 1803. The rebellion shattered Napoleon's dream of a great empire in America dominated by France. Black opposition had made this impossible; indeed, defeating Napoleon made it possible for the United States to expand to the Pacific.

While the revolution of the black slaves was raging in Haiti, President Jefferson was trying to buy New Orleans from Napoleon. Eager to secure that ocean port as a trade depot for American goods, he sent James Monroe and Robert Livingstone to France to negotiate for the southern city and the land to the east of it with ten million dollars. By the time the Americans arrived Napoleon had already lost Haiti, and he feared that the English fleet would take over New Orleans. Consequently, he astounded the American envoys by offering all of Louisiana. Although shocked by Napoleon's willingness to part with the entire territory, the American envoys snatched up all the land between the Mississippi River and the Rocky Mountains for fifteen million dollars. The American nation's size more than doubled overnight.

America's purchase of Louisiana territory in 1803 was followed by a dramatic increase in the population. As the number of settlers moving into new land increased, so did the number of slaves. At the time of the Louisiana Purchase there were 10,340 persons living in Missouri. Blacks numbered 1,320—nearly 13 percent of the total population. By 1810 Missouri's population had increased more than 101 percent to 20,845. During that same period the black population grew to 3,618.

Missouri attracted settlers for many reasons. Most important was its rich soil, especially in the Missouri River bottoms. Thus, it held out the promise for profitable agricultural production. When it became a state in 1821, approximately three-fourths of Missouri's citizens were engaged in farming. The fact that Missouri allowed slavery also made it attractive.

The majority of Missouri's slaves were located in the Mississippi and Missouri River valleys. St. Louis, of course, led the way. The commander of the Missouri territory, Captain Amos Stoddard, reported that there were 667 slaves in the district of St. Louis in 1804 and 740 by 1810. Other areas with high concentrations of slaves in those early days of the territory included St. Charles, Ste. Genevieve, and Cape Girardeau.

Even before the Louisiana Purchase, the number of slaves was large enough to make white settlers afraid of slave uprisings. The French and Spanish had enacted "Black Codes," making it illegal for slaves to leave their owner's property without his permission, to carry guns, to strike their masters, or to own property. Even these rigid rules could not stifle completely the black slave's desire to be free. In 1781 Lieutenant Governor Francisco Cruzat expressed concern about the rowdy and rebellious slaves of St. Louis and called for stricter enforcement of the codes.

The rebellion of Toussaint L'Ouverture and his followers in Haiti had also struck fear in the hearts of southern slaveowners. Within the United States there had been an unsuccessful revolt in 1800 by Gabriel Prosser, who had planned to lead a band of over one thousand slaves on Richmond, Virginia. Many Missourians had migrated from Virginia and carried with them memories of Prosser and of the code that Virginians had enacted to forestall another revolt. Therefore, one of the first things the new territorial government of Missouri did was to enact a new series of Black or Slave Codes, which were patterned closely after those of Virginia.

The code of 1804 in Missouri made no distinction between slaves and other property. Slaves could not testify in court against whites, and they could not leave their owner's farm or plantation without his permission. Likewise, they could not own or carry guns. The code also attempted to define exactly who was a black person. It declared that "any person who shall have one-fourth part or more of negro blood" was to be considered a black person and bound to obey the Black Codes. In other words, a person who had three white grandparents and one black grandparent would be considered black.

From 1810 through 1820 Missouri's population grew even more rapidly than before. Several factors contributed to this growth. The end of the War of 1812 and the Napoleonic Wars in 1815 made migration from the Old World easier. The Industrial Revolution also played a crucial role in making the western territory attractive. Developments in the cotton industry were particularly important to this process. The power loom, an automatic machine used to weave yarn, replaced hand-operated equipment in the early nineteenth century. This advancement, combined with Eli Whitney's invention of the cotton gin, greatly increased the demand for cotton in America. In 1790 approximately seven hundred and fifty pounds of cotton were produced. Seventy years later cotton production in America reached more than two billion pounds.

With such an increase in the demand for cotton, producers quite naturally looked for land on which they could expand their operations. Many people believed that the Louisiana Territory and, in particular, Missouri would provide the added land needed to expand cotton production.

Ultimately, cotton was produced in Missouri, particularly in the southern part, but the state never became a large producer because of its relatively short growing season. Farming was still the main economic stay, however, and the use of slave labor increased its profitability.

In no territory would the issue of slavery and the seeking of statehood be more closely intertwined than in Missouri. Although Missourians could not have anticipated it at the time, their request for statehood would result in one of the most important political battles the country has ever known. By 1820 the Missouri Territory claimed unofficially to have 56,016 white residents and 10,222 slaves. Citizens began clamoring for statehood. The controversy centered around the status of blacks in Missouri. Should they be slave or free? The debate over that question was a rehearsal for the great crisis that eventually split the country into civil war in 1861.

The dilemma created by Missouri's application for statehood was a difficult one to resolve. The North's population was growing faster than the South's, and representation in the United States House of Representatives was based on population. Southerners feared that opponents of slavery in the northern nonslaveholding states would win a congressional fight to restrict or even eliminate slavery.

The slave states had only one chance of avoiding that outcome. Since a bill could not become law unless it passed through both houses of Congress, the South would concentrate on winning its battle in the Senate. Representation in that body was allocated on the basis of statehood with each state, regardless of its size, entitled to two senators. If the South could maintain a balance of slave states equal in number to free states, it could thwart attempts at abolishing slavery.

In March 1818 Missouri's territorial representative, John Scott, petitioned Congress for Missouri's admission to the Union. There were eleven free and ten slave states. Alabama soon balanced the situation, however, by becoming the eleventh slave state. To admit Missouri as a slave state would break the recently achieved Senate balance in favor of the South. To do otherwise would favor the free states. Not to admit it at all would be contrary to the Constitution, which provided that when a territory had a population equal to that of the least populous state it could ask Congress for admission to the Union. Once permission was given, the territory could draw up its own constitution. The next step, after approval of the constitution, was statehood.

Missouri applied for admission into the Union as a slave state. On February 13, 1819, Congressman James Tallmadge of New York proposed that Missouri come into the Union as a slave state but that no more slaves be allowed to enter the territory. He also proposed that the slaves already there be set free whenever they reached the age of twenty-five. Tallmadge's bill barely passed in the House. A combination of southerners and northern proslavery senators defeated it in the Senate.

The issue was raised again in the next session of Congress. By that time, the whole nation was astir with proslavery and abolitionist arguments. It seemed as if the entire nation was holding its breath in anticipation of the outcome. Astute observers of the controversy surrounding Missouri's pending statehood could see that the fight over slavery had only begun and that it would continue to inspire fierce hatred on both sides. To the aged Thomas Jefferson, the Missouri question was as frightening as the sound of a "firebell in the night."

After a furious struggle, Missouri entered as a slave state and northeastern Massachusetts, now known as Maine, entered as a free state. The balance between the number of slave and free states in the Senate was preserved. While Missouri was allowed into the Union as a slave state, all the land north of 36°30′ not located within the boundaries of Missouri was to be forever free.

While the debate over whether or not to admit slavery had been raging in the United States Congress, a similar struggle was played out in Missouri. On March 6, 1820, Congress had authorized the people of the territory to come together and write a constitution for their new state. Those in favor of slavery dominated the convention. When word was brought that Congress was willing to allow slavery to exist in Missouri, the delegates rejoiced. One man even went so far as to try to persuade his fellow Missourians that blacks themselves were exceedingly happy over this bit of news. After all, he argued, the Missouri Compromise meant that blacks would not have to "live in the uncomfortable surroundings of states such as Virginia, Kentucky, and Tennessee; they could be brought to the infinitely more pleasant confines of Missouri."

The Missouri question having finally been resolved, President James

Monroe proclaimed Missouri to be the twenty-fourth state of the Union on August 10, 1821. As a state, Missouri embarked upon a plan of expansion rivaled by few other territories in pre–Civil War America. The black presence had already been strongly felt in Missouri. The complexities of life that accompanied statehood would only cause black and white lives to become more intertwined.

Suggested Readings

The best general work on the origins of Missouri is William E. Foley's *The Genesis of Missouri: From Wilderness Outpost to Statehood* (Columbia: University of Missouri Press, 1989). Foley's work provides much new information on black life in colonial Missouri, as does Carl Ekberg's indispensable *Colonial Ste. Genevieve: An Adventure on the Mississippi Frontier* (Gerald, Mo.: Patrice Press, 1985). Russell Magnaghi's essay "The Role of Indian Slavery in Colonial St. Louis," *Bulletin* 31 (July 1975): 264–72, reveals much about early Indian slavery in the region. Magnaghi's essay should be supplemented with Steven R. Call, *French Slaves, Indian Slaves: Slavery and the Cultural Frontier in the Illinois Country, 1703–1756* (Master's thesis, University of Missouri–Columbia, 1988).

The classic work on black slavery in the Missouri Territory remains Harrison A. Trexler, *Slavery in Missouri, 1804–1865* (Baltimore: Johns Hopkins Press, 1914). It should be supplemented by the following articles: Lloyd A. Hunter, "Slavery in St. Louis 1804–1860," *Bulletin* 30 (July 1974): 233–65; Emil Oberholzer, "The Legal Aspects of Slavery in Missouri," *Bulletin* (January 1950): 540–45; and Arvarh E. Strickland, "Aspects of Slavery in Missouri, 1821," *Missouri Historical Review* 65 (July 1971): 505–26.

The standard work on the Missouri Compromise is Glover Moore, *The Missouri Controversy, 1819–1821* (Lexington: University of Kentucky Press, 1953). Also useful is Ronald C. Woolsey, "The West Becomes a Problem: The Missouri Controversy and Slavery Expansion as the Southern Dilemma," *Missouri Historical Review* 77 (July 1983): 409–32.

Other articles of significance to this period include William E. Foley, "Slave Freedom Suits before Dred Scott: The Case of Marie Jean Scypion's Descendants," *Missouri Historical Review* 79 (October 1984): 1–23; and A. P. Nasatir, "Jacques Clamorgan: Colonial Promotor of the Northern Border of New Spain," *New Mexico Historical Review* 79 (April 1942): 110–12.

2

From Sunup to Sundown
The Life of the Slave

Slavery was, above all else, an economic institution. Masters were interested in getting as much work out of their slaves as they could year round; consequently, the life of the slave was determined largely by this fact. Contrary to what some historians once believed, slavery remained a profitable and viable institution right down to the Civil War. In some regions, such as Callaway County, slavery was the most important factor in maintaining the economy.

Missouri slaves had a wider range of skills and occupations than slaves in the South because of the different types of farming. Although the land was abundant and fertile, the colder weather meant a shorter growing season that was not suitable for growing cotton in large quantities; therefore, Missouri farmers and their slaves practiced mixed farming. Hemp, tobacco, wheat, oats, hay, corn, and other feed grains were the main staples, but Missouri was also known for its fine cattle, sheep, horses, and pigs.

The majority of Missouri's slaves worked as field hands on farms, but many others were valets, butlers, handymen, carpenters, common laborers, maids, nurses, and cooks. Isabelle Henderson from Saline County worked "in the house of my master and mistress. . . . I was taught to sew and had to help make clothes for the other slaves. I nursed all the children of my mistress and one time I was hired out to the white preacher's family to take care of his children when his wife was sick." Emma Knight, born on the farm of Will and Emily Ely near Florida, Missouri, and her three sisters "cut weeds along the fences, pulled weeds in the garden and helped the mistress with hoeing. We had to feed the stock, sheep, hogs, and calves because the young masters wouldn't do the work.

In the evening we were made to knit a finger width, and if we missed a stitch we would have to pull all the yarn out and do it over." Marie Askin Simpson, born about 1854 near Steelville, remembered how her master's family

> kept me busy waiting on them. Carrying water from the spring, hunting eggs and a lot of other little things. . . . Mother did most of the cooking and washing and ironing. In those days they did the washing with battlin' sticks and boards. They layed the clothes on this board and battled them with battlin sticks. . . . We boiled our clothes in big iron kettles over a fire in the yard. We made our own lye and soap.

Richard Bruner, a Missouri slave born about 1840, remembered being "a water-boy to de field hands before I were big enough to wuk in the fields." Another Missouri slave, Mark Discus, born about 1850, recalled: "When I was nine years old I cut all the corn stalks offen a forty-acre field with a hoe. We had to work from sun up 'til dark too." Lewis Mundy, who was born five miles north of La Belle, also worked in the fields as a youth: "When I was small I rode one of the oxen and harrowed the fields. When I was about ten or eleven I plowed with oxen." Gus Smith, born in 1845 near Rich Fountain in Osage County, recalled: "When we didn't have much work, we would get up about five o'clock every morning, but in busy season we had to be up and ready to work at daybreak."

Hiring slaves out was also a profitable gain for Missouri masters. Not only did they receive payment for the slaves' services, but they did not have to feed or house the slaves since that was the responsibility of the hirer. Some slaves found themselves working at the Maramec Iron Works for one hundred dollars a year. When railroads began moving through Missouri, slaves were hired to lay the rails at the rate of twenty dollars a month; brickyards paid a similar sum. Many slaves were hired out to the owners of riverboats where they worked as deck hands, cabin boys, and stevedores for approximately fifteen dollars a month.

Wages for slaves were usually less than those paid to whites for similar work. William Black, a slave from Marion County, recalled that when he was eight years old, he was bonded out to Sam Briggs of New London. "Mr. Briggs was a good master and I had little to do. My duty was to take his children to school and go after them in the evening. In the meantime I just piddled around de fields." Another slave, Margaret Davis of Cape Girardeau, was hired out as a nursemaid to a white family when she was just ten years old. She was so small that she remembered having to stand on a chair in order to wash clothes.

Missouri's population grew rapidly during the decades after it became a state. Attracted by the virgin Missouri soil, people from Kentucky, Tennessee, North Carolina, and Virginia poured into the state. Many of the settlers brought slaves, and those who did not came with the hope that they would one day own slaves. The following figures offer some idea of the rapid growth of slavery in the state before the Civil War:

Missouri's Population, 1810–1860

Year	Total pop.	Whites	Slaves	Free Blacks	% Slaves
1810	20,845	17,227	3,011	607	14.4
1820	66,076	54,903	9,797	376	14.8
1830	140,445	115,364	25,091	569	17.8
1840	383,702	322,295	57,891	1,478	15.2
1850	682,044	592,004	87,422	2,618	12.8
1860	1,182,012	1,063,489	114,509	3,572	9.7

These figures reveal that the white population of Missouri grew by more than sixty-one-fold between 1810 and 1860. The slave population increased more than thirty-seven-fold during the same period. In 1830 slaves represented 17.8 percent of the total Missouri population. By 1860 that percentage had dropped to about 9.8 in large part due to the influx during the 1840s and 1850s of Germans who were against slavery.

In spite of the large numbers of slaves, there were few large slaveholding plantations in Missouri. Only thirty-six of Missouri's 114 counties had one thousand or more slaves. According to Bill Sims, a slave born in 1839 in Osceola, Missouri, "A man who owned ten slaves was considered wealthy." Jabez F. Smith of Jackson County at one time owned 165 blacks. John W. Ragland, the largest slaveholder in Cooper County, owned seventy slaves. Daniel Ligon, the largest slaveholder in Lewis County, owned twenty-six slaves. Most Missourians owned none, and for those who did the average was four blacks per slaveholding family. When there were only one or two slaves, the master and his family often worked alongside them in the fields.

Slaves were not equally dispersed throughout the state. They were most heavily concentrated on the fertile farmlands of the Missouri and Mississippi river bottoms. In 1860 approximately one-third of the state's slaves resided in ten counties: Boone, Callaway, Cooper, Howard, Marion, Lafayette, Pike, Randolph, St. Charles, and Saline.

The treatment of slaves varied greatly, depending upon the moods and attitudes of individual masters. Even the best-treated black slave stood in a servile position to all of white society. From the owner's point of view, slavery was justified on economic, spiritual, and social grounds. Blacks were regarded as inferior. The master argued that he was doing them a favor by enslaving and caring for them. (Some slaveholders even went so far as to argue that blacks were grateful to whites for their enslavement.) Nobody expressed this idea better than United States Senator James Green of Lewis County. In 1849 he wrote that of the two races, "one [was] vastly inferior to the other." As the inferior race, blacks were obligated to be subservient to whites in all things. For the black, this arrangement resulted in an "immense good, an incalculable benefit, both moral and physical." According to Green, blacks were not only inferior to whites, but they were "happy inferiors": "Our Negro is a sleek, fat-sided fellow. He loves to eat and to laugh, and give him his bellyfull and he is as happy as a prince. Work is his element. Meat and bread and the banjo are his happiness." Present scholarship does not accept this description of the slave; it is a stereotype invented by slaveowners in response to attacks by abolitionists upon slavery.

Slavery was an inhumane institution. Slaves were supposed to be protected by law from excessively harsh treatment. Any person found guilty of cruel or inhuman treatment of slaves was fined or sent to jail, but slaveholders paid little or no attention to the law. Cruel treatment, such as a female slave whose master had left her hanging by her thumbs in St. Louis in 1839, was not uncommon.

The harsh system of slavery was able to exist only by forcing blacks to stand in awe of whites. Slaveholders as a group were willing to use whatever means they could to instill fear into slaves. They believed a fearful slave would also be an obedient slave. But fear was a double-edged sword. Masters realized that poor treatment of slaves could inspire resentment. Consequently, they sought an elaborate system of laws to protect themselves, their families, and their communities against any semblance of black resistance. They tried to enlist the support of nonslaveholding whites. Through religion, philosophy, law, and social practice, they tried to convince the lowliest white person that he was better than the most cultured and intelligent black. Whites of all classes were encouraged to believe that they could some day enhance their social status by becoming slaveowners, in spite of the fact that seven out of eight Missouri families would never own slaves.

Missouri's slave codes illustrate the general attitude toward blacks during the antebellum period. Slaves were designated as personal property to be taxed, bought, and sold just like any other property. In 1835 Joseph Hardeman of Cole County offered for sale "one Negro man, one Negro woman, and three children ages 10, 12, and 16." Hardeman noted that the "man is a good plowman, woman and children good field hands." Likewise, in 1851 Edward Lewis and his wife listed a young black with animals and other miscellaneous merchandise they had for sale: "One negro boy named Tom aged about fourteen years, one Bay Mare aged three this spring. One yoke of steers aged three years this spring, three young cows, one yearling mule, sixty barrels of corn all for the sum of nine hundred and fifty-five dollars."

Food, clothing, shelter, and medical attention in most cases rested in the capricious hands of the owners. Whether the slave had sufficient food has always been a highly debated question. One student of Cole County slavery says that blacks had an unbalanced diet of cornbread and potatoes. Another historian says that slaves occasionally had pork, beef, or mutton. Of course, a master might allow the slave a little time on Saturday or Sunday to grow a few vegetables. The enterprising slave might supplement his diet with possums, rabbits, squirrels, or fish. Filmore Taylor Hancock, a slave born near Springfield in 1851, remembered that he and his brothers and sisters got special consideration in terms of food because "our ol' granny was de white folk's cook. . . . We got to eat what de white folks did. Up to de cabins where de odder niggers was, had salt meat, cabbage, 'taters, an' shortenin' bread three times a day. We all had plenty vegetables, we raised ourselves. . . . Onced a week we had hot biscuits." Tishey Taylor, born in New Madrid County described the food given out by her master:

> Some of them slaves cooks in their cabin, not what they wanted but "marse" gibd 'em, most times was beans an' 'tators and corn bread and milk, and some times 'round hog killin' time be pass out the "jowl meat."
> I jest don' member but it seems we did eat three times a day. I wus allays so glad to hear dat bell ring 'else a horn blow. Youse seed that kind of shell like called "Konk horn"—and could that "nigger" blow lowd!

While some of the slaves thought their diet was at least "moderate," they complained about the manner in which they had to eat. Dave Harper, born in Montgomery County, reported:

> We was fed just moderate. Dere was fifteen hands. When day come in at noon, day ate from de big old kettle where de old colored women had cooked de food. De next morning after he bought me, de boss carried me to de old woman and told her to take care of me. Dat morning de kettle was full of spare ribs and de people fished dem out with sticks. I didn't see no knives or forks. Whey dey asked me why I din't get something to eat, I asked 'bout dem and a table where I could eat. De overseer just cried.

Young Dave Harper had been used to eating at a table, but Louis Hill, who was born in Farmington, was not: "All us kids ate on da floor frum da plate an da biggest dog got da mos." But some slaves worried that they and their children would go hungry. Hattie Matthews reported a tale told by her mother:

> De scraps from the white folk's table was all thrown into a kettle. Ma muthur ud stan clos by an she ud grab in the kettle with both hans an eat whatber she got. Den, after all the grown slaves did dis dey wud call 'pot liquor time' an de childr'n ud run to de kettle an drink wat wuz in de bott'm ob de kettle. Dis was generally de juice or water frum greens. Sometimes de childr'n got a

piece ob cornbread. Dis wuz all de childr'n got ta eat an dey was always hungry.

A few slaves claimed they had to eat rotten or spoiled food. Harriet Casey, born in Farmington, related the following: "To eat we had corn-meal and fried meat dat had been eaten by bugs. We had some gravy and all ate 'round de pan like pigs eating slop. And we had a tin cup of sour milk to drink. Sometimes we would have ginger bread—dis was 'bout twice a year. . . . Once it got so cold dat de chickens froze and fell out of the trees and de mistress gave each of us a chicken to eat."

Sometimes the slaves resorted to trickery to get such extras as coffee. Charlie Richardson, born in Warrensburg, reported that slaves would sometimes burn the grain while they were drying it in preparation for making their master's coffee, hoping that he would give the burned grain to them so that they could make coffee for themselves. "Some times they got whupped for burnin' it cause he knowed they burned it too much for his coffee, on purpose—jest so they'd git it."

Housing for slaves varied but was generally inadequate. If only one or two slaves were owned, they might sleep in the master's house. If several were owned, they generally lived in cabins where they cooked, slept, and socialized. Their quarters gave them little privacy and were not spacious by any means. Daniel Ligon of Lewis County had only two houses for ten slaves. The quarters of another owner consisted of small log cabins about twelve-to-fourteen-feet square, an area smaller than most present-day bedrooms. In Cole County, slaves were herded into cramped quarters like cattle. At one point there were 987 slaves in the county sharing only ninety cabins, an average of nearly eleven slaves per cabin. Harriet Casey claimed that the cabin her family lived in consisted of "one room, one door, and one fireplace."

The quality of the slaves' quarters depended on individual masters. Some masters provided barely livable quarters, while others provided roomy and comfortable living space. Typically, quarters were hot in the summer, cold in the winter, poorly lighted, and unsanitary. Windows were often only holes in a wall, lacking glass panes and covered with paper or cloth. Charlie Richardson remembered the construction of the slave cabins as being "made of good old Missouri logs daubed with mud, and the chimney was made of sticks daubed with mud." Annie Bridges, born in St. Francois County, lived in a log cabin with two rooms, a floor, and "a bed, but hit hadn't no mattress; jus' roped an' cord'd—holes wuz in de side ob de bed, soo's de ropes cud go thru."

Some masters clothed their slaves better than others, but most looked for the cheapest solution. Materials used were largely tow cloth, white and striped linsey-woolsey, and heavy brown jeans. Advertisements for a runaway slaves often described how slaves might be clothed: a slave who ran away in 1835 carried with him "two cotton shirts, one pair of linen pants, one green blanket, a coat, one pair of brown pants, and an old fur coat." A newspaper in 1847 stated that R. C. Cordell of Jefferson City, clothed three slaves for seventy-nine dollars: Lydia for twenty-four dollars for two years, Mary Ann for fifteen dollars for two years, and Penney for forty dollars for one year. An old slave related that the Missouri slaves generally received two pairs of trousers, two shirts, and a hat in the summer; a coat, a pair of trousers, and a pair of shoes in the winter.

Boys and girls generally wore a gownlike garment until they were about ten to fourteen years old. Boys who wore such gowns were called "shirttail boys." Louis Hill described the garment as "a straight slip like a night gown and hit fastened round the neck. . . . Tah dis off an we was naked." Many of the slaves reported that their mothers made most of their clothes. George Bollinger's "mammy wus a good cook 'en she cud spin en weave. She made all de clothes we wore. Us chillunns never wore no pants—jes sumpin like a long shirt made o' homespun." Still another slave remembers: "We all wore homespun clothes, made of wool mostly. Mother carded, spun and wove all our clothes."

Some slaves had plenty of clothing; others had barely any at all. Sarah Waggoners had two dresses: one for working and one for dressing up. Annie Bridges, on the other hand, complained about the clothing and the lack of footwear: "We all wore jeans an' wrap'd and ole sack 'round our legs; most time we went barefoot." Many of the slaves complained about having gone barefoot. Of course, during the spring and summer Missouri's climate would allow going barefoot without much fear of ill health. However, during the fall and winter, slaves forced to go barefoot would run a high chance of sickness. Harriet Casey claimed: "We had no shoes even in winter—I can't 'member having good clothes." Another former slave remembered often going after cows barefoot "when dere was more than a foot of snow on de ground."

Blacks who suffered from physical illnesses were generally cared for by their fellow slaves. Sometimes the master might call a doctor. More often than not, however, doctors were not available since the frontier did not lend itself to attracting medical practitioners any more than the rural community does today. The slave midwife generally delivered the children and frequently cared for the master's offspring. Because of the scarcity of doctors, there were often two or three slaves in a surrounding area who served as doctors for the slave population in a county. Many of these slave doctors also treated white patients, such as Gus Smith's grandfather, Godfry, a slave from Osage County, who apparently possessed a rare talent for curing burns. Gus Smith remembered his grandfather as "an old fashion herb doctor. . . . Everybody knew him in that country and he doctored among the white people. . . . He went over thirty miles around to people who sent for him. . . . Lots of cases that other doctors gave up, he went and 'raised them.' He could cure anything." Slave doctors practiced folk medicine using herbs and plants found in the nearby woods, such as white root, remedy weed, sarsaparilla root, cherry tree bark, pennyroyal, chamomile root, and ginseng, to cure an assortment of ailments.

Although Missouri slaves were generally worked from sunup to sundown during the week, they were often allowed Sunday afternoons to themselves. During that time, they might manufacture small articles for sale, perform odd jobs, or tend to a small plot of land adjoining the slave quarters. At times they were allowed to sing, swim, and dance in the evening; occasionally they attended a circus. Days off from work, and the festivities that surrounded them, often fostered a feeling of interdependence and community among the slaves that gave them a sense of identity and sustained them against the dehumanizing conditions of slavery. William Black remembered how the slaves spent the few hours each day that they were allowed to themselves, and how they oftentimes combined work with entertainment: "In the evening when the work was all done we would sit around and play marbles and sing songs. We made our songs up as we went along. Sometimes there would be a corn shuckin' and that is when we had a good time, but we always shucked a lot of that corn."

Mark Discus recalled: "Sometimes we'ud get a little time offen from work if the weather was too bad or on Sunday. We mostly tried to see who could lift the mos'. We would rassel too. Sometimes we pitched horse shoes, and sometimes we went possum huntin'." Gus Smith remembered holidays as a time of music: "We all had good times along with the work. . . . We had quiltin's, dancin', makin' rails, for days at a time. . . . In times of our holidays, we always had our own musicians. Sometimes we sent ten or twelve miles for a fiddler. He'd stay a week or so in one place and then he would go on to the next farm, maybe four or five miles away, and they had a good time for a week."

The slaves' favorite time of the year was Christmas because they would get a week or more of holiday. George Jackson Simpson, born in Crawford County in 1854, remembered his master "let us have what was called 'Christmas Week.' On the fourth of July, the white people's day, we could be at their gatherings, but it was not really our holiday. Christmas was our time. We had big dances and dinners. We celebrated at different houses and places. We danced to fiddle and tambourine music. . . . That was the only holiday we had, but we did well to get that in those days." Malinda Discus, a Missouri slave born in 1859, said: "Christmas was always a time we liked. If we could manage to say 'Christmas gift' to any of the Master's family on Christmas morning before they spoke to us, they would have to give us a gift of some kind. We always mostly were first. The gift might be some clothes or a stick of candy. Store candy—as we called it—was a real treat."

Master and slave generally attended the same church. The structure of religious worship left no doubt in the slave's mind of his inferiority. Generally, slaves were physically separated from their masters and other whites either in a loft above the rest of the congregation or in a special section of pews at the rear of the meetinghouse. They often heard sermons in which white ministers counseled them to be obedient and submissive to their masters. Black communicants participated in the sacraments only after all the whites had partaken. Even in death the races were generally separated. There were almost always "white" and "colored" cemeteries in every area of the state occupied by blacks. Isabelle Henderson remembered that the blacks were segregated at the church she attended: "I remember j'inin' the white folks church in old Cambridge. They had a gallery for the slaves." Henderson also recalled that in church "sometimes the slaves did funny things. There was one old woman named Aunt Cindy. . . . One Sunday she got 'happy' and commenced shoutin' and throwin' herself about. White folks in the seats below hurried to get out from under the gallery, fearin' Aunt Cindy, was goin' to lose her balance and fall on them."

The segregation made another Missouri slave, Malinda Discus, question the contradictions inherent in the slave system: "Yes, our Master took his slaves to meetin' with him. They had one corner where they sat with the slaves of other people. There was always something about that I couldn't understand. They treated the colored folks like animals and would not hesitate to sell and separate them, yet they seemed to think they had souls and tried to make Christians of them." Richard Bruner attended a church that was less segregated: "We went to dey white folks church on Sundays. When we went to camp meeting we all went to de mourners bench together. De mourners bench stretch clear across de front of de Arbor; de whites and de blacks, we all jest fell down at de mourners bench and got religion at de same place."

The Missouri slave codes forbade the marriage of slaves. Sometimes a man and woman just "took up" with each other. Other times they were ordered to live together by the master. As far as whites were concerned, the sale of one or the other of the marriage partners ended the relationship. Mark Discus remembered that his master, a Presbyterian preacher, separated his mother and father and ten brothers and sisters: "Yes suh, there was ten children of we'uns and we was all separated. I was sold when I was four years old, they said, for three hundred and fifty dollars. . . . I seen my brothers and sisters [after being separated] but they had different names. Then I heard my Pappy had died. I don't remember him. My Mammy was sold down South and I never seen her again 'til after the war was over." Discus also remembered that slaves often "just had a ceremony and a preacher or some officer married 'em, but after awhile they made 'em get a license. I don't think my Pappy and Mammy had a license but their master was a preacher, as I said, and he married them alright."

The slave family, although often separated by sale and death, was the stabilizing unit of the slave community. The slave family socialized children, taught them folklore and folk songs and herbal remedies, buffered them against the dehumanizing effects of slavery, instructed them in schemes of resistance, and trained them how to survive in a hostile society as black slaves. In place of blood relatives sold away, the slave community ingeniously devised patterns of "fictive kinship" in which other slaves who were unrelated would care for and provide for orphaned or parentless children as "grannies," "aunts," or "uncles."

Filmore Taylor Hancock remembered his "ol' granny," the masters' cook, "helped look after us" after his mother died. Even in death the bonds of the slave family remained strong. When interviewed in Rolla in 1937, the eighty-six-year-old Hancock desired to be buried with his parents: "If I can leave enough, when I die, I want to be buried at the Union Graveyard in Greene County, Missouri, where my mammy is buried since 1858. . . . My daddy was buried there in 1863." The results of the separation of slave families would play out in dramatic fashion after emancipation as many families and relatives who had not seen one another in years were joyously reunited, and as many others were tragically doomed to search unsuccessfully for their loved ones, never to see them again. The law never recognized slave marriages. It considered them merely moral agreements with no legal force. After the Civil War, Missouri required all ex-slaves in the state who were living together as man and wife to be remarried "legally."

Slaves were degraded by laws that divided them further from the rest of society. Punishments were barbarous. The general crudeness of frontier justice was made even worse by the master's fear of rebellious or disobedient slaves. A slaveowner who was surrounded by free territory on three sides (Illinois, Iowa, and Kansas) was prompted to take strict precautions to keep his slaves secure. To protect the master and community against slave uprisings, Missouri's statutes included restrictions that prohibited slaves from carrying arms without a license from the justice of the peace. If a gun was found on a slave, it could be taken away, and he or she could receive thirty-nine lashes on his or her bare back. Slaves found guilty of crimes such as conspiracy, rebellion, or murder were to be put to death.

The slaveowner had a great deal of discretion in the punishment of his slaves. Gus Smith recalled that his master, Bill Messersmith, "a Pennsylvania Dutchman," was "as good a man as ever lived": "My master let us come and go pretty much as we pleased. In fact we had much more freedom than the most of the slaves had in those days. . . . We had it so much better than other slaves that our neighbors would not let their slaves associate with us, for fear we would put 'devilment' in their heads, for we had too much freedom." But Smith's neighbor "ol' man Thornton" was a cruel master, who

> did not allow his slaves to go anyplace. . . . He was mean to his slaves. He whupped them all the time. I've seen their clothes sticking to their backs, from blood and scabs, being cut up with the cowhide. He just whupped them because he could. . . . I remember he had a nigger woman about seventy years old on his place. The Thorntons did not feed their slaves good; they were nearly starved. One night that ol' woman was so hungry she stole a chicken from her marster—ol' Thornton—and was cooking it in her cabin. He found it out some way and started to her cabin, and caught her, while she had it on boiling. He was so mad, he told her to get a spoon and eat every bite before she stopped. It was scalding hot but he made her do it. She died right away, her insides burned."

Ed Craddock, born about 1858 near Marshall, Missouri, told a story his father had told him about the cruel punishment of a slave: "A slave right here in Marshall angered his master, was chained to a hemp-brake on a cold night and left to freeze to death, which he did." Another slave, Mary Martha Bolden, born in 1861 on John Lindsey's farm six miles east of Troy, Missouri, was a small girl when she saw "the master and two other men whip three men slaves, for running off. The whipping was unmerciful." And Mark Discus's master once "whooped me 'til the blood run offen my heels for breakin' an axe handle. We knowed to step when he yelled at us."

Often a slave was punished in the presence of other slaves as a dramatic lesson of what would happen to disobedient slaves. The most frequent punishment was whipping. The usual instrument was a wooden handle attached to a flat piece of leather belting about a quarter of an inch thick. The number of lashes varied from ten to one hundred. Such a whip caused blisters, frequently drew blood, and sometimes left permanent scars. Occasionally slaves were beaten with sticks or anything else that might come to the master's hand. Usually, however, the master tried to avoid permanently marking a slave. A scarred slave would be regarded by a prospective buyer as mean or having made attempts to escape. His potential value could be lessen considerably.

Slaves were forbidden to have sexual relations with white women. Blacks or mulattoes who assaulted or attempted to assault a white woman could be killed or mutilated, often by castration. Rape of a black woman by a white man was less serious in the eyes of the law, however. Sexual assault of a slave woman by a white man was not considered an offense against the woman: it was only a case of trespassing on the master's "property." Many slave children were the result of interracial sexual unions, sometimes rapes, between white masters and their slave women. George Jackson Simpson was the son of his master: "My mother was quarter Indian. . . . She was only fifteen when I was born. My master, Jim Simpson a white man was also my father. I did not know who my father was until my mother told me when I was seventeen years old. What was done in slavery days, was simply done and not much thought of it."

Slaves who offered resistance to their owners and overseers could receive thirty-nine lashes. A slave guilty of striking a white person, except in self-defense, was to be punished at the discretion of the justice of the peace. The punishment was not to exceed thirty-nine lashes, which was also the penalty for disturbing church service by "noise, riotous or disorderly conduct." Any person providing liquor to a slave got twenty-five lashes on his bare back and time in jail. Blacks were also declared incompetent as witnesses in legal cases involving whites. They could, however, testify against each other.

By 1847 Missouri slaveowners were extremely fearful of slave insurrections. News of uprisings in the southern states further fueled their fears. Convinced that slaves rebelled because they were reading abolitionist literature, whites sought to stop rebellions by adopting an ordinance that specifically prohibited the education of blacks. Anyone operating a school for Negroes or mulattoes, or teaching reading or writing to any Negro or mulatto in Missouri, could be punished with a fine of not less than five hundred dollars and sentenced up to six months in jail. Bill Sims remembered that "slaves were never allowed to talk to white people other than their masters or someone their masters knew, as they were afraid the white man might have the slave run away. The masters aimed to keep their slaves in ignorance." Filmore Taylor Hancock feared being "kotched wid a book, to read or try to be educated." Despite the state law prohibiting the education of blacks, Emma Knight said her "master's girls taught us to read and write."

One of the most important institutions established in the slave states to guard against slave plots and insurrection was the slave patrols. Legislation was designed authorizing each county to set up its own patrols in Missouri in 1823. The patrols were to ensure that slaves were not traveling abroad at night without their master's consent. Patrols also visited slave quarters to guarantee that there were no unlawful assemblies of slaves. Thirty-nine lashes was the punishment for such illegal activity if the patrol took the slave before the justice of the peace; however, without the master's permission punishment by the "patterollers," as some slaves called them, was limited to ten lashes. Richard Bruner recalled: "Whenever us niggas on one plantation got obstreporous, white folks hawns dey blowed. When de neighbors heard dat hawn hyar dey come to hep make dat obstreporous nigga behave."

As the intensity of the antislavery struggle increased in the years immediately preceding the Civil War, strenuous local laws were passed to control the slaves. In most Missouri cities all blacks without a pass had to be off the street at nine o'clock at night unless they were on business for their master. Special permission had to be secured from the master for all special meetings, and all such persons had to be home by ten o'clock. Passes were good for twenty-four hours only, and the city constable had to see that meetings were orderly.

Compensation of patrol members varied. Sometimes they received no pay—except the satisfaction of keeping blacks "in their place." Patrols were mostly made up of poor and working-class whites, young men who excelled in taking undue advantage of blacks, particularly of the women and girls. Occasionally slaveowners served as patrollers. In Cole County, patrolmen were paid eight cents an hour in 1851 and twenty-five cents an hour in 1852. Pay for patrolmen apparently increased as fear engendered by the antislavery movement intensified. Still, five members of the Jefferson City patrol served for the paltry sum of $28.50 for a year's work.

The "intractable" slave always had one major fear that haunted him continuously: the prospect of being sold away from his family, especially "down South." This was the ultimate legal form of social control open to the master. It was also the most brutal. Masters frequently sold intractable or disobedient slaves down South, away from their families. Filmore Taylor Hancock's uncle was sold after a confrontation with his master:

One time my ol marster Hancock, got mad at my uncle, who was a growed up nigger. Ol marse wanted to whup him. He tried to make my uncle put his head twixt his [ol marster's] knees. My uncle didn't offer to fight him, but twisted him roun' an' roun' tryin' to get his head out. He gave one twist dat throwed ol marse down to de groun'. My uncle jumped an' run an' jumped obber de fence. . . . But ol Marse sure got mad when my uncle run. So he sold him to a man named Dokes—a nigger trader ob dat neighborhood. Dokes bought niggers an' sold dem on de block in St. Louis.

The heavy demand for black slaves in the South meant that there was always a buyer from that region ready to purchase a Missouri slave. Several slave dealers carried on the trade in Missouri, buying and selling blacks for the cotton, rice, and sugar fields of the South. St. Louis was the largest slave market in the state. Slave dealers there advertised in various counties for salable slaves. In 1845 W. Edgerton, a St. Louis dealer, advertised in the *Jefferson Inquirer:* "The undersigned proposes remaining a few weeks in this city for the purpose of purchasing a few Negro slaves. Persons having young slaves for sale will find this a favorable opportunity to sell. His rooms are in the national hotel."

St. Louis companies such as Blakey and McAfee kept an agent in the state capital in the early 1850s, offering "highest prices for Negroes of every description." They boasted of their facilities as being "well suited for the boarding and safe keeping of Negroes sent to this market for sale." Competing with them was yet another St. Louis firm, Bolton, Dickens and Company. In 1853 the latter firm advertised in the *Jefferson Examiner* for one thousand slaves.

None of the slave states admitted to the breeding of slaves, and the question of Missouri's involvement in that practice remains debatable. Still, William Wells Brown, an escaped slave who became an antislavery speaker and novelist, argued that slave breeding occurred in Missouri and that the children born of such unions were sold down South. Another former slave claimed that a neighboring master "used to have me come over and father children; you know, I was big and strong and made big strong slaves."

Suggested Readings

Two of the best works on slavery in Missouri are dissertations: Donnie D. Bellamy, "Slavery, Emancipation, and Racism in Missouri, 1850–1865" (University of Missouri–Columbia, 1970); and Robert William Duffner,

"Slavery in Missouri River Counties, 1820–1865" (University of Missouri–Columbia, 1974).

One of the most promising trends in the study of slavery has been the interest shown in local studies. The following articles are good examples: Lyle W. Dorsett, "Slaveholding in Jackson County, Missouri," *Bulletin* 20 (October 1963): 33–34; George R. Lee, "Slavery and Emancipation in Lewis County, Missouri," *Missouri Historical Review* 65 (April 1971): 294–317; James William McGettigan, Jr., "Boone County Slaves: Sales, Estate Divisions and Families, 1820–1865," Parts 1 and 2, *Missouri Historical Review* 72 (January and April 1978): 176–97 and 271–95; Philip V. Scarpino, "Slavery in Callaway County, Missouri: 1845–1855," Parts 1 and 2, *Missouri Historical Review* 71 (October and April 1976–1977): 22–43 and 266–83; and Barbara L. Green, "Slave Labor at the Maramec Iron Works, 1820–1850," *Missouri Historical Review* 73 (January 1979): 150–64.

More recently, R. Douglas Hurt has written about slavery in a seven-county area along the Missouri River, *Agriculture and Slavery in Missouri's Little Dixie* (Columbia: University of Missouri Press, 1992). Also helpful is W. Sherman Savage, "Contest over Slavery between Illinois and Missouri," *Journal of Negro History* 28 (July 1943): 311–45.

The comments from ex-slaves used in this chapter are taken from the following: George P. Rawick, gen. ed., *The American Slave: A Composite Autobiography*, vol. 11 of *Missouri Narratives* (Westport, Conn.: Greenwood Publishing Co., 1972); Rawick, *The American Slave: A Composite Autobiography*, in *Arkansas, Colorado, Minnesota, Missouri, Oregon and Washington Narratives* (Westport, Conn.: Greenwood Press, 1977); and, John W. Blassingame, ed., *Slave Testimony: Two Centuries of Letters, Speeches, Interviews, and Autobiographies* (Baton Rouge: Louisiana State University Press, 1977).

Although not dealing directly with Missouri, Julius Lester's *To Be a Slave* (New York: Dial Books, 1968) is one of the best studies available that gives the reader a detailed sense of what it was like "to be a slave." Michael Tadman, *Speculators and Slaves: Masters, Traders, and Slaves in the Old South* (Madison: University of Wisconsin Press, 1989), found no convincing evidence for the systematic breeding of slaves in Missouri or any other border state.

3

The Slave Strikes Back

The Reaction to Bondage

The Missouri slave was not the docile, happy Sambo that many masters and historians once claimed he was. All of the available evidence suggests that black slaves hated their servile role in the white man's world, and they were quite creative in their protests against the way of life imposed upon them. Their ways of protest were numerous, both nonviolent and violent.

The protest that whites feared most was rebellion. The strength of their numbers meant that at least temporarily the rebelling slaves were unstoppable and able to slay or overcome an individual master or even a small white community. Black rebellion sometimes began with the Africans captured by white slavers and shipped to the New World. While on the ocean voyage, Africans occasionally rose in mutiny against the shipmaster and attempted to kill the entire crew in their effort to return home. The most famous incident was the mutiny aboard the Spanish ship *Amistad* in 1839 when slaves took over the ship but were unable to navigate back to Africa.

Once the slave was sold to his or her master, the chances of collective rebellion lessened. Many slaveowners did not treat their slaves so brutally as to inspire rebellion or other retaliation, but even the kindliest slaveowner feared that his slaves might someday rebel. This fear was heightened by the news of rebellion elsewhere in the United States. In 1831 Nat Turner and sixty to seventy other slaves banded together in Virginia and killed Turner's owner and nearly sixty other whites. But slave rebellions were doomed to fail because the whites had superior forces: the Virginia militia captured and executed twenty of the rebels, including Turner, and whites in the area reacted by murdering another one hundred innocent slaves. Still, slaveowners across the country feared that they, like Turner's master, would be slaughtered before those forces could be deployed. The restrictive and harsh slave codes, especially the denial of education, were designed to suppress any potential uprising. Turner had been an educated preacher, who believed God had given him a mission to free the slaves.

There is no evidence that an armed revolt of slaves ever succeeded in Missouri; indeed, from our vantage point today we can see that the chances of success were fewer in Missouri because blacks comprised a much smaller percentage of the population than in the deep South. There were, however, at least two narrow misses in the state. In November 1849, the McCutchen farm in Lewis County was the scene of potential insurrection that was barely nipped in time. McCutchen was awakened one night by voices coming from a kitchen that was separated from his house by a passageway. Soon a slave from an adjoining farm owned by John Miller approached McCutchen demanding guns. The black man moved toward the gun rack, at which point McCutchen called to his slaves for help. The slaves failed to respond, and McCutchen took his family and fled into the night. He went to the Miller farm where the two slaveowners decided to send out a general alert.

By morning thirty armed whites were approaching the McCutchen farm. They found that slaves from four families had barricaded themselves in the house. The slaves were armed with three guns, butcher knives, and clubs. The slaveowners ordered the blacks to surrender. One of the slaves, John, apparently the leader, came out. Instead of surrendering, however, he threatened Captain Blair with his corn knife. Someone in the crowd shot the slave on John Miller's order, but the slave kept coming at Blair. A second shot killed him.

Once their leader was dead, the other slaves surrendered. Ultimately, all of them were sold down South. For months after the aborted rebellion, controversy raged in Lewis County about what had inspired the Miller and McCutchen slaves. Some argued that a slave woman named Lin was behind the plot. She was alleged to have concocted a strong potion of coffee and tea and given it to the slaves to make them powerful. Others laid the blame for inciting the adults on Henry, Lin's ten-year-old grandson, who had visions of all whites being dead. Still others blamed Senator Thomas Hart Benton, who had been making antislavery speeches in the state the previous spring. Many believed that white abolitionists from a place called Gregory's Landing were helping the rebellious slaves escape, although some speculated their real goal was to get the slaves on board a boat and sell them down South.

In late December 1859, near Bolivar, a group of drunken slaves who had been celebrating Christmas revolted and attacked whites with rocks and clubs. The white community was able to gather a sufficient force to drive the rebellious slaves into the nearby woods. During the pursuit it was reported that both sides freely exchanged gunfire. That same evening the slaves threatened to burn the town, but all their "attempts were foiled." One slave was said to be badly wounded and several others were captured and jailed. A master of some of the rebels was also seriously wounded and barely escaped with his life. During a hastily called town meeting, a "vigilance committee" was appointed to discover which slaves had taken part in the revolt. Meanwhile, a "mounted company" continued to search the woods for other insurrectionists. Several slaves in the area were severely punished as a result of the fear generated by this revolt.

Although Missouri slaves rarely united to rebel violently against their masters, many did strike out in other ways at the institution of slavery and the whites who enforced it. Because slavery was basically a profit-motivated economic system, slaves sometimes sought to make slavery as unprofitable as possible by breaking the master's tools, by crippling or killing his livestock, and by slowing down the pace of their work. Others feigned illness or ignorance of how to do a particular job, allowed the animals to stray, or pulled up plants instead of weeds.

Tony, a Boone County slave, took out his frustrations on his master's livestock. He had been accused of stealing a hog. He worked at a University of Missouri laboratory as a janitor, so in anger he stole a bottle of acid and poured it on his master's mules. He confessed to the deed following his arrest. The court convicted Tony and sentenced him to thirty-nine lashes on his bare back. He was taken before a meat market, where observers could readily watch, and then strung up and whipped. Every blow, it is said, drew blood or raised a blister. Later he was freed by his master and went to Iowa. In 1857 another slave named Gilbert allegedly cut the throat of a mare belonging to Charles Crane. Gilbert was brought to trial and convicted. Fortunately for Gilbert, the Missouri Supreme Court later overturned his conviction on a legal technicality.

Stealing by slaves was also a common practice. To the slave, "taking" from his master or any whites was regarded as a form of compensation for his or her unpaid labor. A Missouri slave named Joe was arrested for stealing a fiddle and other goods worth a total value of two dollars. He was tried before a justice of the peace, convicted, and whipped. Another such crime occurred in Callaway County in 1841. A slave named Carter broke into a store at night and took about sixteen dollars. He was brought to trial in that county and found guilty. His punishment was not mentioned, but his master was obliged to pay all costs.

Arson was a popular form of slave protest. Arsonists could start fires in buildings belonging to whites who had inspired their wrath, and the whites would have a difficult time fixing the blame on a particular individual. In Howard County in 1847, a slave owned by Mr. Reed was arrested for burning his master's property. He was convicted and exiled for twenty years. Nine years later, a female slave belonging to Mr. Towler in the same county was accused of burning a stable belonging to Mr. Phillips, who brought suit against Towler for damages. During the trial the slave had been allowed to testify, although Towler's counsel had objected to the use of her testimony. Towler meanwhile died, and the suit was continued against the administrator of his estate. In 1844 a slave named Sam was said to have entered the house of John G. Koenig of Jefferson County, struck him with a club, robbed him, and set fire to the house. This case is unusual because Sam was acquitted for lack of evidence, in spite of the fact that he had in his possession some of Koenig's belongings.

Other slaves struck at their masters by daring to engage in what whites considered to be one of the most heinous of crimes: sexual relations with white women. Elaborate legal codes had been devised to protect white women from the slaves. A slave found guilty of raping a white female could expect to be castrated or even killed.

In mid-August of 1853, Hiram, a Boone County slave, was accused of attempting to rape a fifteen-year-old white girl. Two justices tried Hiram and found him not guilty, but local residents were convinced the slave was guilty and refused to accept the judgement. A new trial began in Columbia on August 20, 1853, with James S. Rollins, a founder of the University of Missouri and future congressman, retained by Hiram's owner to serve as the slave's defense counsel. During the proceedings, a mob rushed the courtroom and dragged the slave into the street, intent on lynching him. However, Rollins and several other prominent Columbians persuaded the mob that the slave deserved the right to a fair trial. The next day Hiram confessed to the crime. Meanwhile, some angry and impatient residents organized a citizen's committee to deal swift punishment to the slave. Led by Eli E. Bass, the largest Boone County slaveholder, the citizen's committee removed Hiram from the county jail and lynched him on the outskirts of Columbia. The state prosecutor, Odon Guitar, later a Union general, reportedly urged the vigilantes to hang Hiram "cooly, and do it decently in order." The antebellum extralegal murder of Hiram set a bloody precedent for mob lynchings in Missouri during the last half of the nineteenth and first half of the twentieth centuries.

The most extreme form of protest against enslavement was murder. On occasion, a Missouri slave sought to break the shackles of bondage by killing his or her master. In 1848 Patsy, a Boone County slave, was convicted of attempting to poison her mistress by putting arsenic in her milk. She was sentenced to receive thirty-nine lashes on her bare back "well laid on" and to be jailed for sixty days. Seven years later another slave tried to poison her master's child; he too was sentenced to thirty-nine lashes "well laid on."

In 1838 a slave woman named Fannie allegedly murdered two boys belonging to William Prewitt of Lincoln County. The boys had received permission to pick some peaches in an orchard owned by Fannie's master, and it was the last time the boys were seen alive. Four days later the sheriff arrested Fannie, her husband, and their young son. The officer resorted to threats of dire punishment to force Elick, Fannie's son, to incriminate his mother as the murderer. According to Elick, the sheriff and another man threatened to hang him unless he turned informer. Strung up, with a rope around his neck, the terrified youth accused his mother of killing the boys when they came for peaches. Elick made that statement, however, only after the sheriff had assured him that the remainder of the family had already been hanged. Although Fannie was convicted and sentenced to be hanged, no concrete incriminating evidence against her was found. A stick with what was supposed to be blood and the two naked bodies of the victims were all the evidence against Fannie. However, the brutal manner in which a child was forced to condemn his mother was too much for the state supreme court to accept. The court reversed the decision.

Once the mere threat of punishment inspired murder. In Boone County, 1837, James T. Paints hired William Robinson's slave Joe to split rails and sent Joe to the woods alone. Upon his return, Paints asked him how many rails he had split. Paints later inspected Joe's work and discovered the slave had lied concerning the number of rails split. The following day Paints accompanied Joe to the woods where the two began splitting rails. When they sat down to rest, Paints began telling the slave how severe the punishment was for lying, implying that Joe was going to be whipped. Joe seized an ax and struck Paints upon the head, killing him instantly; then he hid the body and fled. After his arrest, he confessed to the crime and was lodged in the county jail to await trial. The verdict was guilty, and the slave was sentenced to death by hanging. The sentence was carried out on November 13, 1837.

In 1860 Miss Susan Jemima Barnes had remained at home in Callaway County while the rest of her family went for a visit. Upon returning they found her dead upon the floor. Practically all of her facial and cranial bones had been crushed, and she had been stabbed a number of times as well. After the coroner's inquest, suspicion was cast upon Teney, a female slave, who, it was charged, was usually impudent and insolent unless a white man was around. Teney denied the accusation first but later confessed when one of her bloodstained dresses was found hidden in a cornfield. The county constable had started to Fulton with Teney in custody when he was overtaken by an outraged mob. The mob threatened the constable and forced him to turn Teney over to them. They immediately hanged her from a nearby tree.

The first and youngest female to be executed for murder in Missouri was a seventeen-year-old slave named Mary. Mary was charged with drowning Vienna Jane Brinker near Steelville in 1837. On May 14, 1837, Brinker had sent his teenage slave Mary after wood. Mary took the child Vienna with her, but when she returned the child was nowhere in sight. Mary was questioned about the missing child but denied any knowledge of her whereabouts. Mary then ran off in the direction of a small stream of water and that area was searched by Brinker and a couple of his neighbors. The body of the drowned child was soon discovered. What appeared to be a mark from a blow was spotted on the child's head. Mary was tied to a log and further questioned by one of the neighbors. The neighbor then began to act as though he was going to whip Mary, which made her confess that she had thrown the child in the water. When the child rose up in the water, Mary struck her with a stick.

Mary was brought before the Crawford County justice of the peace where she again confessed. She was held at the Potosi jail until her trial began some three months later. The court appointed three attorneys to represent Mary. The court even instructed the jury of twelve white men that Mary's confession was only admissible if made "of her own free will and not under the influence of hope or fear, torture or pain." The trial began on August 16, 1837, and by August 18 the jury found her guilty of first degree murder. The next day the judge dismissed a defense motion for a new trial, and sentenced Mary to hang on September 30, 1837. Her attorney filed an appeal with the Missouri Supreme Court.

In September the supreme court overturned Mary's conviction and granted her a new trial. The grounds for the new trial were that the prosecution did not clearly state if the mode of death was drowning or the blow to the head, and that the prosecution had examined the witnesses even after agreeing with Mary's attorneys that the evidence be closed. Because of an unsuccessful change of venue motion, Mary's second trial was delayed until 1838. Mary was found guilty again, and there were no appeals. On August 11, 1838, she was executed in a public hanging by the Crawford County sheriff.

In the case of the *State v. Celia, a Slave,* Celia, a black slave girl of fourteen, was purchased by Robert Newsom, a wealthy large landowner of Callaway County. Newsom was some sixty years of age and a grandfather in 1850. There is considerable evidence that Newsom, an active churchman, raped the girl on their way home after he purchased her in Audrain County. Moreover, he visited her cabin regularly for sex. Celia did not view these visits favorably, especially after her slave lover, George, told her he would no longer have anything to do with her unless she stopped engaging in sex with the master. Celia lived with her two children, fathered by Newsom, in a cabin very close to his house. On the night of June 23, 1855, Newsom visited Celia's cabin despite her repeated warnings to stay away. Celia had earlier told her master that she "would hurt him if he did not quit forcing her while she was sick." Celia had been pregnant for some months with her master's child. This time when the master advanced toward her, she struck him on the head with a stick and killed him. She then burned his body in the fireplace of her cabin, carrying out the ashes the next morning.

A search of the ashes by local officials revealed buttons and bits of bone. An inquest was held, and Celia was jailed until her trial in October. Celia was found guilty and sentenced to hang on November 16, 1855. Her counsel requested a new trial, which was denied. In the meantime, Celia escaped from the Fulton jail but was recaptured. Her execution was delayed until the birth of her stillborn child. On December 13, 1855, she was taken to the gallows and hanged at the young age of nineteen.

Near Fulton, Missouri, there lived a young slave boy of eleven named Mat. On July 9, 1855, Mat's master sent him to the neighboring Womack farm to borrow a piece of equipment. Later that same day Allen Womack found his son, Virgil, in a semiconscious state. Virgil told his father that Mat had attacked him. On August 10, Virgil died of wounds to his head. To obtain a confession, three neighbors took Mat into a stable and questioned him about the blood on his shirt. A rope was put around Mat's neck, and he was drawn up some four or five times. Mat was then taken to a nearby barn. There he was stripped naked and whipped until blood ran from his back in several places. Mat confessed to striking the child. He was taken to the Callaway County jail and charged with first-degree murder. The presiding judge appointed two attorneys to defend Mat during his trial, which was held on October 14, 1855. Mat's attorneys could not get the forced confession thrown out. He was found guilty and condemned to hang but escaped before the sentence could be carried out.

Slaves also committed crimes against each other. In some instances, slaves who felt powerless to rebel against the oppressive life imposed upon them vented their frustrations violently against their fellow slaves. Violence committed against another slave was seen as a crime against the master's property more than a violation of the rights of the victim. When a slave killed another slave or a free black, punishment was usually a whipping, or the owners themselves settled the matter out of court. For example, Lorine, a slave woman who possessed an ugly temper, fought with, and threw Marianne, another slave, into a hole she had chopped in the ice for fishing. Another slave saved Marianne from drowning, but the furious Lorine grabbed and threw her into a fire, burning her severely. Lorine's punishment was one hundred lashes to be administered on two separate days. Later, a Clay County slave who had murdered another slave was given thirty lashes and sold out of the state.

Slaves sometimes mutilated themselves to protest their condition. Their purpose was to depreciate their value, to make slavery less profitable, and to avoid being sold down South. Women might even, although rarely, kill their children. A case in point was Margaret of Cole County. Her master found her one morning in 1848 foaming at the mouth. Upon talking with her, the master believed that the slave had miscarried. However, a search revealed part of the baby's body had been eaten by hogs, and a blood-stained knife was found nearby. Margaret was arrested and indicted for murder. A doctor testified the knife had been used to sever the umbilical cord. The court found Margaret guilty, although extant records make no mention of her punishment.

Other slave mothers reacted violently when their children were sold away. One instance occurred in 1834 in Marion County. A slave trader bought three small children from a planter. The mother became so violent that she had to be tied up. During the night she broke free and killed her sons with an axe, chopping off their heads. She then turned the same ax on herself, ending her own life. Reportedly, the slave trader's only comments reflected his sorrow at having lost a financial investment. Another Boone County slave tried to thwart his master's selling him South by cutting the fingers off of his left hand.

Delicia Patterson, born in 1845 at Boonville, recalled her personal attempt on the auction block to influence who her new master would be:

> When I was fifteen years old, I was brought to the courthouse, put up on the auction block to be sold. Old Judge Miller from my county was there. I knew him well because he was one of the wealthiest slave owners in the county, and the meanest one. He was so cruel all the slaves and many owners hated him because of it. He saw me on the block for sale, and he knew I was a good worker. So, when he bid for me, I spoke right out on the auction block and told him: "Old Judge Miller don't you bid for me, 'cause if you do, I would not live on your plantation. I will take a knife and cut my own throat from ear to ear before I would be owned by you." So he stepped back and let someone else bid for me.

Despite successfully escaping being purchased by Judge Miller, Patterson's plan backfired. "My own father knew I was to be for sale, so he brought his owner to the sale for him to buy me, so we could be together. But when my father's owner heard whad I said to Judge Miller, he told my father he would not buy me, because I was sassy, and he never owned a sassy nigger and did not want one that was sassy. . . . So I was sold to a Southern Englishman named Thomas Steele for fifteen hundred dollars." Resistance to slavery could be double-edged.

A slave by simply running away could deprive their master of his investment as well as the economic gain he expected from it. To add insult to injury, the absconding slave frequently carried away some of his master's property. Masters often placed advertisements in newspapers to alert other whites to assist in recapturing their escaped slaves. These advertisements generally carried a description of the runaway and included his or her name, age, occupation, clothing, and any identifying scars or physical characteristics. One Boone County advertisement of July 7, 1832, read "$100 reward. Lost on night of 6 and 7 of April last. . . . A Negro woman and her four children. Her name is Betsy. Complexion is yellow, with a good supply of clothing for a servant. Her bedding, box, cooking utensils, etc. The children range from 9 months to 6 years of age."

Runaway slaves employed a variety of methods in their efforts to escape. A runaway in 1840 who lived twenty miles from Jefferson City "rode away on [his master's] sorrel horse with two white hind feet, 15 hands high and somewhat white in the forehead." The slave was identified as being "23 years old, slender, yellow, having broad teeth set far apart, scar on one cheek and the ball of one eye yellow." Gus Smith recalled that runaways used Indian turnip to confuse the dogs tracking them: "They would take this and dry it, pulverize it and tie it in big quantities around their feet to keep off the trail of the bloodhounds. No bloodhound could trail a bit further after smelling it. It was strong like red pepper, burns like everything and colored folks running away use it all the time."

One famous Missouri runaway was William Wells Brown. Brown, who had worked on Mississippi River boats before he ran away, became an ardent abolitionist, received a college education, and lectured extensively abroad. He wrote a letter on November 23, 1849, from London to his former master, Captain Enoch Price of St. Louis, challenging the law that had made him Price's slave. The letter, published in the *Libertarian* on September 14, 1849, declared: "The United States had disfranchised me and declared that I am not a citizen, but a chattel: her Constitution dooms me to be your slave. But while I feel grieved that I am maligned and driven from my own country, I rejoice that in this land I am regarded as a man."

Many masters felt that the runaways were being facilitated by the Underground Railroad, a system by which sympathetic whites provided way stations for runaways who were fleeing North. Allegedly, St. Louis was a central depot for the Underground Railroad, with a home on Spoede Road and on the Helfenstein plantation in Webster Groves serving as principal asylums. Although it seems likely that the Underground Railroad did help some Missouri slaves to escape, it is unlikely that it had the effect on Missouri slavery that contemporary masters believed.

Many slaveowners did not treat their slaves brutally, but regardless of the abuse the slaves were still held captive. Often slaves turned to religion and found comfort believing in a God who would reward their patient suffering in an afterlife. Nowhere was this sentiment better expressed than in the spiritual that speaks of heaven as the slave's real home:

> This world is not my home.
> This world is not my home.
> This world's a howling wilderness,
> This world is not my home.

In most instances, slaves were forced to worship with their masters so they could be supervised. Back in the slave quarters, however, they often had their own religious service, which might include the ridiculing of their masters. Sometimes they expressed the hope that a just God would "take care of" the whites who abused them, as was the case in this song collected in *Negro Folk Rhymes*:

> My ole mistress promised me
> Before she died she would set me free . . .
> Now she's dead and gone to hell,
> I hope the devil will burn her well.

Indeed, songs and stories were two important ways in which slaves could try to insulate themselves from the harshness of their lives. They could recount to each other the unlimited exploits of Brer Rabbit, who always managed to defeat Brer Fox by cunning and trickery. Such exploits were also celebrated in songs sung out of the master's hearing:

> I fooled Old Master seven years,
> Fooled the overseer three.
> Hand me down my banjo,
> And I'll tickle you bel-lee.

Slaves might even indulge in criticism of one of their own who had been assigned the responsibility of supervising them:

> O, de ole nigger-driver!
>   O, gwine away!
> Fust ting my mammay tell me,
>   O, gwine away!
> Tell me 'bout de nigger-driver,
>   O, gwine away!
> Nigger-driver second devil,
>   O, gwine away!

Many slaves realized that their survival depended upon a togetherness, a sense of community, which would allow them to draw upon each other's emotional and psychological strength. Contrary to what historians once supposed, the black family was strong during slave times; it served as an island of familiarity and love in a sea of hostility and hate.

Thus blacks responded to slavery in a variety of ways: sometimes they protested vigorously against it, either violently or nonviolently, and other times they simply tried to make the best of a bad situation. Whatever the case, virtually all of them yearned to be free, a status that could be attained by only a fortunate few.

Suggested Readings

Many of the older studies on slavery have to be read with care because of the tendency to view the institution from the perspective of the master rather than the slave. Only in the last few decades have scholars concentrated on the reaction of the slave to his bondage. Writing from the slave's perspective is difficult, largely because of the paucity of literary sources left behind by slaves who were denied an education.

Two studies that devote much attention to the slave's nonviolent resistance to slavery are Eugene D. Genovese, *Roll, Jordan, Roll: The World the Slave Made* (New York: Pantheon Books, 1974), and Lawrence W. Levine, *Black Culture and Black Consciousness* (New York: Oxford University Press, 1977). The most extensive treatment of violent resistance to slavery remains Herbert Aptheker, *American Negro Slave Revolts* (New York: Columbia University Press, 1943).

Other successful efforts to tell more of the slave's side of the story include Stanley Feldstein, *Once a Slave: The Slave's View of Slavery* (New York: William Morrow, 1971), and John W. Blassingame, *The Slave Community: Plantation Life in the Antebellum South,* rev. and enl. (New York: Oxford University Press, 1979). In addition, the volumes edited by Blassingame and Rawick and cited at the end of chapter 2 contain many interviews with Missouri slaves, who talked about resistance to slavery.

William Wells Brown's experiences are retold in his *Narrative of William Wells Brown: A Fugitive Slave* (1848; repr. Reading, Mass.: Addison-Wesley, 1969). Also helpful in studying Brown is William Edward Farrison, *William Wells Brown: Author and Reformer* (Chicago: University of Chicago Press, 1969), and William L. Andrews, *To Tell a Free Story: The First Century of Afro-American Autobiography, 1760–1865* (Chicago: University of Illinois Press, 1986). Henry C. Bruce, *The New Man: Twenty-Nine Years a Slave, Twenty-Nine Years a Free Man* (York, Pa.: P. Anstadt and Sons, 1895), is another autobiography by a Missouri runaway slave. The sad case of the slave Celia is detailed in Hugh P. Williamson, "The State against Celia, a Slave," *Midwest Journal* 8 (Spring–Fall 1956): 408–20. More recently, Melton McLaurin has written the provocative *Celia, a Slave* (Athens: University of Georgia Press, 1991). The case of Mary, the slave executed in 1838, is told in Harriet C. Frazier, "The Execution of Juveniles in Missouri," Part 1, *Journal of the Missouri Bar* 46 (December 1990): 633–42.

The songs quoted in this chapter are taken in order from the following sources: William E. Barton, *Old Plantation Hymns* (1899; reprint, New York: AMS Press, 1972); Thomas W. Talley, *Negro Folk Rhymes* (New York: The Macmillan Co., 1922); Norman R. Yetman, ed., *Voices from Slavery* (New York: Holt, Rinehart and Winston, 1970); and Thomas Wentworth Higginson, *Army Life in a Black Regiment* (Boston: Fields, Osgood, and Co., 1869).

The Louisiana Territory

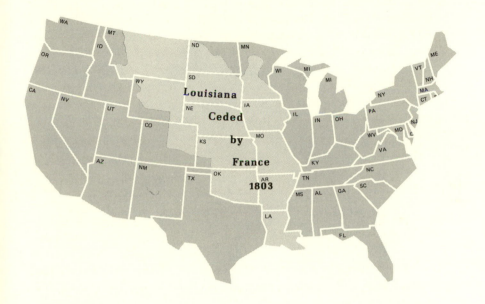

Percentage of Slaves by County, 1860

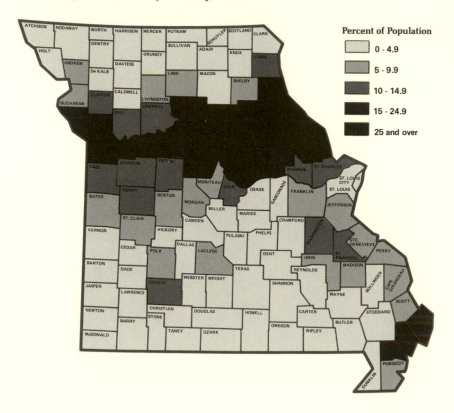

Logan Bennett,
member of the Sixty-
fifth Colored Infantry
(Inman E. Page
Library of Lincoln
University, Jefferson
City).

The Reverend Moses Dickson, prominent St. Louis minister and one of the organizers of the Missouri Equal Rights League in 1865 (State Historical Society of Missouri, Columbia).

James Milton Turner, 1839–1915. Born a slave in St. Louis, Turner became Missouri's most prominent post–Civil War black leader. (Inman E. Page Library of Lincoln University, Jefferson City.)

Joseph Penny, a Kentucky native who migrated to Saline County in the late 1860s and established a town that bore his name. (Kalen and Morrow Collection.)

Slave nurse Louise and owner H. E. Heyward, ca. 1858 (Missouri Historical Society. Ambrotype negative Por H-0004).

Bob Wilkinson, bar-
ber at the Southern
Hotel, St. Louis.
Daguerreotype by
Thomas M. Easterly.
(Easterly Collection
193m, negative East-
erly 193, Missouri
Historical Society.)

William Wells Brown;
engraving from *Nar-
rative of William Wells
Brown: A Fugitive
Slave,* 1847. (Missouri
Historical Society.
Negative L/A 0308.)

Elizabeth Keckley, engraving from frontispiece of *Behind the Scenes*, 1868. (Missouri Historical Society. Negative Por K-0060.)

4

Slaves without Masters
Free Blacks before the Civil War

The black men and women who finally gained their freedom at the end of the Civil War in Missouri were not the first black freedmen of the state. A free Negro class, distinct and separate from either whites or slaves, existed throughout the period of slavery in Missouri, although the distinction between free blacks and slaves was often vague.

There were approximately four hundred and eighty-eight thousand free blacks and four million slaves in the United States in 1860. Free blacks were a concern in all slave states, and reactions to their existence revealed a uniform response. This was as true for Missouri, which had slightly more than one hundred thousand slaves, as it was for South Carolina and Virginia, which had more than four hundred thousand slaves, respectively. Missouri's free black population, like its slave population, remained smaller than either South Carolina's or Virginia's. In 1860 Missouri had 3,572 free blacks, compared to nearly ten thousand in South Carolina and fifty-eight thousand in Virginia.

The larger the slave population, the harsher the treatment of the free blacks, for their very presence threatened to undermine the foundation upon which slavery was built. The continuation of the slave system was based upon whites exercising indisputable control over blacks. Freedmen, regardless of the theoretical rights and equalities that freedom implied, could not be allowed to subvert the system by expecting the same rights and privileges as whites.

It was necessary, therefore, for Missouri and other slave states to conduct a campaign of suppression against free blacks in order to "keep them in their place." Free blacks had to be maintained as a separate and inferior class so that, among other things, they could be more easily observed. Whites were convinced that free blacks instigated many of the attempts made by southern slaves to break the bonds of servitude. Consequently, the more vocal freedmen were, the more fearful whites became of their holding "tumultuous and unlawful meetings" during which secret plots and conspiracies were hatched.

This widespread fear of the free black class manifested itself in laws and social customs designed to institutionalize black, rather than merely slave, inferiority and subjugation. South Carolina, for example, made very little legal distinction between slaves and free blacks. Any free black caught trespassing could be adjudged guilty of a misdemeanor. He could be punished at the discretion of the court so long as the court did not kill or maim him. Additional laws enacted to control free blacks in South Carolina included laws against employing them as clerks or salesmen and even a law forbidding whites to gamble with free Negroes. Likewise in Virginia, legislators made it clear that free blacks would have few privileges forbidden to slaves. Blacks were prohibited from testifying against whites, from learning to read and write, and from carrying firearms.

Free blacks in Missouri faced equally stringent legislation. First of all, the state tried to make it difficult for blacks to gain their freedom. A black person was not considered legally free without a deed of manumission, written and certified by the state or county authorities. Such legal trappings hindered the ability of a slave to gain his or her freedom. Children fathered by a free man, black or white, remained slaves unless their mother was also free; children always followed the status of their mother to be counted as additions to the slaveowner's property.

As early as 1817, the territorial government of Missouri hoped to check slave insurrections by passing an act that prohibited free blacks from traveling and from gathering in meetings. As a result, it became illegal for freedmen to assemble even for purposes of education, although at this time there was no formal decree against the education of blacks. In 1847, however, the Missouri General Assembly passed a law forbidding blacks, slave or free, to be taught even the rudiments of reading and writing. This act, too, was a reflection of a slaveholder's fear that literacy might lead to rebellion.

Other statutory attempts in Missouri to subjugate freedmen included a law of 1825 that declared blacks to be incompetent as witnesses in legal cases involving whites. That law indicates the low-esteem in which free blacks were held: it permitted slaves, who were considered totally irre-sponsible before the law, to testify against them. In 1835 it became illegal for a free black or mulatto to possess a firearm "or weapon of any kind" without first having acquired a license from a justice of the peace in the county where he or she resided. The license, of course, could be granted and revoked at the discretion of the justice.

One of the most restrictive laws enacted against free blacks in Missouri was passed in 1835. It required county courts to bring before their benches all free Negroes and mulattoes between the ages of seven and twenty-one and bind them out as apprentices or servants—in short, to enslave them by another name. It was further legislated that no black apprentice could be placed in the company of a white worker except by the consent of the parent or guardian of the white apprentice. To place a black person along-side a white person while learning the same trade was considered a dan-gerous first step toward the emancipation of the slave.

Fear of free blacks manifested itself in another way in 1835. In that year, the Missouri legislature tried to restrict the movement of free blacks into and within the state. The legislature declared that in order to reside in a Missouri county a free Negro had to obtain a license from the county court. The license was, in effect, a permit to remain in the county so long as the free black behaved. To get the permit, the black applicant had either to post a bond ranging from one hundred to one thousand dollars or to get some white person to act as security for him. The license granted to Celia James in 1847 was typical. The Cole County court ordered that "Celia James . . . is hereby licensed to remain in the State of Missouri during good behavior, and thereupon she enters into bond in the sum of three hundred dollars with John D. Curry as Security which is approved and ordered to be filed."

The whole question of free licenses keenly reflects the attitude of pol-icymakers toward blacks in general and free blacks in particular. The burden of proof always rested upon the black person, for "color raised the presumption of slavery." It was assumed that all blacks were slaves until they could prove otherwise. Brought before a justice of the peace, the freedman who was unable to persuade the court that he was free could be jailed as a common runaway or sold back into slavery.

In 1846 the constitutionality of the pernicious free-license law was sustained by Judge John M. Krum of the Circuit Court of St. Louis.

Krum denied the claim that blacks were citizens of the United States "in the meaning of the word as expressed in the Constitution." His decision offered a portent of things to come. His argument followed the same line of reasoning adopted later in 1857 by the Supreme Court when it rejected the Missouri slave Dred Scott's petition for equal protection under the laws of the United States: whites were not obligated to respect the rights of blacks, slave or free.

When legal means seemed insufficient to restrict free blacks' behavior, whites sometimes turned to extralegal means. In April 1836, a St. Louis mob lynched Francis McIntosh, a free mulatto steamboat cook from Pittsburgh who had allegedly stabbed one constable to death and seriously wounded another. The mob lashed McIntosh to a tree and burned him alive on the outskirts of the city. The abolitionist Illinois newspaper, the *Alton Telegraph,* carried a graphic account of the brutal lynching:

> After the flames had surrounded their prey, and when his clothes were in a blaze all over him, his eyes burnt out of his head, and his mouth seemingly parched to a cinder, some one in the crowd more compassionate than the rest, proposed to put an end to his misery by shooting him, when it was replied, that it would be of no use, since he was already out of his pain. "No," said the wretch, "I am not, I am suffering as much as ever,—shoot me, shoot me." "No. No," said one of the fiends, who was standing about the sacrifice they were roasting, "He shall not be shot; I would sooner slacken the fire, if that would increase his misery," and the man who said this was, we understand, an *officer of justice* [emphasis in original].

At the inquest into McIntosh's murder, the presiding judge, ironically named Luke Lawless, condoned the self-appointed executioners' lynching of the free mulatto as an act "beyond the reach of human law." The brutal lynching and the inaction of authorities to bring the lynchers to justice gave St. Louis a national reputation for lawlessness and barbarism.

Five years later when four black men were charged with a double murder, burglary, and arson, civic-minded St. Louisans saw an opportunity to redeem their city's notorious reputation by assuring the defendants a fair trial. In May 1841, St. Louis authorities arrested three free blacks, Charles Brown, James Seward, and Alfred Warrick, and a slave, Madison Henderson, and charged them with the murders of two white bank tellers, bank robbery, and arson. In order to secure a fair hearing for the accused, the court appointed three prominent white attorneys to serve as their defense. The four accused men, however, were found guilty and sentenced to death by hanging. In July 1841 an estimated crowd of twenty-thousand—which, as Mary E. Seematter notes, was "approximately three-quarters of the St. Louis population"—watched the execution of the four convicted murderers at nearby Duncan Island. Excursion steamboats had carried passengers the short distance out to the island to witness the event.

Despite these legal and extralegal restrictions and other obstacles, the free black population increased in Missouri for a number of reasons. Generally, however, a slave gained his freedom only after the master agreed. According to Harrison Trexler, an early authority on slavery in Missouri, there were generally two motives that entered into the act of liberating a slave: financial consideration and sentiment.

Most frequently, slaves purchased their freedom. This meant that the cash payment they offered the master had to be worth more than he would receive from their continued servitude. The cost of freedom depended upon several variables, among them sex, age, health, skills, and the availability of a ready market for slaves. Occasionally, the price was as low as two hundred dollars, as it was when Jonathan Ramsey manumitted his slave girl Chaney in 1839. Ramsey, however, indicated that the money was not his only motive; he was also prompted by "benevolence and humanity."

More often the purchase price ran high. In 1857, for example, forty-year-old John Lane of Jefferson City paid twelve hundred dollars for his freedom. Lane was perhaps the most self-sufficient black man in the capital city and was to remain a prominent figure in black affairs in the state for another thirty years. He was one of the few free blacks who held any property in Cole County during the antebellum period, and in the early postwar years he became one of the strongest supporters of Lincoln Institute, later known as Lincoln University. For many years after the Civil War, he and another black man, Howard Barnes, operated a restaurant and hotel that was one of the most popular dining places in Jefferson City.

Occasionally, free blacks who were able to purchase their freedom turned around and purchased the freedom of other members of their family. One such example is Violet Ramsey, who first raised the money to purchase her freedom by taking in washing and ironing. She then saved money for the purchase of her husband, Elijah. Ultimately, both of them pooled their resources and purchased the freedom of their son, Elijah, Jr., or "Cudge."

Other slaves took advantage of the California Gold Rush. A Cole County slave named Joe traveled to California with his master in 1849. While there, he saved enough money to pay his master sixteen hundred dollars for his freedom. He also earned enough (two thousand dollars) to buy the freedom of his wife and children. St. Louis slave Jesse Hubbard accompanied his master to California and returned with fifteen thousand dollars. Subsequently, Hubbard purchased his freedom and bought a farm in the St. Louis area.

Occasionally, Missouri's free blacks would themselves become slaveholders. In some instances, their motives were similar to those of their white counterparts: they wanted the use of slave labor to make money. Often, however, their goal was to allow their slaves an opportunity to earn money for self-purchase. One of the most famous of the antebellum free blacks in the state who engaged in this practice was John Berry Meachum. Meachum was born a slave in Virginia and worked under a skilled craftsman from whom he learned carpentry, cabinet making, and coopering (barrel making). After he earned enough money to purchase his freedom, he married and followed his wife's master to St. Louis. There he found employment and was soon able to purchase his wife and children. Meachum's industriousness allowed him to save enough money to open a barrel factory, which became a training ground for freedom. Between 1826 and 1836 he purchased approximately twenty slaves whom he employed in his factory until they had learned a trade and saved enough money to buy their freedom.

In addition to being a businessman, Meachum was also an ordained minister. He was the founder of the First African Baptist Church of St. Louis, located on Third and Almond streets. In his *History of Black Baptists in Missouri,* David Shipley describes Meachum's church as "the first black Protestant congregation west of the Mississippi River." In the years before the legislation of 1847 outlawed black education, Meachum was in the forefront of efforts to educate blacks, both slave and free. He constantly encouraged those he taught to view education as the key to their success as freedmen. When opposition to the education of blacks surfaced, Meachum went underground. Initially, he taught slaves and free blacks to read and write under the guise of conducting a Sunday School. When whites became aware of what he was doing, he switched tactics. He built a steamboat, equipped it with a library, and anchored it in the middle of the Mississippi River, which was subject to federal, not state, law. Each morning he transported students to his school on a skiff and, once having gotten them on board, proceeded to teach them in defiance of state law. Meachum's "floating" school continued until his death in the late 1850s and became famous throughout the nation. One of the countless numbers of black children who received an education there was the young James Milton Turner, later a prominent St. Louis lawyer and United States minister resident and consul general to Liberia.

There were other, if somewhat less dramatic, efforts to educate blacks in antebellum Missouri. Timothy Flint, a northern white missionary, conducted a school in St. Charles from 1816 to 1826. White college students at Marion College in northeast Missouri taught blacks in the 1830s, and a number of schools for blacks run by St. Louis Catholics operated with varying degrees of success throughout the antebellum period.

Other schools operated by free blacks in the state included one headed by the Reverend Tom Henderson of Hannibal, who was a Methodist minister. During the Civil War, his school was taken over by another free black, Blanche K. Bruce, who later became the second black person in the history of the country to serve in the United States Senate. He was the only black to be elected to a full term in the Senate until the election of Edward Brooke of Massachusetts in 1966. The only other black man to serve in the Senate during the nineteenth century, Hiram K. Revels, was also associated with antebellum black education in Missouri. Revels opened a school in St. Louis in 1856, enrolling approximately one-hundred-and-fifty freedmen and slaves at a cost of one dollar per pupil per month. Later, Revels left Missouri and took up residence in Mississippi. In 1870 he was chosen to occupy the seat previously held by Jefferson Davis of Mississippi, the former president of the Confederacy.

One of the most important institutions in the Missouri free black community was the church. The church provided freedmen with a source of stability and social strength in an otherwise hostile society. Moreover, black churches provided one of the few forums in which potential black leaders could develop and refine their leadership skills. Unfortunately, the same sentiment that led blacks to establish their own churches caused whites to fear them. Therefore, blacks who wished to worship often had to do so in white churches, physically separated from the rest of the congregation.

St. Louis, where nearly half of the state's free blacks resided on the eve of the Civil War, was the only place in the state where the organized black church achieved any measure of success. By 1860 there were three Baptist and two Methodist churches in the city. White anxiety about possible slave rebellions led the Missouri General Assembly to pass a law in 1847 that required a county official to attend and supervise all religious services conducted by blacks. Just how strictly that law was enforced is not known.

Employment for free blacks, like education and religious worship, was also a problem. Some stayed with their masters after receiving their freedom and continued to work as farm hands or common laborers. Skilled freedmen stood a better chance of getting a job, but even they found employment difficult in rural areas. Quite naturally free blacks in the state tended to migrate to the cities, especially St. Louis; it had in 1860 1,755 "free men of color" out of a total free black population of 3,572. These former slaves worked as wagoners, blacksmiths, carpenters, house servants, cooks, waiters, draymen, stone masons, watchmen, carriage drivers, painters, gardeners, hostlers, stable keepers, store owners, chambermaids, washwomen, ironers, and seamstresses. Undoubtedly, Missouri's most famous black seamstress was Elizabeth Keckley, who saved the earnings from her trade to purchase her freedom in 1855. Later she left her native St. Louis to become the employee and confidante of Mary Todd Lincoln in Washington, D.C.

Throughout the state, free blacks demonstrated their ability to fit into a free society despite the restrictions placed upon them. In the early days of the state many free blacks became trappers, hunters, mountain men, and leaders of wagon trains going West. Jean Baptiste Pointe DuSable, the founder of Chicago, was a mulatto fur trapper, who subsequently settled in St. Charles, Missouri. James P. Beckwourth, another black trapper, accompanied General William Henry Ashley's fur expedition in 1823. He spent four decades as a scout, trapper, explorer, and ranger. Among his many accomplishments, he discovered the famous pass over the Sierra Nevada that bears his name.

Another free black Missourian who caught the western expansion fever was George Bush. Bush left Missouri for Oregon and returned several times to lead settlers to that region. He also helped finance white settlers who were migrating there. Bush later moved to what would become the state of Washington and helped secure the United States's claim to that territory. Subsequently, his son was selected to serve as a member of the first legislature in the state of Washington. Likewise, George Washington, a Macon County freedman, was a wealthy sawmill operator and landowner who later moved to the Oregon Territory and is generally credited with being the founder of Centralia, Washington.

Yet another black entrepreneur who both contributed to and prospered from westward expansion was Hiram Young. Young was born about 1812 in Tennessee and came to Missouri as the slave of George Young who settled in Greene County. As historian William O'Brien has discovered, "It was said that he earned his freedom and that of his wife Matilda by whittling and selling ox yokes." Young purchased his wife's freedom before his own because he knew their children would be free only if their mother was no longer a slave.

Soon after Young gained his freedom in 1847 he moved to Liberty in Clay County. By 1850 he had settled in Independence, the "outfitting center" for the Santa Fe Trail. Young began making yokes and wagons, "principally freight wagons for hauling government freight across the plains." Over the course of the next decade he produced thousands of yokes and more than eight hundred wagons per year. By 1860 his business had become one of the largest industries in Jackson County, and he was one of the county's wealthiest citizens. Young owned a 480-acre farm east of Independence and employed as many as eighty workers in his business, including several slaves, freed blacks, and Irish immigrants.

Then Young's business was interrupted by the Civil War. In 1861 he and his family fled to Fort Leavenworth where Young continued his business on a much smaller scale until after the war. In the late 1860s he returned to Independence and resumed his business there, although he never again enjoyed the same level of prosperity that he had known before the war. A decade later Young sued the federal government in an effort to collect damages for property belonging to him that had been destroyed by Union troops during the war, but he died before his claim could be settled.

Nowhere were there more of these individual success stories than in St. Louis. In fact, there emerged in that city during the years preceding the Civil War what Cyprian Clamorgan, a contemporary, called "the Colored Aristocracy." Clamorgan, himself a freedman, claimed in 1858 that free blacks in St. Louis controlled several millions of dollars worth of real and personal property. According to Clamorgan, Mrs. Pelagie Nash owned nearly the whole block where she lived. Mrs. Sarah Hazlett, a widow, possessed a fortune of $75,000. Samuel Mordecai, with a business at Fourth and Pine streets, had amassed $100,000. Albert White, a barber who came to St. Louis with $15,000, took his wife to California and returned with an even bigger fortune. William Johnson, a realtor who started with a barber shop in 1840, commanded an estate of $125,000 in 1858. A cattle dealer, Louis Charleville, owned a business worth $60,000, and another wealthy cattle dealer, Antoine Labadie, controlled a business worth $300,000. James Thomas, born in Tennessee, occasionally served as a barber aboard the steamboat *William M. Morrison;* he was worth a reported $15,000.

This colored aristocracy was made up primarily of light-skinned mulattoes who principally resided around several streets: Seventh, Rutger, Third between Hazel and Lombard, Fourth and Pine, and Fifteenth near Clark Avenue. As a class, they looked down on their darker and enslaved fellows and sisters, tended to lead separate social lives, married within their own ranks, attended different churches, sent their children to elite northern and European schools—all in an effort to maintain as close a connection with white society as the lightness of their skin would allow. Henry Clay Bruce, a former Missouri slave and the older brother of Senator Blanche K. Bruce, asserted, "The free fellows felt themselves better than the slave, because of the fact, I suppose, that they were called free, while in reality they were no more free than a slave." After Emancipation, the antebellum free black elite continued to distinguish themselves from the former slaves. As one former slave recalled, the "freeborns" applied the derogatory term *contraband* to the newly freed blacks.

But the hostility and racism of white society often led black Americans to minimize their class distinctions and cultivate a campaign of racial solidarity. White society generally refused to distinguish color or class among the black community when imposing slave codes and racial segregation—restrictions that limited the social mobility of free people of color, despite their status, wealth, education, and skill. Thus, the free black elite often realized that divorcing themselves from the black masses amounted to racial suicide, and they recognized that their political struggle for equal rights in a hostile American society was inextricably bound to the "uplift" of the entire race.

The fact that a number of free blacks were able to rise above the obstacles placed in their paths by a persistently racist society caused Missourians to continue to hate and fear free blacks as a class right up to the Civil War. The clearest manifestation of this hostility was the continuous effort to colonize freedmen outside of the state or even the nation. The American Colonization Society, established by slaveholders in 1816, founded Liberia on the west coast of Africa to rid the country of free blacks.

Ironically, an abolitionist might also be a racist. For instance, many Missouri emancipationists were willing to endorse the abolition of slavery in the state only if the freed blacks were transported out of the country. Emancipationists were particularly eager to send Missouri freedmen to Liberia. Many prominent free blacks in Missouri endorsed the colonization efforts of the society, including John Berry Meachum. Another free black from St. Louis, N. D. Artist, attempted to "raise a company of one hundred men and their families for the purpose [of] emigrating to Liberia and then settling a 'colony' to be known as 'Missouri.'" In an 1849 letter to the American Colonization Society, Artist pined for Liberia: "I long to be there. For a long time I have believed that Liberia is the country for me and all those of my cast who are not content with the mock freedom for the colored man in the United States and who have not lost all love of liberty and mental elevation." Artist's scheme never matured, and he left St. Louis for Burlington, Iowa, in the 1850s. However, a handful of other ventures succeeded. According to historian Donnie D. Bellamy, a total of eighty-three Missouri blacks had emigrated to Liberia by 1860. Most free blacks, however, claimed America as their home and resisted emigration, and the movement in Missouri and elsewhere failed.

Whether wealthy and successful like the St. Louis "aristocrats," or struggling like so many other free blacks, in the long run freedmen prospered in Missouri even under stifling limitations and strictures. They proved a living refutation of the black's "inferiority" and alleged inability to live in a racist white society. By establishing churches and schools, by entering into businesses, and by putting to use skills learned in slavery, they demonstrated both their ability and their willingness to move into the mainstream of society.

Suggested Readings

There has been no book-length study of free blacks in Missouri; so perhaps the best place to begin is with Harrison A. Trexler's book, *Slavery in Missouri, 1804–1865* (Baltimore: The Johns Hopkins Press, 1914). Trexler devotes a chapter to "Manumission, Colonization and Emancipation." Trexler's work is best supplemented by several articles by Donnie D. Bellamy: "Free Blacks in Antebellum Missouri, 1820–1860," *Missouri Historical Review* 67 (January 1973): 198–226, a study that, while not definitive, certainly points the way for future studies of the Missouri free black community; "The Education of Blacks in Missouri Prior to 1861," *Journal of Negro History* 59 (April 1974): 143–57; and "The Persistence of Colonization in Missouri," *Missouri Historical Review* 72 (October 1977): 1–24.

The story of freedmen in St. Louis, where the heaviest concentration of free blacks resided, is told by Judy Day and M. James Kedro in "Free Blacks in St. Louis: Antebellum Conditions, Emancipation, and the Postwar Era," *Bulletin* 30 (January 1974): 117–35. The major achievements of Meachum's career are detailed by N. Webster Moore, "John Berry Meachum (1789–1854): St. Louis Pioneer, Black Abolitionist, Educator, and Preacher," *Bulletin* 29 (January 1973): 96–103. David O. Shipley's *History of Black Baptists in Missouri* (National Baptist Convention, USA., 1976) is helpful. Likewise, one can gain insight into antebellum free black life in St. Louis by reading Elizabeth Keckley's autobiography, *Behind the Scenes: Thirty Years a Slave and Four in the White House* (1868; reprint, New York: Arno Press, 1968). Another contemporary document of great importance is Cyprian Clamorgan, *The Colored Aristocracy of St. Louis,* ed. Lawrence O. Christensen, *Bulletin* 30 (October 1974): 3–31. Also useful are Janet S. Herman, "The McIntosh Affair," *Bulletin* 26 (January 1970): 123–43, and Mary E. Seematter, "Trials and Confessions: Race and Justice in Antebellum St. Louis," *Gateway Heritage* 12 (Fall 1991): 36–47.

The role that blacks played in buying their own freedom is treated by Lorenzo J. Greene in his "Self Purchase by Negroes in Cole County, Missouri," *Midwest Journal* 1 (Winter 1948): 83–85. Likewise, the role of religion in the life of antebellum freedmen is touched upon in Gaston Hugh Wamble, "Negroes and Missouri Protestant Churches before and after the

Civil War," *Missouri Historical Review* 61 (April 1967): 321–47. Finally, the participation of Missouri blacks in the westward movement is covered in two works by W. Sherman Savage: "The Negro in the Westward Movement," *Journal of Negro History* 25 (October 1940): 531–39, and *Blacks in the West* (Westport, Conn.: Greenwood Press, 1976).

Hiram Young's extraordinary accomplishments are chronicled in William O'Brien, "Hiram Young: Black Entrepreneur on the Santa Fe Trail," *Wagon Tracks* [Santa Fe Trail Assoc. Newsletter] 4, no. 1 (November 1989): 6–7. Loren Schweninger, ed., *From Tennessee Slave to St. Louis Entrepreneur: The Autobiography of James Thomas* (Columbia: University of Missouri Press, 1984), edits the first-person account of a free black man who arrived in St. Louis in 1857 and worked as a waiter and barber on a luxury steamboat.

5

The Sable Arm
Blacks in the Civil War

On April 13, 1861, the Confederates fired on Fort Sumter in Charleston harbor. By the afternoon of the next day the Union stronghold fell, and the bloodiest war in American history was underway. President Abraham Lincoln, unwilling to submit to any compromise, called for seventy-five thousand volunteers to suppress the rebellion. Jefferson Davis, president of the newly formed Confederate States, called for one hundred thousand. Neither figure was adequate; when the war ended in 1865, the combined casualties of both sides totaled more than one million.

The Civil War pitted two vastly different forces against each other. Eleven southern states seceded from the Union—states inferior in number, population, and resources to their northern neighbors who were firmly committed to maintaining the Union. Between these two sides stood the border states Kentucky, Maryland, and Missouri, which were essential pawns in the overall war strategy: neither side could win without them. In 1861 President Lincoln stated that if the border states seceded, the job of preserving the Union would be "too large for us."

Lincoln was especially concerned about Missouri, which he described as the key to the West because Missouri was a border slave state. Many of its population of nearly 1.2 million had migrated from the South. According to the 1860 census, over half of the 431,397 Missourians born outside of the state came from slaveholding states, primarily from Kentucky, Tennessee, Virginia, and North Carolina. With more than one hundred thousand slaves in Missouri, many of the state's residents felt psychologically tied to the South. Ironically, many of the slaveholders had strong Union ties because they were engaged in hemp production; so many, in fact, that Missouri became the second-largest hemp-producing state in the country.

Missouri's internal division between northern and southern sympathizers encouraged guerilla warfare. Killing, burning, and plundering became common events. Pro-Union Kansas Jayhawkers, led by Jim Lane and Colonel Charles "Doc" Jennison, laid waste the western counties of Missouri. Meanwhile, the distracted and divided state sent its sons into both armies. While 109,000 Missourians fought for the Union, 30,000 were fighting for the Confederacy.

When the war began in 1861, Lincoln denied any intention to interfere with slavery—to do so would risk losing the crucial border states to the Confederacy. He did realize, however, that something had to be done about slavery. The president tried to persuade border state congressmen to pass legislation paying masters for freeing their slaves. His proposal included a scheme for sending the freedmen out of the country to Haiti or Liberia, but Lincoln failed to convince these leaders that slaves in their states should be free.

Lincoln's hand was quickly forced. Just six months after the war began, his commander of the Western Department, John C. Frémont, declared martial law throughout Missouri and on August 30, 1861, issued a proclamation freeing the slaves of prosouthern Missourians. The president reacted quickly and rescinded what he considered to be Frémont's bold and reckless proclamation. But over the next year political pressure from the Radical wing of Lincoln's own Republican party, as well as the recognition that black soldiers were needed to win the war, forced him into action. His solution, the famous Emancipation Proclamation, was a stroke of political genius. As of January 1, 1863, it freed all of the slaves residing in states that were still rebelling against the Union. Slaves in the border states were not affected, and most Radical Republicans were satisfied. Lincoln also tacked on a provision making slaves eligible for military service.

Missouri remained a slave state loyal to the Union. The first effective challenge to slavery in Missouri came as a result of the debate over whether or not blacks should be enlisted in the Union army. The pressure on Lincoln was intense: slaveholders in the border states feared enlisting blacks, but abolitionists, black and white alike, vigorously urged the president to enroll blacks. Perhaps most persuasive of all was the argument of the famous black leader Frederick Douglass, who likened Lincoln's refusal to use blacks to the plight of a man forced to fight with one arm tied behind his back. On July 31, 1863, Lincoln ordered that all available able-bodied blacks between the ages of twenty and forty-five be allowed to enlist into the armed forces. The decision was momentous because all black volunteers and draftees into the Union army were to be forever free.

Despite a variety of impediments to black recruitment, more than one hundred and eighty thousand blacks served in the Union cause, comprising about 10 percent of the total Union enlistments. These men are credited with taking part in five hundred military actions and nearly forty major battles. More than 20 percent of their number gave their lives—almost thirty-seven thousand. In addition, some twenty-nine thousand blacks served in the Union navy; they represented 25 percent of that service's manpower. Seventeen black soldiers and four black sailors were awarded the nation's highest military decoration, the Congressional Medal of Honor.

Although the official figures state that there were 186,017 black troops in the Union army, the exact number will probably never be known because records of black troops were carelessly kept. In order to draw a dead man's pay, white officers often filled the place of a dead black soldier with a new recruit who answered to the same name. Joseph T. Wilson, author of *The Black Phalanx* and himself a member of both the Second Louisiana Native Guard Volunteers and the Fifty-fourth Massachusetts Volunteers, wrote in 1885: "If a company on picket or scouting lost ten men, the officer would immediately put ten new men in their places and have them answer to the dead men's names. I learn from very reliable sources that this was done in Virginia, also in Missouri and Tennessee." Wilson concluded that because of this procedure, probably two hundred and twenty thousand black men served in the Union army.

While President Lincoln and his government struggled with the important questions about slavery and black soldiers nationally, Missouri had to deal with these and other questions locally. In January 1861, Governor Claiborne Jackson asked the Missouri General Assembly to convene a state convention to determine whether Missouri would secede. A special election of delegates was held in February, with 110,000 votes going to candidates who supported the Union and only 30,000 votes going to secessionists. The convention was held in March and was presided over by former Governor Sterling Price, a southern sympathizer.

Unionists controlled the proceedings, so the convention refused to support secession. But when Lincoln fixed Missouri's quota of volunteers for the Union army at four thousand men, Governor Jackson refused to comply. Instead, he tried to lead the reluctant state into the Confederacy and set out to raise a rebel militia of fifty thousand men. Jackson was forced to abandon his plan and to flee the capital when Union forces under General Nathaniel Lyon entered Jefferson City in mid–1861.

With the governor in exile and his administration in shambles, Union sympathizers held another convention in July 1861. They declared all state offices vacant and elected pro-Union conservative Hamilton R. Gamble as their provisional governor. The last serious military threat to the state was a bloody battle at Pea Ridge, Arkansas, on March 6–8, 1862. Union forces won that battle, and thereafter Missouri remained loyal to the United States.

Once the Union decided to use black soldiers, earnest attempts were made to enlist them. In May 1863, Adjutant General Lorenzo Thomas was sent into the Mississippi Valley to recruit black soldiers. Later in the fall, his jurisdiction was extended to include Maryland, Tennessee, and Missouri. By that time, Lincoln was convinced that the use of black soldiers was necessary for the salvation of the Union. Accordingly, as historian V. Jacques Voegeli has reported, Lincoln wrote Governor Andrew Johnson of Tennessee: "The colored population is the great available and yet unavailed of force for restoring the Union. Fifty thousand armed and drilled black soldiers upon the banks of the Mississippi would end the rebellion at once."

There were drawbacks, however, which discouraged would-be black enlistees, not the least of which was unequal pay. General Orders No. 163, June 4, 1863, set the pay of black soldiers at ten dollars a month and one ration, three dollars of which was to be used for clothing. This was the wage scale for army laborers, set by the Militia Act of July 17, 1862, and was paid to black combatants and noncombatants alike. In contrast, white volunteers received thirteen dollars a month, three dollars of which was for clothing. The pay scale was finally equalized in June 1864, retroactive to January of that year, but arrears in payments to black soldiers for those early months of 1864 were not made until after the war was over.

Closely associated with wages was the matter of bounty. From the outset of hostilities, the federal government paid one hundred dollars bounty to any person volunteering for two years or for the duration of the conflict. Supplementing this were state bounties, ranging from three hundred dollars in Connecticut to five dollars in Wisconsin. County, local, and even private organizations added to the volunteers' incentive. In most instances, blacks saw none of this money. If the slave was drafted, the master received the bounty of one hundred dollars. If the slave volunteered, the master received three hundred dollars, the equivalent of a sort of compensated emancipation. Many people, President Lincoln included, felt that blacks had so much to gain by being taken into the army that they should be willing to join under any circumstances. The muster rolls of various Missouri black companies for 1863 through 1865 show different amounts under the heading "Entitled to Bounty." Sometimes the amount is one hundred dollars; sometimes three hundred. In many cases no amount is indicated. Not until the summer of 1864 were black soldiers entitled to a bounty of one hundred dollars.

Lincoln was correct in his assessment—military service was the passport from slavery to freedom. Missouri slaves, like those in other states, enthusiastically embraced the opportunity to join the army. Discrimination followed black soldiers into the services, however. Often they were given inferior weapons and supplies, and they usually received inadequate medical care. At first, they were likely to be killed by the Confederates, if they were captured, until Lincoln and Grant threatened to treat captured rebels in a similar manner. But the chance for freedom far outweighed the drawbacks.

Newspaper articles recruited black soldiers from Boston to St. Louis to fill the ranks of the prestigious Fifty-fourth Massachusetts Regiment. Likewise, when Missouri blacks heard that the First Kansas Colored Volunteer Infantry Regiment, which included Missouri blacks, had defeated a guerrilla force at Mound Island in Bates County, Missouri, on October 29, 1862, their eagerness to join increased. Regimental adjutant, Lieutenant Richard J. Hinton, praised the black soldiers' valor as "nothing I have ever seen, read, or heard, in the annals of war, surpasses the desperate personal valor exhibited by each and every man."

The army began recruiting the first black Missouri regiment in June 1863 at Schofield Barracks in St. Louis. By June 10, the *St. Louis Tri-Weekly Democrat* announced that more than three hundred blacks had enlisted. The ranks of the First Regiment of Missouri Colored Infantry were virtually complete by the end of 1863. This unit became the Sixty-second U.S. Regiment of Colored Infantry. By January 1864 another regiment was being organized. According to General Schofield, commander of the military district of Missouri, the First and Second Missouri Infantries of African Descent were among the 4,486 officers and enlisted men at Benton Barracks, St. Louis.

During 1864 Grant's Wilderness Campaign and Sherman's March through Georgia increased the demand for additional soldiers, and throughout the year Lincoln made repeated calls for more men. Black troops were needed to help fill the quotas assigned Missouri. As a result, 1864 saw the largest recruitment of Missouri blacks. By February 2 of that year, forty-six assistant provost marshals in as many towns had enrolled 3,700 black men: St. Louis provided 670; Jefferson City, 399; Louisiana, 356; Troy, 343; Macon, 292; Lexington, 272; Tipton, 267; Mexico, 213; Hannibal, 206; Glasgow, 193; Fayette, 172; Sedalia, 169; Marshall, 167; Carrollton, 165; Chillicothe, 105; and Columbia, 103. Liberty, Potosi, Ironton, Kingston, St. Charles, Cape Girardeau, Springfield, Pilot Knob, and Washington sent at least forty soldiers. Howard County reported that six hundred of its nine hundred black men of military age had enlisted in the Union army.

Generally, the Missouri militia was restricted to white men, but at least one independent colored militia company was formed at Hannibal in the fall of 1864. This company, captained by C. W. A. Cartlidge, had ninety-nine members and was raised for emergency duty to guard prisoners being transported to and from headquarters. It was active for only two months, but the men were not paid until ten years later.

Not all blacks were volunteers; some had to be drafted. On November 14, 1864, 164 men from Boone County were called before the draft board of St. Charles. Since this county had failed to meet its draft quota by eighty-two men, this number was taken from the 164. Of those drafted, twenty-two were black. George Jackson Simpson gave this account of how his uncle ended up in military service: "When the war broke out, my uncle was 'pressed' into service under Lieutenant Krantz, at Salem, Mo., who took him to St. Louis and put him in a colored regiment and ran that company down south. The first battle he fought was at Fort Massacre. My uncle was killed, in fact nearly all that company were killed. I had two uncles killed in the war, one in New Orleans, we never knew exactly where, anyhow he never came back."

Despite the generally enthusiastic response of blacks to enlistment opportunities, several factors operated to slow down their enrollment in Missouri. Many persons vigorously opposed blacks serving in the armed forces. Masters were particularly hostile, since enlistment was practically a writ of emancipation. T. M. Allen of Boone County summed up this sentiment in a letter dated February 12, 1864, to his representative in Washington, James S. Rollins: "I think Missouri has been badly treated by the Administration. No State in the Union has made the sacrifices for peace as we have. . . . Was it just to issue an order to enlist the slaves of Union men as well as Rebels? Was not this virtually issuing an edict emancipating forthwith our Negroes?"

Conservative officials also sought to block the recruitment of slaves, for they felt that it would incite them to rebellion. Judges of circuit courts charged grand juries in Marion County and in western parts of the state to invoke Article 1 of the *Revised Missouri Statutes,* which provided the death penalty for anyone convicted of "inciting rebellion or insurrection among slaves, Mulatoes, or free Negroes."

Guerrillas terrorized blacks to retard enrollment. The infamous guerrilla leader William Quantrill threatened to kill anyone answering Lincoln's call for volunteers. He and other leaders of bushwhacking bands often frightened blacks away from recruiting stations. Sometimes terrorism resulted in murder. The official records and newspapers report many cases of blacks being killed by guerrilla bands. Several hangings and shootings in the fall of 1863 were capped by what contemporary sources describe as a "massacre" of three blacks in Boone County on November 18, 1863. According to county Provost Marshal C. F. Russell, these killings were intended as a warning for all blacks to leave the county in ten days or be killed by raiders.

Some whites grudgingly consented to the use of black soldiers and even encouraged black recruitment as a way of saving white soldiers' lives. The commanding officer of the First Kansas Colored Volunteers, whose troops were mostly fugitive slaves from Arkansas and Missouri, declared, "I believe the Negro may just as well become food for powder as my son." In the period of one week in November 1863, the Union army provost marshal enrolled seventy blacks at Lexington. The *Lexington Weekly Union,* which championed black recruitment in Lafayette County, hoped "to see every negro in the county put in the service. Every negro received saves a white man, and we must confess that our sympathies are decidedly for the white man. We advise all the owners of slaves to put them at once into the service taking a receipt therefore."

In all, seven Negro regiments were enrolled in Missouri. The official figures place the total number of men at eight thousand, or almost one-twelfth of the total number of troops sent from Missouri to the Union army, with 665 serving as substitutes for whites who had been drafted. But even this figure does not accurately reflect the number of black Missourians actually sent to the Union army. Many Missouri blacks served in out-of-state regiments. This was especially true in the First Iowa Regiment of African Descent and the First and Second Regiments of Kansas Colored Volunteers. Richard Bruner, a Missouri slave, explained: "Well you see I wus a runaway nigga; I runaway when I wus about grown and went to Kansas. When de wah broke out I jined de 18th United States Colored Infantry, under Capt'n Lucas. I fit three years in de army. My ole Marsa's two boys jist older than me fit for de south." Others enlisted in Illinois, Ohio, and even Massachusetts units. Missouri ranked fifth in the number of black troops furnished, behind Louisiana with 24,052, Kentucky with 23,703, Tennessee with 20,133, and Mississippi with 17,869. Of the total 186,017 blacks in the Union army, Missouri contributed 4.4 percent.

Black Missourians saw action in a number of contests. Members of the Eighteenth Regiment fought at the Battle of Nashville and pursued Confederate General John B. Hood to the Tennessee River in 1865. The Sixty-second saw action in Texas, which included a skirmish at White's Ranch, the last battle of the war. The Sixty-seventh spent most of its time in Louisiana and participated in a battle at Mount Pleasant Landing in May 1864. The Sixty-eighth helped to make up the force that assaulted and captured Fort Blakely, Alabama, in April 1865. The Sixty-fifth performed mostly fatigue duty in the Louisiana swamps where sickness claimed the lives of six officers and 749 enlisted men.

Blacks performed other valuable services for the Union army besides fighting: they worked as teamsters, cooks, builders of breastworks, and in other noncombatant capacities. Many black women also served as cooks, nurses, and laundresses in the camps of both the Union and the Confederacy. They also acted as informants and spies, pointing out the locations of bushwhackers and guerrillas. Historian Michael Fellman has observed that in Missouri Union soldiers discovered that blacks "provided the most trustworthy military information. Because Union soldiers trusted the freedmen rather than white Southern sympathizers, they raised their estimate of the black character." Often blacks who provided information were protected by the troops they helped. In March 1862, Lieutenant Colonel Arnold Krekel succeeded in killing three members of a guerilla band in large part because of the help of a young black man. Krekel wrote his superior: "A negro boy gave valuable information in conducting the command, and I would ask for permission to retain him until the war is over, as he cannot safely return." Blacks who provided information to Union troops were routinely given sanctuary.

The existence of armed black soldiers, most of whom were ex-slaves, in the state had a tremendous psychological effect on the slaveowners. Richard C. Vaughan, a Lafayette County slaveowner, wrote to James O. Broadhead, U.S. district attorney in St. Louis, telling him of the fear in his county of black regiments: "Our wives and daughters are panic stricken, and a reign of terror as black as hell itself envelops our country." In at least one instance a slaveowner's worst fear was realized when he came face-to-face in battle with his ex-slave. In September 1861, a veteran of the Battle of Boonville reported that the slave of Colonel William O. Brown had shot and killed his master at the battle. According to the witness, the ex-slave showed no regret; indeed, he was "tickled almost to death."

Blacks played a vital role in the Union victory, and Lincoln himself acknowledged the importance of their participation. A skeptic at first about the worth of black soldiers, Lincoln later became enthusiastic in describing their contributions. The president openly declared that the nation could not be saved without them.

Psychologically, the Civil War had a tremendous effect upon the black soldier. In general blacks—particularly soldiers—identified the Civil War as their own American Revolution. The war transformed and regenerated them. The black soldier went into the army as a despised and degraded chattel, mere property, having no name except the one given to him by his master. He came to the recruiting station as "George," "Andy," or "Primus." He came out as a man, as "George Washington," "Andrew Jackson," or "Primus Davis." Putting on the uniform of the United States enhanced his self-esteem and his dignity. It gave him a sense of identity with the struggle for human freedom and fired him with the conviction that he was sharing in a great humanitarian crusade larger than himself. As historian Leon Litwack has pointed out, Sergeant Prince Rivers, a black soldier of the First South Carolina Volunteers, spoke for black soldiers everywhere when he summed up what the war meant to him: "Now we sogers are men—men de first time in our lives. Now we can look our old master in de face. They used to sell and ship us, and we did not dare say one word. Now we ain't afraid, if they meet us, to run the bayonet through them."

For many black soldiers, the greatest boost they had gotten out of the freedom struggle was proving their manhood. Or, as one black soldier, who served with Thomas Wentworth Higginson, put it:

> We can remember, when we fust enlisted, it was hardly safe for we to pass by de camps to Beaufort and back, lest we went in a mob and carried side arms. But we whipped down all dat—not by going into de white camps for whip um; we didn't tote our bayonets for whip um; but we lived it down by our naturally manhood; and now de white sojers take us by de hand and say Broder Sojer. Dats what dis regiment did for de Epiopian race.
>
> If we hadn't become sojers, all might have gone back as it was before; our freedom might have slipped through de two houses of Congress and President Linkum's four years might have been passed by and notin' been done for us. But now tings can neber go back, because we have showed our energy and our courage and our naturally manhood.

As the events of the Civil War unfolded during the more than four years of bloody strife, black people in Missouri and elsewhere prepared for what they believed would soon be the day of freedom. The war uprooted many of them. Wartime chaos in Missouri prompted many masters to transport their slaves to Arkansas or even Texas in an attempt to salvage something from their investment. Sometimes guerrillas kidnapped slaves for resale down South.

Thousands of slaves simply abandoned their masters, particularly if there were Union troops in the immediate vicinity. Many carried with them as many of the master's possessions as they could handle—"spiling the Egyptians," they called it. Some wandered to towns such as Columbia, Jefferson City, or St. Louis. Others sought the more secure borders of free states such as Kansas, Illinois, Iowa, or Michigan. It has been estimated that of the more than one hundred thousand slaves in Missouri in 1860, only eighty-five thousand were still in bondage in 1862 and not more than twenty-two thousand in 1864. The precariousness of slave property was reflected in a drastic drop in price, from approximately thirteen hundred dollars in 1860 to one hundred dollars in 1864.

Some idea of what happened in one town can be gleaned from a report by Sheriff Bruns of Cole County in January 1865. Sheriff Bruns was asked by local officials to take a census of the county. He discovered that there were 565 blacks in Jefferson City, a marked increase over the 333 of 1860. Moreover, despite the fact that only three of the 565 black residents were described as free, all of them were virtually so, "belonging either to the class called contrabands, or to the number whose master had ceased to make any effort to control them."

As the war drew to a close, many black and white leaders, aware that slavery was a dying institution, tried to arrange educational opportunities for slaves and free blacks alike. They viewed education as the single most important key to black integration into the mainstream of American life. Black and white educational efforts on behalf of blacks were so large in St. Louis that a black board of education was established. The unofficial board had charge of four schools with a total of four hundred students. By 1865 the system had eight teachers and six hundred pupils.

In 1865 the Western Sanitary Commission, a white benevolent association, operated a high school in St. Louis for about fifty blacks in the basement of a local church. The commission also organized classes for black soldiers at Benton Barracks. The instruction, mostly in reading and writing, continued during the war in the black regiments. The officers of the black outfits, many of them college-trained, often taught the former slaves around the campfires.

The federally sponsored Freedmen's Bureau was also effective in offering financial support for local black education near the end of the war. During the war years, however, the most important single force supporting black education was probably the American Missionary Association. In the late 1850s, the AMA had unsuccessfully tried to convert the Missouri slaveholder to the abolitionist gospel. Forcefully and violently driven out of Missouri at the start of the Civil War, the AMA returned in 1862. This time the main thrust of the organization was to provide the former slaves with a Christian education.

Despite black eagerness to receive education, the AMA encountered constant opposition to its efforts. In 1863 an AMA school that served sixty black pupils in St. Louis was burned by a group of whites. The school had been open for only three days. By 1865 AMA agents were located in several Missouri communities, including Jefferson City, Warrensburg, Kansas City, Carondelet, and Holt County. The society's teachers, many of whom were women, were often intimidated and threatened with physical violence. In Carondelet the AMA school was closed after only nine weeks because the female teacher could no longer secure living quarters in the unfriendly white community. Alma Baker later reopened this school, but she suffered much abuse for boarding with a black family; so the grateful black community paid her rent out of their own meager resources.

In Jefferson City AMA agent Mrs. L. A. Montague was labeled the "nigger teacher," and the resistance did not stop at name calling. School books and furniture were destroyed by local whites, and Montague's black students were stoned on the way to school. Although several white citizens of Jefferson City encouraged Montague to continue her work and to stand her ground, in general most moral and financial support for these efforts came from the black communities. In Carondelet, Warrensburg, Jefferson City, St. Louis, and other localities blacks raised money for the teachers' board, for the rent on school buildings, and, insofar as they were able, for the teachers' salaries.

Throughout the former slave states, blacks believed a new day had dawned. The end of the war and of slavery had turned their world upside down. They were uncertain about what it all meant and about what the future held for them. Signs of optimism abounded—a new status as freedmen, a new sense of belonging and worth, new opportunities in education—all proof that whatever lay ahead was better than what had gone before.

Suggested Readings

Thomas Wentworth Higginson's *Army Life in a Black Regiment* (New York: Collier Books, 1962) is an important contemporary account that provides insight into the life of black Civil War soldiers. There have been a number of excellent books on the meaning of the Civil War for black Americans. They include Benjamin Quarles, *The Negro in the Civil War* (Boston: Little, Brown, 1953); V. Jacques Voegeli, *Free but Not Equal: The Midwest and the Negro during the Civil War* (Chicago: University of Chicago Press, 1967); James McPherson, *The Negroes' Civil War* (New York: Pantheon Books, 1965); James McPherson, *The Struggle for Equality* (Princeton: Princeton University Press, 1964); and Dudley T. Cornish, *The Sable Arm: Negro Troops in the Union Army, 1861–1865* (New York: W.W. Norton, 1966).

President Lincoln's goals in issuing the Emancipation Proclamation are the subject of John Hope Franklin's *The Emancipation Proclamation* (Garden City, N.Y.: Anchor Books, 1965). Emancipation at the state level is the subject of John W. Blassingame's "The Recruitment of Negro Troops in Missouri during the Civil War," *Missouri Historical Review* 68 (April 1964): 326–38.

The politics of Missouri are thoroughly treated in William E. Parrish, *The Turbulent Partnership: Missouri and the Union, 1861–1865* (Columbia: University of Missouri Press, 1965). Guerilla warfare in Missouri is treated in Richard S. Brownlee, *Gray Ghosts of the Confederacy: Guerilla Warfare in the West, 1861–1865* (Baton Rouge: Louisiana State University Press, 1958); and Michael Fellman, *Inside War: The Guerilla Conflict in Missouri during the Civil War* (New York: Oxford University Press, 1989). Fellman's essay "Emancipation in Missouri," *Missouri Historical Review* 83 (October 1988): 36–56, is also useful.

The support of black education during the war is covered by Joe M. Richardson, "The American Missionary Association and Black Education in Civil War Missouri," *Missouri Historical Review* 69 (July 1975): 433–48.

6

Forty Acres and a Mule

Reconstruction in Missouri, 1865–1877

The Civil War drastically altered black life in America. Former slaves were thrust into a fundamentally new social, political, and economic situation. Innumerable obstacles presented themselves as they sought to adjust to a new way of life for which slavery had ill-prepared them. Without money, property, or education, they tried to move into the mainstream of a highly competitive, literate, and capitalistic society.

The blacks' initial response to the ending of slavery was influenced very little by the problems that lay ahead. Missouri's slaves were freed on January 11, 1865, an action that was pushed through a state convention dominated by members of the Radical Unionist party. Thus, Missouri blacks gained their freedom eleven months before the ratification of the Thirteenth Amendment to the Constitution ended the institution of slavery nationally. Blacks throughout the state rejoiced. On Sunday, January 14, thousands took to the streets of St. Louis, Jefferson City, and other communities with flags and banners proclaiming their joy at finally having achieved their most sought-after dream. Others celebrated more privately, often thanking God for deliverance from their bondage. Such was the case of a black servant whose joy at gaining her freedom was recorded by contemporary writer Laura Haviland:

I jump up an' scream, "Glory, glory, hallelujah to Jesus! I's Free! Glory to God, you come down an' free us; no big man could do it." An' I got sort o' scared, afeared somebody hear me, an' I takes another good look an' fall down on de groun', an roll over, an' kiss de groun' fo' de Lord's sake, I's so full a' praise to Masser Jesus. He do all dis great work. De soul buyers can neber take my two chillen lef' me; no, neber can take 'em from me no mo'.

Blacks would soon realize, however, that because slavery had largely confined them to performing menial or farm laborer tasks, they were now just additional unskilled workers thrown upon an already overcrowded job market.

The uncertainty that the freed men and women felt with emancipation was revealed in a "Freedom Song" sung by many ex-slaves:

> No more peck o' corn for me
> No more, no more,—
> No more peck o' corn for me,
> Many thousand go.

> No more driver's lash for me,
> No more, no more,—
> No more driver's lash for me,
> Many thousands go.

The phrase "No more driver's lash" expresses the joy of their new won freedom and the realization that they no longer had to suffer slavery. But "No more peck o' corn" signifies their anxiety and doubts about supporting and providing for themselves now that they could no longer depend upon their masters' care.

The diversity of the response to freedom is clearly documented in the WPA interviews with surviving ex-slaves conducted during the 1930s. Many blacks were too consumed with trying to reunite families to be concerned with thoughts of making a living. Often former slaves traveled the South searching for their lost relatives. The fortunate ones were reunited with their families and able to start a new life together; others searched in vain for their loved ones. Margaret Nickens, raised on a farm six miles from Paris, Missouri, in Monroe County recalled: "My Father came from Virginia and my mother from Kentucky when they were little. They never saw their parents any more. They watched for a long time among the colored people and asked who they were when they thought some body looked like their parents, but never could find them. They were so small when they left, they didn't even remember their [parents'] names."

Other former slaves remembered clearly that they began their new lives with almost nothing and that they struggled to find places to live and work. William Black, a former slave from Marion County remembered that after being "freed our master did not give us anything, but some clothes and five dollars. He told us we could stay if we wanted to, but we was so glad to be free that we all left him." Malinda Discus's owners were southern sympathizers and tried to influence their slaves: "Oh yes, they tried to make us believe that we couldn't take care of ourselves if we were free." Malinda's husband, Mark Discus, added:

Ol' master wanted to see us free when he saw how things was goin', but his oldest son had took charge of things and he said 'No.' Hit was right funny. Ol' master had refused to sell me for twelve hundred dollars, so young master loaded me and four others of the best slaves in a wagon and linked our hands together and started South with us to sell us. We got within twelve miles of the Texas line when we met some soldiers and they said to turn the niggers loose. Freedom had come. That made young master mad as a hornet, but he let us go right there and then.

George Jackson Simpson was twelve years old when his slave uncle bound him out to a Scotch-Irish man named Sammy Wilson until he was twenty-one. "I could have been free at the close of the war, but did not know it, I thought I had to stay with my new boss until I was twenty one. I was not exactly enslaved, but when my uncle 'bound me out', he agreed with my boss that I was to work for him until I was twenty-one, and then I was to get a horse, saddle, bridle, two suits of clothes and six months schooling. All I actually got when I became of age was one suit of clothes and $40 in money for eight years work."

Marie Askin Simpson remembered that after her father died

my mother did the best she could. The war ended, everybody was mad or suspicious of each other and it was hard to find places to live. My mother stayed on with her white folks. We made out the best we could make a living. Then they found me a place to stay with a family in Steelville, taking care of the children, scrubbin floors, and scouring knives and forks. I was only a little girl and got fifty cents a week, with my board.

Gus Smith said: "After slavery, we did not know what to do. Most of the slaves just left, went first one place and then another. Some lived out among the neighbors. You see, your marster couldn't hold you and if you continued to work for him, it was expected that he had to pay you."

An even more serious problem than the lack of preparation and training was the persistence of antiblack sentiment in the state. Slavery died hard in Missouri, and the slave code mentality lived on for many years after the Civil War. Conservative counties, like the Kingdom of Callaway—so-called because so many of its citizens continued to support the Confederacy even after the state of Missouri took a formal pro-Union stance during the early days of the Civil War—hated emancipation.

The last year of the war in Missouri saw a sharp increase in guerilla activity, a violent response to the frustration that southern sympathizers felt. Often the guerrillas vented their wrath upon innocent freedmen who had become a symbol of all that the bushwhackers detested. One of the more infamous of the lawless bandits was Jim Jackson. He led his gang into Boone County in mid-February of 1865 and lynched one of Dr. John Jacobs's black hired hands as a warning both to blacks who sought work and to whites who hired them. Referring to racial violence, General Clinton B. Fisk wrote the following account in March 1865 of what he had seen during his travels throughout the state:

Slavery dies hard. I hear its expiring agonies and witness its contortions in death in every quarter of my district. In Boone, Howard, Randolph, and Callaway the emancipation ordinance has caused disruption of society equal to anything I saw in Arkansas or Mississippi in the year 1863. I blush for my race when I discover the wicked barbarity of the late masters and mistresses of the recently freed persons of the counties heretofore named. I have no doubt but that the monster, Jim Jackson, is instigated by the late slave owners to hang or shoot every negro he can find absent from the old plantations. Some few have driven their black people away from them with nothing to eat or scarcely to wear. The consequence is, between Jim Jackson and his colaborers [*sic*] among the first families, the poor blacks are rapidly concentrating in the towns and especially at garrisoned places. My hands and heart are full. I am finding homes for them in Northwest Missouri, Kansas, Illinois, and Iowa. There is much sickness and suffering amoung them; many need help.

Attitudes such as the one expressed on September 7, 1867, in the *Lexington Weekly Caucasian,* a white supremacist newspaper, were widespread in Missouri:

We want to see them [ex-slaves] all quietly and happily settle in Liberia, where they may indeed enjoy the full blessings of liberty, . . . equality, and fraternity. . . . Here, these blessings can never be enjoyed by the African, and he is an enemy to the race who would legislate enactment, or by persuasion, induce him to believe otherwise. . . . The position of the negro is that of vassalage here; there it would be, if he chose to make it, a condition of real independence. Here he must deteriorate and finally disapear or go back to bondage; there he might multiply and replenish the land, and contribute toward building up a government and civilization that would ennoble him.

Many black Missourians did respond to such racial hostility by fleeing the state, if not for Liberia, at least for other parts of the country. In fact, in spite of natural increases, there were fewer blacks in the state in 1870 than there had been ten years before—a decline from 118,503 to 118,071. Some of those who stayed tried to find jobs with their former masters or other whites. Often their pay was only room and board. By 1870 more than two-thirds of the black males employed in the state were still working as farm laborers. In 1870 blacks in Lafayette County were virtually propertyless. Of the 128 black families in Lexington Township, only two owned property. Most of the women who worked outside of the home were domestics.

Most blacks throughout the state continued to work at relatively low-paying, unskilled jobs. In some places, blacks came together as economic and social units simply to survive. Such was the case in the communities of Pennytown, Eldridge, and Three Creeks. Pennytown was a freedmen's hamlet in Saline County, south of Marshall, on land that was originally purchased by the town's black namesake, Joseph Penny, in the early 1870s. Community members survived in large part by sharing resources and responsibilities. Some members raised cows, others raised hogs, and still others raised chickens, and the produce was bartered within the group. Even child-rearing responsibilities were shared; elderly community women cared for the children while parents of both sexes worked in Marshall as domestic servants, gardeners, and general laborers. A similar situation existed in Laclede County in the 1880s after a community grew up on and around land owned by former Tennessee slave Alfred Eldridge. A third community of freedmen grew up in the vicinity of the Bass, the Bonne Femme, and Turkey creeks in Boone County, an area that came to be called Three Creeks.

Even if blacks were able to find employment, they faced other burdens. Although Missouri escaped much of the segregation legislation that would later dominate the South, there were informal codes of behavior designed to ensure that blacks kept their place. For example, streetcar companies in St. Louis prohibited blacks from riding inside their cars. In 1867 Caroline Williams, a black woman, pregnant and holding a baby, tried to board a car only to be shoved into the street by the conductor. She and her husband sued the company. They won their suit but were awarded damages of only one cent. Nevertheless, a principle of law had been established that effectively ended the practice of keeping blacks off the streetcars.

One of the most sought after goals of the ex-slaves was education. When George Jackson Simpson came to Rolla in the 1930s, he "went to 'Free School' for twenty days. I learned to read and write just by picking up all I could and having people show me. . . . When I got to writing my own name, I thought I was flying." Efforts by blacks to obtain education often met with arson. In 1866 a school for blacks at Linneus in northwest Missouri was set on fire by whites, but the fire was extinguished before major damage was done. In January 1867, white youths burned a new school for blacks in Fulton, and in the same year a drunken band of whites fired pistols into a black Christmas Eve congregation at St. Paul's AME Church in Columbia. They killed one person and wounded another. In August 1869, arsonists set fire to Robert Stokes's school for blacks in New Madrid and left a note "warning off" Stokes "under pain of being 'treated' in 'the same way'." Similar acts of violence occurred in other parts of the state.

Nationally, the Radical Republicans were trying to enact legislation that would at least ensure blacks equal protection before the law and the right to vote. While they never provided the legendary "forty acres and a mule" that many blacks were led to believe would be forthcoming, the Radicals did advance the black cause. Under the congressional leadership of men such as Charles Sumner and Thaddeus Stevens, they pushed through three important amendments to the Constitution. The Thirteenth Amendment (1865) abolished slavery forever. The Fourteenth Amendment (1868) guaranteed blacks equal protection of the laws and all civil liberties enjoyed by white persons, and the Fifteenth Amendment (1870) granted the black men the coveted right to vote.

Another way the federal government hoped to assist the ex-slaves was by encouraging them to save their money in order to secure a stronger economic position in the social order. As a result, it created in 1865 the National Freedmen's Savings and Trust Company, better known as the Freedmen's Bank. In 1868 a St. Louis branch was established under the presidency of the Reverend William P. Brooks, who served for the entire six years of the bank's existence. Born a slave in Virginia in 1826, Brooks moved to Missouri in 1842, purchased his freedom in 1846 for one thousand dollars, and became actively involved in the Underground Railroad and black education. He conducted a wood and coal business in St. Louis from 1855 to 1865. In 1865 he sold his business for three thousand dollars after deciding that he wanted to spend more time in the ministry. The St. Louis Freedmen's Savings and Trust Company was a marginal operation at best, largely because black Missourians had so little money to save. It later fell victim to the financial crisis that swept the country during the Panic of 1873.

The Radicals also established the Freedmen's Bureau, a national organization to help both whites and blacks adjust to the new situation. Bureau agents came to Missouri in the spring of 1865 and began setting up schools for blacks; legalizing marriages among the freedmen, which had been prohibited under slave law; providing the destitute with food, medicine, clothing, and shelter; and arranging labor contracts with farmers. It is estimated that more than one thousand Missouri blacks received some form of direct aid from the Freedmen's Bureau in the immediate postwar period. Another white philanthropic organization serving the freedmen was the Western Sanitary Commission established in 1861. The commission was especially active in the St. Louis area where it set up four elementary schools and one high school. The commission also established a Freedmen's Orphans' Home for abandoned children of slaves.

Radical Republicans tried to assist blacks at the state and local level as well. Although many Missouri Radicals who favored emancipation also endorsed the removal of freedmen from the state, they drew up a constitution in 1865 that was relatively progressive. Although emancipation was quickly granted, the exact nature of the rights that the freed blacks were to enjoy caused much more difficulty. The issues centered on three questions: whether blacks could testify against whites in court cases, whether they could vote and hold office, and whether they could receive educational opportunities at the state's expense.

The first question was resolved by deciding that no person could be denied the right to testify because of his or her race. The Radicals then cleared the way for state-established black schools by including a provision in the constitution stating that the General Assembly could establish schools "for children of African descent." Funds for all public schools were to be appropriated "in proportion to the number of children without regard to color."

However, the Radicals moved more cautiously on the suffrage issue. The vast majority of Missourians remained hesitant about allowing black men the right to vote. Even the Radical leader Charles Drake was skeptical about including a black suffrage plank in the constitution, for fear that it would cause the entire document to be rejected by Missouri voters. Consequently, voting and office holding were initially limited to qualified white men.

Because the convention that drafted the new state constitution rejected black men's right to vote or to hold office, blacks in Missouri felt they lacked an essential freedom. The result was the organization of Missouri's first black political activist movement, the Missouri Equal Rights League. The organizational meeting of the league in October 1865 was held at a St. Louis church on the corner of Green and Eighth streets. It was dominated by black St. Louis religious leaders, although freedmen from other parts of the state were present.

The blacks gathered in St. Louis called attention to their plight as freedmen who lacked the rights and privileges of the elective franchise and charged that such a condition was little better than the oppression they had suffered as slaves. They pointed out that they too had borne arms in defense of the Union and stated that their future safety and prosperity would be best ensured by the state declaring all people—regardless of color—equal before the law.

Before adjourning, league members chose a seven-member executive committee to work toward this goal. The committee members were Henry McGee, Colonel Francis Robinson, Reverend Moses Dickson, J. Bowman, Samuel Helms, Dr. George Downing, and George Wedley. Specifically, the committee was charged with the responsibility of providing for a series of mass meetings throughout the state, which included procuring black speakers and preparing an address on the plight of black people to the citizens of Missouri.

The Reverend Moses Dickson, a prominent black St. Louisan, was probably the best known of these men. His involvement with the Equal Rights League represented the continuation of a struggle for black freedom that he had begun long before. After traveling throughout the South from 1840 to 1843 and observing the plight of slaves, the Reverend Mr. Dickson recruited twelve men and formed a secret organization called the Knights of Liberty to enlist and arm southern slaves for a general rebellion. At one point, the Knights claimed to have forty-seven thousand members. The group set the year 1856 as the time for revolution. As the year approached, however, the antislavery struggle increased in intensity, so Dickson counseled his followers to wait for what he felt certain would be a civil war. When the war came and black troops were authorized, Dickson and many of his followers took up arms for the Union cause. Later, a fraternal organization known as the International Order of Twelve, Knights of Tabor, was founded to continue the struggle for equality. This organization still exists today.

Two weeks after the Equal Rights League executive committee was appointed, a twenty-seven-hundred-word *Address to the Friends of Equal Rights* appeared in local newspapers and as a pamphlet. It was an elaborate expression of the concerns and aspirations that had been voiced at the October organizational meeting. The major plea was for the right to vote. The petitioners reminded their readers that they were citizens of the state and nation and that their toil had enriched both. They also recalled that nine thousand black soldiers had "bared their breasts to the remorseless storm of treason, and by hundreds went down to death in the conflict while the franchised rebel . . . the . . . bitterest enemy of our right to suffrage, remained . . . at home, safe and fattened on the fruits of our sacrifice, toil and blood." The address warned that its readers should take seriously the plea of black Missourians and emphasized that the question of what to do with black people would become the greatest issue before the republic.

The committee hired John M. Langston of Ohio, a well-known black orator and lawyer, to tour the state in support of its petition. Langston began his journey by delivering a talk in St. Louis in November 1865. He followed that speech with trips to Hannibal, Macon, Chillicothe, St.

Joseph, Kansas City, Sedalia, and Jefferson City. Everywhere he went the message was the same: he pleaded with members of both races for black suffrage and for black access to education.

Langston was not the only black spokesman touring the state. Another was James Milton Turner, who was only twenty-six years old when the Civil War ended. Turner was one of the most important black leaders in post–Civil War Missouri. Born a slave in 1839, he gained his freedom in 1843 when his mother was freed. Educated in St. Louis schools and at Oberlin College in Ohio, Turner was a fiery orator who emerged as secretary of the Missouri Equal Rights League in 1865. Throughout that winter he traveled around the state, especially in the southeast, advocating education and the ballot for black men. Turner encountered his strongest opposition in southeast Missouri, a region that had remained strongly sympathetic to the rebel cause. On one occasion he was forced "to escape for his life at midnight, barefooted in the snow, leaving his shoes behind him."

The executive committee also circulated a petition throughout the state, imploring the legislature to provide suitable schools for black children. It also sought an amendment to the constitution that would remove the word *white* and, in so doing, guarantee the legal equality of all the state's citizens. The petition gained the signatures of four thousand blacks and whites. It was then turned over to the Honorable Enos Clarke, state representative from St. Louis, to present to the legislature. Despite Clarke's strong endorsement of the petition, the legislature refused to act favorably upon it. In fact, the result of all the activism in Missouri was disappointing. Success came only in 1870 after the Fifteenth Amendment to the Constitution guaranteed the right to vote without regard to "race, color, or previous condition of servitude."

The black citizens who made up the Equal Rights League had known that the fight to secure full political and civil rights was not going to be easy. Accordingly, they placed great emphasis on education to advance the progress of blacks and to refute arguments against black suffrage that were offered by white opponents. They realized that many freedmen were unprepared for participatory democracy. In its address the executive committee emphasized, "We mean to make our freedom practical," adding that it regarded education as the chief means by which full freedom could be achieved. Convinced that the responsibilities of citizenship could be best fulfilled by an educated citizenry, the league sought to establish schools for the freedmen wherever possible.

James Milton Turner, the Equal Rights League secretary, was the most active and effective black advocate of education for the former slaves. He taught in two of the earliest black public schools in the state: Kansas City and Boonville. Turner was appointed an agent of the Freedmen's Bureau in 1869, and his major responsibility was traveling around the state to set up black schools. During the same year he received a similar appointment from Radical state superintendent of public schools, Thomas A. Parker. When Turner submitted his report to the Freedmen's Bureau in early 1870, he revealed that he had traveled "between eight and ten thousand miles." His efforts, he stated, had assured black children that approximately eight thousand dollars of public funds annually would be applied toward their education. In addition, he was instrumental in opening thirty-two schools and erecting at least seven new school buildings.

Turner's task was not easy. One of the biggest obstacles he faced, he wrote, was "in such sections where the largest number of colored people are found there is a preponderance of disloyal and former slave holding peoples, who in most cases are opposed to the establishment of these schools." Another problem was finding qualified black teachers since blacks had been denied education in antebellum Missouri. Many Missourians, black and white, were opposed to white teachers teaching black students—especially women. Discrimination in salaries further complicated the issue.

The need for black teachers did not go unnoticed by government officials in Jefferson City, for Parker had written of the desperate need for black teachers in his annual report of 1869. He suggested that the need could be met by providing state support for the newly established Lincoln Institute in Jefferson City. The idea of the institute had originated with the black Missourians who served in the Sixty-second United States Colored Infantry. As Lieutenant Richard B. Foster, a white officer of that regiment, recounted the story, a number of soldiers were told in January 1866 that they would soon be sent home. They were happy at the thought of returning home, and many felt satisfied that they had at least learned the basics of reading and writing while in the service. Nevertheless, there was great anxiety among them that what little knowledge they had gained would be lost if they were not able to continue their education back home.

The soldiers began raising money for a school back in Missouri. Money quickly poured in. The lieutenants gave fifty dollars each, officers of higher rank gave one hundred dollars, and enlisted men gave what they could afford. Meanwhile, Foster was appointed traveling agent for the soldiers and sent to ask the men of the Sixty-fifth Infantry, many of whom were black Missourians, for additional contributions. The seriousness of the commitment these black soldiers felt toward education is exemplified by Private Samuel Sexton of the Sixty-fifth, who gave one hundred dollars, although his annual salary totaled only $156.

The total collected from the Sixty-second was $5,000, and more than $1,300 was collected from the Sixty-fifth. Foster was designated as the agent to carry the money to Missouri and to set up a school there. He was a logical choice, for his abolitionist and humanitarian credentials were impeccable. Foster was born and raised in Hanover, New Hampshire, graduated from Dartmouth College, and was well-steeped in the Congregationalist tradition. He had also taught school in Illinois and Indiana prior to the Civil War and had demonstrated his abolitionist sentiments as early as 1856 by assisting John Brown in a raid on Fort Titus, Kansas. He entered the service of the Union army in 1862 as a private of the First Nebraska Regiment. When President Lincoln authorized the formation of black regiments, Foster volunteered to join the Sixty-second United States Colored Infantry.

Foster took the money and the trust of the black soldiers and headed for Missouri. Upon his arrival there in the summer of 1866, he was beset by problems. He made an unsuccessful attempt to establish a school in St. Louis before he moved west to Jefferson City where he encountered additional difficulties. His plight is best summed up in his efforts to find a place to house the school. "I applied to the colored Methodist Church for their house," he wrote in 1871, "but the minister refused, alleging as a reason that the teacher would be white. . . . I applied to the white Methodist Church," he continued, "but the minister refused, alleging as a reason that the scholars would be black."

Foster had to settle for an old log cabin on the outskirts of Jefferson City at a place called Hobo Hill. The building had previously been used as a white school but had since been declared unfit for human occupancy. He later gave this account of the school's beginning:

> The rain is pouring in torrents. As I approached the schoolhouse, I am stopped by a creek, the bridge over which has been swept away—usually fordable, but now impassable by . . . the flood. A half hour's detour, and the scrambling of several fences brings me to the sanctuary of learning. What a sanctuary! The rains pour through the roof scarcely less than outside. I could throw a dog through the side in twenty places. There is no sign of a window, bench, desk, chair, or table. In this temple of the muses I meet two pupils. On the next day the same scene is repeated. The third day the rain has ceased, the creek has become fordable, and seventeen pupils are enrolled: and for more than six weeks, new names are added to the register every day.

Foster named the school Lincoln Institute. The school struggled along barely making ends meet until 1870 when the Radicals Republicans' self-interest meshed with black aspirations. James Milton Turner, whose activities on behalf of black education had made him a well-known leader throughout the state, called for a convention of blacks to meet in Jefferson City in January 1870 to petition the legislature for support of Lincoln Institute as a training school for black teachers.

The Radical Republicans were in trouble in Missouri by 1869 and 1870. They still had control of the state government largely because they continued to deny the vote to former "rebels." Yet, there was a growing sentiment within the party to restore the franchise to the rebels, a position that stalwart Radicals fought against. Congress passed the Fifteenth Amendment on February 26, 1869, and sent it to the states for ratification. Once it was ratified, many Radicals believed that they could neutralize any rebel threat by wooing the soon-to-be enfranchised blacks. Their support of black causes, however, were utilitarian and short-sighted and reflected more the instability of Missouri politics than a genuine concern for black people.

The Radicals' strategy was to identify and latch on to a black leader who they believed could deliver black votes, and the man they turned to was James Milton Turner. Turner aspired to become United States minister to Liberia, and in mid–1869 many Radicals, including Governor Joseph W. McClurg, endorsed his candidacy. When Turner convened the January 1870 gathering of black leaders in Jefferson City, the Radicals quickly came to his aid. In February they passed a law granting five thousand dollars annually to Lincoln Institute on the condition that the trustees first agree to convert the school into a facility for the training of black public school teachers. On March 10, 1870, the Radicals opened the Hall of Representatives to Lincoln principal Richard B. Foster and his students for a public recitation. The gathering was designed to attract contributions to the institute. Governor Joseph W. McClurg and other highly placed Radical officials set the stage for the proceedings by giving one hundred dollars each.

Radical support for Lincoln Institute did not guarantee a warm reception for black students in Jefferson City. In 1874 several Institute students were turned away from a reading by a Jefferson City author because they were black. Such overt racial discrimination prompted black instructor Lizzie Lindsay to write an eloquent but futile protest:

> These were students thirsting for knowledge, and hearing that Mrs. Siddons' readings were worth attending, they went for the purpose of gaining instruction, yet were subjected to insult merely on account of their color. The cry is heard from the Lakes to the Gulf, from the Orient to the Occident, educate the colored people: and how are they to be educated advantageously if colored teachers, students and persons of culture are insulted and outraged by those who consider themselves their superiors?

The Radical Republicans's endorsement of the black suffrage and education further convinced Turner and others that the Radicals were the blacks' best benefactors. Subsequently, twenty thousand blacks voted the Radical ticket in 1870. Unfortunately, the continued division within Republican ranks in Missouri over rebel reenfranchisement split the party into stalwart conservative and liberal factions. Consequently, a coalition of dissident liberals and Democrats ousted the Radicals from power in Missouri in 1870. Nationally, the Radicals still held some sway, and President Grant appointed Turner to the Liberian ministership. Turner held that position from 1871 to 1878, making him the second black person in the history of the country to become a diplomat.

Although Radical Reconstruction was over in Missouri by the early 1870s, Radical Republican rule had given both urban and rural blacks the right to vote. In addition, a commitment to public education for blacks had been established. These two things would be the major vehicles that blacks would use for the next one hundred years in traveling down the narrow and treacherous path in search of full equality.

Suggested Readings

One of the best general accounts of the immediate post-slavery period is Leon F. Litwack, *Been in the Storm So Long: The Aftermath of Slavery* (New York: Alfred A. Knopf, 1979). Laura Haviland, *A Woman's Life-Work: Labors and Experiences of Laura S. Haviland* (Cincinnati: Walden and Stowe, 1882), offers interesting contemporary observations of the slaves' response to freedom.

Any discussion of black life during Reconstruction Missouri must begin with two books by William E. Parrish: *Missouri under Radical Rule, 1865–1870* (Columbia: University of Missouri Press, 1965), and *A History of Missouri 1860 to 1875,* vol. 3 of *A History of Missouri,* sesquicentennial edition (Columbia: University of Missouri Press, 1973). Parrish devotes chapters in each of these books to blacks in the immediate postwar period.

Black education during this period is the subject of Antonio F. Holland and Gary R. Kremer, "Some Aspects of Black Education in Reconstruction Missouri: An Address by Richard B. Foster," *Missouri Historical Review* 70 (January 1976): 184–98. Other articles on black education include W. Sherman Savage, "The Legal Provisions for Negro Schools in Missouri from 1865 to 1890," *Journal of Negro History* 16 (July 1931): 300–321; and Henry S. Williams, "The Development of the Negro Public School System in Missouri," *Journal of Negro History* 5 (April 1920): 137–65. The story of the founding of Lincoln Institute is told in Savage, *The History of Lincoln University* (Jefferson City: The New Day Press, 1939); and in Antonio F. Holland et al., *The Soldiers' Dream Continued: A Pictorial History of Lincoln University of Missouri* (Jefferson City: Lincoln University, 1991).

The career of prominent black politician James Milton Turner is detailed by Gary R. Kremer, *James Milton Turner and the Promise of America: The Public Life of a Post–Civil War Black Leader* (Columbia: University of Missouri Press, 1991). Also useful is Lawrence O. Christensen, "Schools for Blacks: J. Milton Turner in Reconstruction Missouri," *Missouri Historical Review* 76 (January 1982): 121–35.

The role of the Freedmen's Bureau in Missouri is covered by W. A. Low, "The Freedmen's Bureau in the Border States," in Richard O. Curry, ed., *Radicalism, Racism, and Party Realignment: The Border States during Reconstruction* (Baltimore: Johns Hopkins University Press, 1969). Other essays of interest include Michael Fellman, "Emancipation in Missouri," *Missouri Historical Review* 83 (October 1988): 36–56; and John Starrett Hughes, "Lafayette County and the Aftermath of Slavery, 1861–1870," *Missouri Historical Review* 75 (October 1980): 51–63. Another important county study is Suzanna Maria Grenz, "The Black Community in Boone County, Missouri, 1850–1900" (Ph.D. dissertation, University of Missouri–Columbia, 1981).

The intriguing stories of Pennytown and Eldridge are told by Gary R. Kremer and Lynn Morrow, "Pennytown: A Freedmen's Hamlet, 1871–1945," *Missouri Folklore Society Journal* 11 and 12 (1989–1990): 77–92; and Kremer and Ann Jenkins, "The Town with Black Roots," *Missouri Life* (July–August 1983): 11–14. For the Three Creeks area, see Frances Maryanne Jones-Sneed, "The Bottom of Heaven: A Social and Cultural History of African Americans in Three Creeks, Boone County, Missouri" (Ph.D. dissertation, University of Missouri–Columbia, 1991).

7

Separate and Unequal
Reconstruction to World War I

Although there were disappointments for freedmen during the first decade after emancipation, black people remained generally optimistic during those years. Radical concessions to their cause, both nationally and locally, nurtured the dream that equality for all was attainable. There were disturbing trends in the former slave states, however. More and more old-line southern Democrats were rising to positions of power. These "Bourbons," as they were sometimes called, promised to "redeem" the South from northern problack control. The process was capped in 1877 by the famous compromise that brought President Rutherford B. Hayes to the White House. Hayes narrowly defeated the Democratic challenger, Samuel J. Tilden, in an election that was ultimately decided by a congressionally appointed commission. Hayes won the contest only after agreeing to certain concessions to the South (among which was the withdrawal of federal troops). With that accomplished, black rights could be violated with impunity.

Many southern blacks responded to this turn of events by fleeing the South for the "promised land" of Kansas. St. Louis, located on the Mississippi River near the mouth of the Missouri, became a way station for the voyage West. By early March 1879, the first group of the more than six thousand blacks who would come to St. Louis during the next four months arrived.

The problems faced by these "exodusters" were legion. The first obstacle was to secure money for boat fare up the Mississippi. It cost from three to four dollars per adult to travel from the vicinity of Vicksburg, Mississippi, to St. Louis. Children under ten years of age were transported for half price, and a small amount of baggage could be carried free of charge. Consequently, a family of five needed from ten to fifteen dollars just to get up the river, an amount that, in many cases, blacks had to raise by a hasty and unprofitable sale of most of their household goods.

Many exodusters arrived in St. Louis with their money already spent and no way to secure passage to Kansas, but the black community of St. Louis quickly responded to the exodusters' needs. Charleton H. Tandy, a prominent black leader, organized and spearheaded the relief effort. Tandy helped the men find jobs and arranged for impromptu food and shelter for that first group of several hundred. His efforts to solicit the aid of whites in St. Louis were largely unsuccessful; indeed, Mayor Henry Overstolz discouraged attempts to aid the migrants, lest other destitute southern blacks be attracted to the city. Realizing that whites were going to be of little use, Tandy organized a group of fifteen persons that later grew to a committee of twenty-five. The committee assumed the responsibility for seeing to the needs of the migrants, including the arrangement and supervision of their transportation to Kansas.

Most of the money raised in this relief venture came through the black churches of St. Louis. Between March 17 and April 22, St. Louis blacks provided the exodusters with nearly three thousand dollars of goods and services, making it possible for the vast majority of them to travel on to Kansas. Many migrants stopped again in Kansas City where B. B. Watson, pastor of the African Methodist Episcopal Church, organized a similar relief effort. In contrast to his counterpart in St. Louis, Mayor George M. Shelley supported Kansas City's aid to the freedmen.

The Radical Republican fall from power in Missouri had begun with the 1870 election. Black voters had supported the Radical Republican gubernatorial candidate, Joseph W. McClurg, in 1870. McClurg was defeated, however, after a split in the Republican party's ranks formed a coalition of liberal Republicans and Democrats to elect B. Gratz Brown, Missouri's twentieth governor. He was replaced in 1872 by Democrat Silas Woodson of St. Joseph. A Republican governor of Missouri was not elected again until Herbert S. Hadley took office in 1909.

Even if the Republicans had maintained control of state politics, blacks could have expected little from them. The endorsement of black political rights, which had been characteristic of the party in the late 1860s, gave way to concern about economic issues in the 1870s and 1880s. In 1878 James Milton Turner, who had recently returned from a seven-year appointment as minister to Liberia, sought the Republican nomination for a seat from Missouri's Third Congressional District. Turner's candidacy was flatly rejected by the Republicans; so, too, was an effort to increase black representation on the Republican State Central Committee.

St. Louis was the only place in the state that blacks could expect any kind of support from the Republicans. There Chauncey I. Filley, long-time party leader and the St. Louis postmaster in the 1870s, appointed a few blacks to menial patronage positions in the post office. To many black Missourians, this token gesture was simply not enough.

As the national election of 1880 approached, a delegation of black Missourians, calling itself the Missouri Republican Union, traveled to the White House for a meeting with President Hayes. Led by James Milton Turner, these black leaders sought to persuade Hayes that the black vote in Missouri was still important and that the national Republicans should make greater efforts to reward their black supporters.

The lame-duck president did nothing, of course, and the Missouri Republican Union turned its attention to Hayes's successor, James A. Garfield, who could not have been elected without the black vote. Union members demanded patronage jobs for leaders of their race and protection for southern blacks. Turner and his colleagues tried to organize a national meeting in Washington, D.C., to dramatize their demands. Despite efforts by Union members, the meeting in Washington never materialized, largely because many blacks in the country thought that such a gathering held little promise. Alternatively, the Missouri Republican Union turned its attention away from national politics and focused once again on affairs within the state.

In August 1882, the Union sponsored a statewide black convention in Jefferson City. One of the major objectives of this convention was for the state of Missouri to establish a mechanical or industrial school for black youths. A petition to that effect was presented to the House of Representatives, but it failed to gain the approval of the committee on education. The meeting in Jefferson City revealed a growing dissatisfaction among blacks with the Republican party. Members present passed what they called a "new Monroe Doctrine," announcing that the black vote could no longer be colonized and appropriated by the Republicans. Rather, blacks would henceforth support the party that showed the greatest promise of helping them.

But there was no political party that showed any real interest in helping black people. Even the courts refused to offer any assistance. In 1883
the U.S. Supreme Court declared the Civil Rights Act of 1875 unconstitutional. One of the last vestiges of Radical Reconstruction, the law of
1875 had attempted to ensure blacks access to public accommodations
such as restaurants and theaters. Its nullification in 1883 touched off a
series of new segregation laws by the Democratically controlled southern
states, which effectively deprived the freedmen of their constitutional
rights.

Black Missourians had been fighting segregated education for years.
Missouri's constitution of 1875 provided for separate school facilities for
blacks and whites. In 1881 black leaders James Milton Turner and J. H.
Murray met with Democratic Governor Thomas T. Crittenden in an
effort to encourage him to support integrated schools. Crittenden, however, refused to endorse any such move. Some schools continued to
admit both blacks and whites. In 1887, however, a white teacher in Grundy
County refused to admit black students to a white school that had previously been open to them. Parents of the children sued the teacher on
the grounds that the young pupils were being denied rights guaranteed
to them by the Fourteenth Amendment.

While the courts debated the question, the Missouri legislature met
the issue head-on. In 1889 it passed a law ordering separate schools to
be established "for the children of African descent." The next year the
Grundy County case finally reached the Missouri Supreme Court, which
ruled against the black students. Justice Francis M. Black wrote the unanimous decision, declaring that "color carries with it natural race pecu-
liarities" which justified the separation of blacks and whites. Moreover,
he proclaimed the court to be of the opinion that these racial differences
could never be eliminated. Six years later the U.S. Supreme Court, in the
famous *Plessy v. Ferguson* case, declared separate but equal accommodations for blacks to be constitutional; segregation had become the law of
the land. Although Missouri did not pass segregation laws covering public accommodations, custom prohibited blacks from joining whites in
facilities such as hotels, restaurants, theaters, and hospitals.

The black population of Missouri changed dramatically during the last
half of the nineteenth century by moving to the cities. By 1890, 47
percent of the state's black population lived in cities; by 1900 the figure

jumped to 55 percent. Social, political, and economic changes for blacks came in the wake of these demographic shifts: their increased number and their tendency to live near each other within a few political wards influenced city elections when they voted as a bloc.

Political leaders in Kansas City and St. Louis began to take notice of this change. In St. Louis Dr. George Bryant, a black delegate to the St. Louis Republican convention, persuaded the delegates to nominate Walter M. Farmer, a black lawyer, for the position of assistant prosecuting attorney for the Court of Criminal Correction. Another black man, W. C. Ball, was also nominated for the position of constable. Both men were defeated by Democrats. Three years later, Farmer became the first black lawyer to argue a case on behalf of a black client before the Missouri Supreme Court.

In Kansas City there was a similar token acknowledgment of potential black political power. E. L. Hamlin, a wealthy black contractor, was nominated in 1890 for a seat on the city council. The Republican mayoral candidate, Joseph J. Davenport, endorsed Hamlin in return for the promise of black support at the polls. Both Hamlin and Davenport were defeated, however.

The nomination of three blacks for elective office in Missouri's two major cities certainly did not change the status of black people in the state. As the decade of the 1890s wore on, the frustration and helplessness of blacks increased. The neglect of black people by political leaders led many lawless whites to feel that they had a license to harass them. This oppression was manifested most clearly in the growing prevalence of lynching throughout the state and the nation during the late nineteenth and early twentieth centuries.

The late nineteenth century was a violent period in American history. Industrialization spawned social and economic changes that shattered the agrarian life-style of the nation. Labor unrest, financial panics, and a tremendous increase in the number of immigrants who challenged native whites for jobs caused Americans to search for scapegoats for the country's problems. When scapegoats could be found, lynching blacks was the chief form of violence. Nationally, of the 3,224 persons who were lynched between 1889 and 1918, 2,522 of them were black. During this same period, mobs lynched eighty-one persons in Missouri, fifty-one of whom were black. This number exceeded lynchings in the southern states of Virginia (seventy-eight) and North Carolina (fifty-three) and was dramatically more than the bordering states Illinois (twenty-four) and Kansas (twenty-two). Mob leaders generally escaped punishment, often with the complicity of legal authorities.

In 1892 a number of Missouri's most prominent black citizens called attention to this crime of violence. They hoped that educating whites to the realities of black life would make things better for them. James Milton Turner, Peter Clark, George B. Vashon, Walter Farmer, Albert Burgess, E. T. Cottman, Moses Dickson, R. H. Cole, J. H. Murray, John W. Wheeler, and a host of others circulated an address throughout the country to call attention "to the wrongs that were being heaped upon" their fellow blacks. They declared May 31, 1892, a national day of "humiliation, fasting, and prayer" to emphasize their plea. On that day fifteen hundred blacks solemnly gathered in St. Louis for what they called a "lamentation day."

Neither prayer nor fasting could stop lynching; indeed, mob murders increased. Perhaps the most flagrant example of this tragic violence against blacks occurred in Springfield in 1906. The black community of Springfield had grown in both number and prosperity during the generation after the Civil War. According to Katherine Lederer, author of *Many Thousand Gone: Springfield's Lost Black History,* one-quarter of Greene County's population was black in 1875. By 1890 one-third of the county's registered voters were black. Three black men served on the Springfield City Council between 1870 and 1900: Julius Rector, James Stone, and Alfred Adams. The latter also served for a time as the Greene County coroner. Springfield blacks also served on the local school board. Indeed, one of the black board members, Burton Hardrick, owned what Lederer has described as "the largest grocery store in the city." The Hardrick Brothers grocery store used twelve delivery wagons in the early 1900s to deliver to middle- and upper-class white residents of the city.

Another prominent black business in Springfield at the turn of the century was the Gatewood Shoe Store, which was operated by Bill Gatewood whose parents Will and Narcissa were among southwest Missouri's most interesting post–Civil War black entrepreneurs. Will Gatewood had been a slave born in Kentucky but later was sold to a man named McIlroy from Fayetteville, Arkansas. Gatewood worked as a handyman for the McIlroys and also made shoes and kept a garden. He was allowed to keep part of his earnings from the sale of shoes and garden produce and eventually purchased his freedom. Subsequently, he married Mrs. McIlroy's maid, Narcissa, and began saving money to buy her freedom. Soon, however, in the midst of the Civil War when federal troops occupied Fayetteville, Will and Narcissa left the town for Springfield where they used the money that Will had saved to start a freight-hauling business. Later, they expanded into the shoe business and prospered for many years.

Perhaps Springfield blacks were too prosperous and too numerous in the early years of the twentieth century; whites in the city obviously felt threatened by them. On April 13, 1906, Good Friday, a white Springfield woman claimed that she had been raped by two young black men. Two black suspects were arrested the next day but were released for lack of evidence. Later the same day the men were again arrested and placed in jail. That night a mob of white men and boys broke into the jail, dragged the two black men out, and lynched them on the town square. They hung the men and burned their bodies beneath a burning replica of the Statue of Liberty before an estimated crowd of six thousand people. Having killed two victims, the mob returned to the jail and lynched another black man. The Springfield black community was never the same again. Hundreds of blacks fled the city over that Easter weekend, and by the 1980s Springfield's black population fell to less than 2 percent of the city's total population.

The excitement surrounding this despicable event was so great that Governor Joseph Folk ordered the state militia into the city to quell the riot. The governor was eager to have the guilty parties sentenced to death and sent state officials to assist the local prosecuting attorney in the trial. After a lengthy trial, however, the leader of the mob was acquitted.

Despite the growing concentration of blacks in the cities, the Republican party continued to pay little attention to them. In 1892 former Radical William Warner gained the party's gubernatorial nomination by running on a "new Missouri" platform, which emphasized the state's need for industrial development but ignored black problems. When Chauncey I. Filley, one of the last Republican advocates of patronage jobs for blacks in St. Louis, fell from power in 1896, Republican abandonment of blacks was complete.

As the elections of 1898 approached, black St. Louisans contemplated a break with their old political affiliates. Two decisive events moved them to action. They had expected eight hundred of the eight thousand patronage jobs available in the city; instead, they received only seventy-six. Moreover, although there were no black candidates in the city in 1898, blacks wanted David Murphy, a sympathetic judge of the Court of Criminal Corrections, renominated. The Republicans rejected their appeal. By ignoring blacks as a constituency, Republican disregard prompted them to form an independent political organization and to move toward the Democratic party.

The Democrats were themselves divided during these years. Missouri farmers turned increasingly to third-party movements in the 1880s and 1890s. Obsessed with rolling back the power of encroaching industrialists, they advocated issues such as free silver. When the Democratic party failed to hear their cry, the farmers abandoned it.

Internal squabbling caused perceptive Democrats to realize that the party needed new members, and they quickly discovered that disaffected blacks could be wooed into the fold. A slate of black candidates was offered for several elective positions, and the Democrats, led by Governor Lon V. Stephens, began making overtures to black voters. Stephens wrote to several black St. Louis leaders promising patronage jobs, law enforcement jobs, and a strong antilynching law.

Stephens also knew he could gain black support by endorsing programs for Lincoln Institute in Jefferson City, so he persuaded the legislature to appropriate money for a new dormitory. In return, he expected employees of the institute to form a nucleus of support for the Democratic party. The president of Lincoln Institute, Inman E. Page, refused to cooperate with Stephens, and he was quickly removed by the governor in 1898. Soon after his dismissal, support for Democratic candidates throughout the state came from the school.

Democrats dominated the election in black wards of Kansas City and St. Louis in 1898 and again in 1900. In St. Louis, Democratic ward boss Ed Butler and his son, Jim, organized black support. They were aided by a new machine organization in the city known as the Jefferson Club, which was run by the commissioner of the St. Louis Police Board, Harry B. Hawes. Through Hawes's efforts, an auxiliary Negro Jefferson Club was formed with C. C. Rankin, Crittenden Clark, W. H. Fields, and James Milton Turner as leaders. The Negro Jefferson Club rallied behind

Democrat Rolla Wells and helped him win the mayoral contest in St. Louis in 1901. In Kansas City, blacks organized a Negro Central League and supported James Reed, the Pendergast organization's candidate for mayor. Reed won the contest and gave a number of jobs in the fire department to blacks.

The growing influence of blacks on urban Democrats was more than the rural members of the party could take. Racism among this so-called Confederate faction had always been present, but it soared to new heights in the early twentieth century. In 1903 rural Democrats tried to pass new segregation laws, particularly for railroad travel, but urban Democrats joined with Republicans to defeat the bill.

Despite their loss on the issue of segregation, rural Democrats remained strong in the party and made race a political issue in 1904. Democratic antiblack rhetoric, combined with President Theodore Roosevelt's open courting of the black vote, caused many blacks to return to the Republican fold. Consequently, Democratic urban machine organizations declined in power during these years. The rural Democrats attempted to capitalize on the decline and tried repeatedly, but unsuccessfully, to pass segregation laws and to limit the ability of blacks to vote.

The election of Governor Herbert S. Hadley in 1908 brought a more favorable state response to the plight of blacks than had existed for nearly forty years. Republican Hadley appointed blacks to patronage jobs, made efforts to improve the health of black Missourians, and fought strongly against lynching. But blacks were not to be so easily bought off this time. They realized that white restrictions on where they lived gave blacks a power base in the cities. In St. Louis, black leaders Joseph E. Mitchell, Charles Turpin, Homer G. Phillips, and George L. Vaughn formed the Citizens Liberty League to endorse black candidates. Turpin was elected as a St. Louis constable in 1910, becoming the first black candidate elected to a public office in Missouri.

Political bosses and party machines dominated city affairs from 1910 to 1920: the Republicans in St. Louis and the Democrats in Kansas City. The increasingly urbanized blacks of the state found themselves more and more closely attached to these machines. Still, the masses of blacks received few benefits from either party.

The movement of blacks into narrowly defined sections of cities may have provided them with potential political power, especially in closely contested elections, but it also had a negative aspect: it meant that blacks were thrust together in terribly overcrowded neighborhoods. By 1910 nearly 67 percent of Missouri's blacks lived in the cities, almost three times the national average. They were confined to crowded urban ghettos where unsanitary conditions, crime, and vice prevailed. In the 1890s blacks in St. Louis lived in areas where the population density averaged eighty-two persons per acre, as opposed to the overall city average of only twelve persons per acre.

Slum districts took on characteristics of their own and became known by such descriptive names as Clabber Alley, Wild Cat Chute, and Hog Alley. In 1882 Jefferson City's Hog Alley was quarantined when a local physician mistakenly diagnosed smallpox among neighborhood residents. Local officials placed armed guards at the entrances to the alley to limit movement into and out of the alley in the hope of avoiding the spread of the disease throughout the city. Subsequently, the physician's erroneous diagnosis was discovered, although the scare created a public outcry against the filth and squalor of Hog Alley. A local newspaper offered this assessment:

Hog alley to Jefferson City is what Clabber alley is to St. Louis. It is a disgrace to the city; all that is filthy, low, mean and vicious of the colored population can at one time and another be found in this alley. It reeks with filth and crime and wickedness. In its confines are to be found the vagabonds, thieves and prostitutes of the colored population. Innumerable cutting and shooting scrapes, broils and rows of all kinds and varieties have occurred there. The recent scare about the smallpox had its origin there and attracted the attention of the whole city to it. Now is a good time to talk about what action should be taken to rid the city of this blot. The old rookeries of the alley should be declared nuisances by the city authorities and abated if it can be done; if not, the city should buy the old houses and tear them down. We don't know who they belong to, but whoever owns them owes it as a duty to their fellow-citizens not to rent them to the vile class that now occupy them and bring disgrace upon the city.

Soon after, the city council did authorize the razing of several alley buildings.

In Kansas City, as late as 1915, most blacks lived in two- and three-story brick tenement houses on the Bowery. Most of the buildings were arranged in two- and three-room apartments, and nearly all were poorly constructed and crowded closely together. The overcrowded condition was suffocating: twenty-two blocks in that area had a population of 4,295. Housing was even worse in southeast Missouri and in semi-rural places and in small towns.

Substandard housing greatly increased the need for health services, but low incomes made it difficult for blacks to purchase these services. White physicians often refused to treat black patients, and hospitals refused to admit them. Consequently, black doctors set up their own hospitals in former private dwellings. In November 1910, Dr. J. E. Perry set up a fifteen-bed hospital in Kansas City called the Perry Sanitarium and Nurse Training Association. In 1915 it became Provident Hospital and Nurse Training Association. The following year Perry led a community effort to purchase and remodel an old Catholic school into Wheatly-Provident Hospital. But, in spite of growth, such hospitals were unable to deal adequately with all the health problems of urbanized blacks.

Proportionately, many more blacks were dying younger than whites. In 1911 Kansas City officials commissioned a report on the health of the city's residents. The study spanned a period of seven months, and during each of those seven months deaths exceeded births among blacks. The black population of the city was actually declining while the white population was growing at a rate of 15 percent. Aside from death, part of the reason for the decline was that blacks were leaving the state. During the thirty years from 1880 to 1910, Missouri's black population grew by only 8 percent, from 145,350 to 157,452. By contrast, the white population grew by 55 percent, from 2,022,826 to 3,134,932. From 1900 to 1910, Missouri's black population actually declined by 2.3 percent. The white population, in contrast, grew by 6.5 percent during that same period.

At this time, Americans generally held the position that public funds should not support unemployed, elderly, and disabled people. Those who stayed tried to cope with their terrible living conditions in a variety of ways. State chapters of the newly formed Urban League and the National Association for the Advancement of Colored People (NAACP) were established in urban areas to promote better job opportunities and legal and social services for blacks. Black fraternal groups and lodges became extremely popular during this era as well. They provided social cohesion, solidarity, and relief for destitute members when it was unavailable elsewhere. The Ancient Free and Accepted Masons of Missouri established a Masonic home near Hannibal, Missouri, in 1908 to care for elderly and impoverished masons and orphans of masons. It remained a mainstay of the Masonic community until the mid-twentieth century.

The same sentiment toward racial solidarity that caused the lodges to flourish also contributed to the prosperity of a number of black businesses, which catered almost exclusively to a segregated clientele. There were many black businessmen and professionals in St. Louis: Charles C. Clark ran Clark and Smith Men's Furnishing Goods Store, H. S. Ferguson owned the successful St. Louis Delicatessen Company, and C. K. Robinson was proprietor of the Robinson Printing Company. Yearly sales of black businesses such as these totaled more than one million dollars. Yet this impressive figure represented only about 8 percent of the estimated annual earnings of black St. Louisans. More than 90 percent of the black wage earners worked as domestics, factory workers, and common laborers.

In outstate Missouri, most rural blacks were still engaged in farming. State statistics reveal that Missouri blacks owned nearly thirty-eight hundred farms in 1913 worth an estimated $27.7 million. In 1907 Nathaniel C. Bruce, the son of Virginia ex-slaves, established an agricultural school near Dalton in Chariton County "to train the negro youth 'back to the land' and for efficient service in the home and on the farm." By 1911 Bruce reorganized his school as the Bartlett Agricultural and Industrial School after the substantial contributions of white philanthropists, which included Mr. and Mrs. Herschel Bartlett, Judge and Mrs. W. K. James, and Mr. and Mrs. Adolphus Busch I, enabled him to purchase twelve acres and to build classrooms and a dormitory.

A former student of Booker T. Washington, Bruce modeled his school after his mentor's Tuskegee Institute in Alabama, billing it as "the Tuskegee of the Midwest." While hundreds of thousands of blacks were leaving the rural South for northern cities, Bruce advocated a vocational and agricultural training for blacks so that they could achieve economic independence as a means to political and social rights. By 1914 the hard work of Bruce, his staff, and their students began to pay off. In spite of a drought, their entry in a statewide agricultural contest won them the *Missouri Ruralist* first prize for the highest corn yield. The following year the school again won first prize for the highest corn yield and finished second nationally in corn production at the Panama-Pacific International

Exposition held in San Francisco. "Place Missouri black boys on Missouri black land, behind the world-famed Missouri mule," Bruce boasted, "and nothing can beat the combination for raising corn or other crops." By 1920 over five hundred students had enrolled in the school since its inception. The Bartlett School also sponsored the annual Missouri–Mid-Western States Negro Farmer's and Farm Women's Conference, which sometimes attracted as many as fifteen hundred rural blacks to its farm and produce exhibits.

In southeast Missouri, Charles and Bettie Birthright achieved economic prosperity as farmers during the late nineteenth and early twentieth centuries. The Birthrights, both born slaves in Virginia, had moved to Missouri with their master in the 1850s. After Emancipation they moved to Clarkton, Missouri, where Charles worked as a barber and a farmer, and Bettie worked as a seamstress and cook. The couple began to purchase land in the late 1870s, and by 1879 the Birthrights owned ninety-six acres in Dunklin County, including four town lots in Clarkton. By 1909 the couple owned 426 acres in Dunklin County and an additional ninety-three acres in New Madrid County.

Black newspapers of this era catered to and tried to promote black solidarity in the face of oppression. Publishers of black newspapers usually had very limited capital with which to start. Consequently, they were often short-lived enterprises. One of the most successful of the black newspapers during these years was the *St. Louis Palladium*, founded in 1884 and edited by John W. Wheeler from 1897 to 1911. Wheeler advocated black advancement through industry and self-reliance, a philosophy eminently consistent with that of his contemporary, Booker T. Washington. Wheeler shied away from the politics of confrontation and refused to abandon the Republican party when others of his race were doing so in the 1890s and the early 1900s.

Perhaps one of the most positive contributions of the years of betrayal was the flowering of black music in the segregated honky-tonks and dance halls of the state. John William "Blind" Boone of Warrensburg was a musical savant. Born in 1864, he was attacked with what was described as "brain fever" when only six months old. A Warrensburg doctor removed his eyes to relieve the pressure on his brain. Boone began playing publicly while still in his teens, and in 1879 he was taken to Columbia by John Lange, Jr., a black contractor who managed his act for thirty-five years. Boone had the uncanny ability to reproduce, note for note, even the most complicated pieces after only one hearing. Current musicologists believe that Boone's music, some of which is preserved today on player-piano rolls, reveals much about early ragtime music.

Blind Boone's better-known contemporary, Scott Joplin, lived for several years in Sedalia and later moved to St. Louis. Joplin was born in 1868 and left home to become a pianist at age fourteen. Two of his most famous pieces were "The Maple Leaf Rag" and "Treemonisha." The latter is an opera in which education is offered as the key to social advancement of black people. Other turn-of-the century black musicians who made musical history in Missouri included Tom Turpin, Arthur Marshall, Scott Hayden, James Scott, Louis Chauvin, and W. C. Handy. It was Handy who composed the still-popular "St. Louis Blues."

Perhaps Handy's title summed up the feeling of Missouri blacks generally during this mournful period. By the time America entered World War I, blacks were leaving the state in inordinately large numbers. Those who remained became increasingly urbanized, moving to the cities to find jobs and upward social mobility. Instead, most found segregation and squalor and, at best, an uneasy alliance with machine politicians.

St. Louis tried desperately to segregate blacks in 1916. Local citizens, unable to work effectively through the party machinery, used the initiative-referendum procedure to place a segregation ordinance on the ballot. St. Louisans passed the ordinance by a three-to-one majority, although it was later declared unconstitutional by the U.S. Supreme Court.

Despite the court's ruling, the sentiment of white St. Louis and the rest of Missouri toward blacks was obvious. A report in 1914 by the Missouri Association for Social Welfare summed up the situation. Writing for the association, white Missourian Roger Baldwin declared, "So much of the problem lies in the unthinking, inconsiderate attitude of white people that no specific remedies for present conditions can be proposed which in themselves offer any solution." The future looked bleak indeed.

Suggested Readings

The exodus of 1879 has been the subject of numerous books and articles, among them the following: Nell Irvin Painter, *Exodusters: Black Migration to*

Kansas after Reconstruction (New York: Knopf, 1977); Susanna M. Grenz, "The Exodusters of 1879: St. Louis and Kansas City Responses," *Missouri Historical Review* 73 (October 1978): 54–70; and Arvarh E. Strickland, "Toward the Promised Land: The Exodus to Kansas and Afterward," *Missouri Historical Review* 69 (July 1975): 376–412.

Black education during this period is covered in W. Sherman Savage, "The Legal Provisions for Negro Schools in Missouri from 1865 to 1890," *Journal of Negro History* 26 (July 1931): 309–21. Information about the black press can be gleaned from the following articles: George Everett Slavens, "The Missouri Negro Press 1875–1920," *Missouri Historical Review* 64 (July 1973): 535–47; and Lawrence O. Christensen, "The Racial Views of John W. Wheeler," *Missouri Historical Review* 67 (July 1973): 535–47.

The story behind Missouri blacks' involvement in the development of ragtime music is told in Rudi Blesh and Harriet Janis, *They All Played Ragtime: The True Story of an American Music* (New York: Oak Publications, 1966). More recently, William Barlow's *Looking Up at Down: The Emergence of Blues Culture* (Philadelphia: Temple University Press, 1989) is helpful, as is William E. Parrish's essay "Blind Boone's Ragtime," *Missouri Life* (November–December 1979): 17–23. "Blind" Boone is also the subject of Jack A. Batterson, "Life and Career of Blind Boone" (Master's thesis, University of Missouri–Columbia, 1986).

The story of the Bartlett Agricultural and Industrial School for Negroes, later the Dalton Vocational School, is told in Patrick J. Huber and Gary R. Kremer, "Nathaniel C. Bruce, Black Education and the 'Tuskegee of the Midwest,'" *Missouri Historical Review* (October 1991). The exodus of blacks from Springfield after the Easter weekend lynchings is the subject of Katherine Lederer, *Many Thousand Gone: Springfield's Lost Black History* (Springfield: Published by the author, 1986).

Black St. Louis is the subject of Lawrence O. Christensen, "Black St. Louis: A Study in Race Relations, 1865–1916" (Ph.D. dissertation, University of Missouri–Columbia, 1972); his "Race Relations in St. Louis, 1865–1916," *Missouri Historical Review* 78 (January 1984): 123–36; and Katharine T. Corbett and Mary Seematter, "Black St. Louis at the Turn of the Century," *Gateway Heritage* 7 (Summer 1986): 40–48. Christensen is also the author of an article about the fascinating Birthright family, "The Popular Image of Blacks vs. the Birthrights," *Missouri Historical Review* 81 (October 1986): 37–52. The public life of prominent black Missourian James Milton Turner is chronicled in Gary R. Kremer, *James Milton Turner and the Promise of America* (Columbia: University of Missouri Press, 1991).

Private William E.
Chenault, Springfield,
Missouri. Photograph
originally appeared in
the 1919 *Greene
County Honor Roll.*
(Missouri Depart-
ment of Natural
Resources, Missouri
State Museum.)

Richard Baxter Foster, an officer in the Sixty-second Colored Infantry and first principal of Lincoln Institute (Inman E. Page Library of Lincoln University, Jefferson City).

Wendell Pruitt, Lincoln graduate and decorated veteran of the Ninety-ninth Fighter Squadron in World War II (Inman E. Page Library of Lincoln University, Jefferson City).

Bettie and Charles Birthright (Dunklin County Museum; Courtesy State Historical Society of Missouri, Columbia).

Cropperville was home for about sixty-five black families after sharecroppers had been evicted from the Bootheel in 1939. (Western Historical Manuscript Collection, University of Missouri–St. Louis.)

The average family income for Cropperville residents was only $50 per year.

The Reverend Will Driver, Sr., Eldridge, Missouri, preacher, 1909. Driver was a pioneer in the Laclede County town named for the black settler Eldridge. (Courtesy Gary R. Kremer.)

Missouri Industrial Home for Negro Girls. Established in 1916, this facility continued to operate as a reform school for black girls into the 1950s. (Courtesy Gary R. Kremer.)

"Colored" Baptist Church, Bunceton, Missouri, 1914 (Courtesy Gary R. Kremer).

Tom Bass of Mexico, Missouri. Bass was an internationally known horse trainer. (State Historical Society of Missouri, Columbia.)

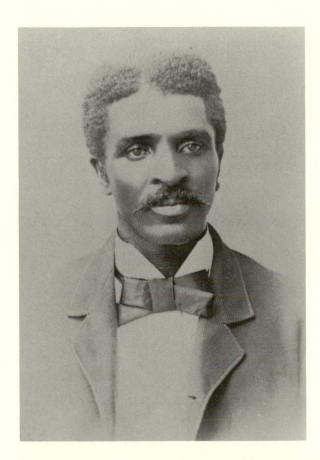

George Washington Carver (Inman E. Page Library of Lincoln University, Jefferson City).

Streetworkers on Grand Street in Kansas City, ca. 1910 (Missouri Valley Special Collections, Kansas City Public Library, Kansas City, Missouri).

128

Belvidere tenement house, ca. 1910 (Missouri Valley Special Collections, Kansas City Public Library, Kansas City, Missouri).

Nathaniel C. Bruce with prize-winning corn (State Historical Society of Missouri, Columbia).

Graduates of Lincoln High School, Springfield, Missouri, June 1906 (Courtesy of Katherine Lederer).

Hardrick Brothers Grocery Store, Springfield, Missouri, ca. 1905 (Courtesy Katherine Lederer).

Private Myrl Billings, Springfield, Missouri, flanked by two unidentified soldiers, World War I. (Courtesy Katherine Lederer.)

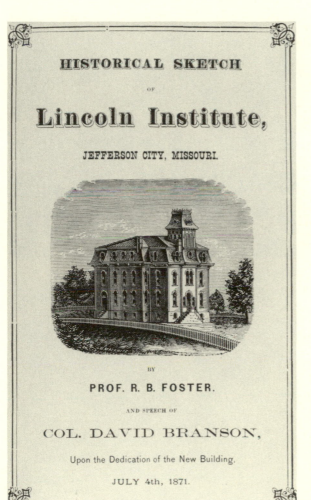

Photograph of the cover of a brochure commemorating the dedication of the first building erected on the Lincoln Institute campus in 1871. (Inman E. Page Library of Lincoln University, Jefferson City.)

Bennie Moten Orchestra, Kansas City, 1931. Count Basie is third from right.
(*Kansas City Star*.)

John William
"Blind" Boone
and his wife,
Eugenia (State
Historical Soci-
ety of Missouri,
Columbia).

Annie Turnbo
Malone, founder of
Poro Beauty College
in St. Louis (Chicago
Historical Society).

Josephine Baker, international entertainer *(St. Louis American)*.

St. Louis tenement homes, 1937 (Charles Treft Collection, State Historical Society of Missouri, Columbia).

Lynchings in the United States, 1909-1918

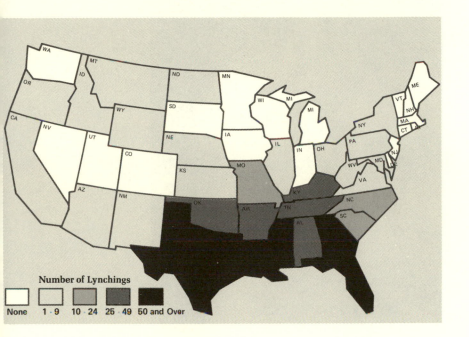

Satchel Paige in
Kansas City
Monarch's uniform
(Courtesy of
John Holway).

Kansas City Monarchs in 1908, *l to r:* Bill Houston, Bert Wakefield, Twitty McAdoo, West Wilkins, Bill Lindsey, Tom McCampbell, Chick Pullam, Frank Evans, Tom Sterman, Ernest McCampbell, Fred Lee, and "Frog" Lindsey. (Courtesy of National Baseball Library, Cooperstown, New York.)

Kansas City Monarchs pitching staff in 1942, *l to r:* Hilton Smith, Jack Matchet, Booker McDaniel, James Lamar, Cozzie Johnson, and Satchel Paige. (Courtesy of National Baseball Library, Cooperstown, New York.)

8

Hope Betrayed
Between the World Wars

The era of World War I brought hope and disillusionment for black Americans. The war effort required all Americans to make sacrifices in winning the struggle. When the war ended, blacks expected to share equally in the fruits of victory. Instead, they found that their nation grew increasingly hostile toward them during the 1920s. Likewise, when economic depression struck in the 1930s, they found that they were hit the hardest.

This was a particularly bitter irony in view of the fact that World War I was to have been an especially idealistic confrontation. President Woodrow Wilson proclaimed its noble purpose when he declared that it was a war "to make the world safe for democracy." Although black Americans were still victimized by white racism when the war began, they were urged by black leaders to support the war effort in spite of the way they had been treated. W. E. B. Du Bois's "Close Ranks" editorial in the NAACP's official magazine *The Crisis* in July 1918 summarized the argument:

> We of the colored race have no ordinary interest in the outcome. That which the German power represents spells death to the aspirations of Negroes and all dark races for equality, freedom, and democracy. Let us not hesitate. Let us, while this war lasts, forget our special grievances and close our ranks shoulder to shoulder with our white fellow-citizens and the allied nations that are fighting for democracy.

Many blacks believed that prejudice against them would be lessened if they joined the fight. Less than twenty years before, that sentiment had led a number of black Missourians to volunteer for service in the Spanish-American War. The black 70th Regiment of the Immunes was mustered in on September 16, 1898, at St. Louis with forty-two officers and 953 enlisted men.

World War I saw a similar response from the black community. Nation-wide, over four hundred thousand blacks joined the army, including 1,353 commissioned officers, 9 field clerks, and 15 army nurses. There were 9,219 black Missouri soldiers inducted into the service between June 5, 1917, and November 11, 1918. Despite his willingness to fight, however, the black soldier was used primarily as a noncombatant, usually in loading and unloading ships and driving trucks. When he did receive an opportunity to fight, he acquitted himself well. Two black infantry divisions, the Ninety-second and Ninety-third, served in France. The Ninety-second Division served on the battlefront with the U.S. Second Army in an assault on the Hindenburg line. In September 1918, *The Crisis* carried the following assessment of black soldiers in a recent battle:

American Negro troops proved their value as fighters in the line east of Verdun of June 12. . . . The Germans attempted a raid in that sector but were completely repulsed by the Negroes. The Boches began a terrific bombard-ment at one minute after midnight (throwing over between 3,000 and 4,000 shells from guns ranging in size from 67 to 340 millimeters). The bombard-ment was concentrated on small areas. Many of the shells made holes from ten to fifteen feet across. In the midst of this inferno the Negroes coolly stuck to their posts, operating machine guns and automatic rifles and keeping up such a steady barrage that the German infantry failed to penetrate the American lines. The Americans miraculously sustained only two wounded.

Obviously, the black soldier was fighting for a victory that was both national and personal; he wanted victory for America and hoped that upon his return he would receive the full rights of citizenship that had thus far eluded him.

When the war broke out, Governor Frederick D. Gardner asked a number of black leaders in the state how blacks could become a more efficient and productive part of the state and nation. Tired of the lack of response to their problems from both Democrats and Republicans, a number of leaders responded that black self-reliance was the only answer. They proposed the idea of a Missouri Negro Industrial Commission that would be run by blacks and would allow black citizens to prove their merit. As historian Tom Baker has pointed out, the Missouri Negro Industrial Commission became the first state agency to be primarily concerned with the welfare of black Missourians. After being criticized by black leaders for not appointing any blacks to state positions, Governor Gardner organized the commission on February 12, 1918 (Abraham Lincoln's birthday), appointing sixteen commissioners and charging them to "have a voice in their own upliftment and to discover, ferret out, survey and recommend remedies for their own betterment." Governor Gardner, a Democrat, apparently created the commission to strengthen his reputation with the increasingly important black voters and also to avoid appointing blacks to the white patronage positions in the state government.

The Missouri Negro Industrial Commission's first goal was to organize black Missourians, especially farmers, behind the war effort by selling war bonds, teaching better agricultural methods, increasing acreage under cultivation and crop production, and conserving food and materials. By late 1918 the commission had sold over six hundred thousand dollars in Liberty and Baby Bonds. Missouri was among the first states to organize a black commission to support the war effort. New York, Georgia, Texas, Alabama, Mississippi, and several other southern states quickly followed with Negro councils of defense modeled after Missouri's organization.

The first commissioners of the Missouri Negro Industrial Commission were not salaried, were all loyal Democrats, and were all champions of Booker T. Washington's philosophy of accommodation and self-improvement. Nathaniel C. Bruce, the commission's first chairman, reported in late 1918 that the commissioners had held over forty meetings statewide "urging and stimulating our race's old time loyalty, fidelity and hearty, persistent labor. We have also time after time, gone about especially emphasizing the value of good manners, quiet, gentle, courteous and patience in overcoming evil." The members of the Missouri Negro Industrial Commission probably realized that given the racism and racial attitudes of the period, deference to whites would reap the greatest benefits for black Missourians within the political system.

The commission, however, was politically powerless. It could only make recommendations to the governor and to the General Assembly and had no enforcement powers. Although it made numerous recommendations to the General Assembly throughout the years, that body rarely endorsed its initiatives. Two significant recommendations that were acted upon by the state legislature included the creation of the position of Negro Inspector of Schools, and in 1923 the all-black Bartlett Agricultural and Industrial School in Chariton County was reorganized with a state appropriation as a demonstration farm and agricultural school for black youths. It was placed under the general control of the University of Missouri's College of Agriculture and renamed the Dalton Vocational School.

Some of Missouri's most prominent and finest black leaders were at one time commissioners, including C. C. Hubbard, the principal of Lincoln High School in Sedalia; Tom Bass, the world-famous horse trainer of Mexico; and Aaron E. Malone, president of Poro College in St. Louis. The law creating the Missouri Negro Industrial Commission expired in 1928, and although the General Assembly originally intended the commission to operate as a permanent organization, it was allowed to die quietly.

In spite of the commission's relative lack of success, World War I gave blacks all over the country an opportunity to improve their conditions. When fighting broke out in 1914, European immigration, averaging approximately one million people a year, virtually stopped. With Europe torn apart by the war, the United States became the workshop of the world. White employers, badly in need of workers for mines, railroads, shipyards, automobile factories, and flour and meat packing houses, turned to a major new source of labor—southern blacks.

Blacks began to stream north by the thousands to fill the labor gap. Census figures revealed that in 1910 there were 552,845 blacks in the country engaged in industrial pursuits; that number jumped to 960,039 by 1920. Many idle or underpaid Missouri blacks left the state for Detroit, Pittsburgh, New York, Cleveland, and Chicago where they could earn five dollars a day in factories, foundries, and shipyards. Rural blacks, hearing of better economic and social opportunities in the cities, moved to Kansas City and St. Louis.

Serious problems emerged, however, when the black migrants who had been attracted to urban industry stayed in the cities, thereby adding to the general unemployment that the end of the war raised to dangerously high levels. Greater numbers of blacks living in cities meant that two things would happen. First, the all-black neighborhoods of the cities became more crowded, more unsanitary, and more crime-ridden. Second, the all-black neighborhoods could no longer house the increased population, so blacks began seeking places to live in all-white neighborhoods. Many white families resented living next door to blacks: some moved away, others threatened black families, and others resorted to violence. A period of extreme reaction set in, and immigrants, Jews, Communists, blacks, and a host of others outside the mainstream of American life were attacked as alien to the American way.

Black relocation into white neighborhoods was often vigorously resisted. In 1905 pastors of five white churches in St. Louis joined together to stop the sale of the white Central Presbyterian Church to the black congregation of Memorial Methodist Episcopal Church. In 1908 a white St. Louis newspaper carried the following headline: "The Negro Must Go, Is Cry: West End Citizens Bitterly Resent Invasion of Blacks." Samuel R. Hopkins, the black president of the Square Deal Realty and Loan Company, tried in 1925 to move into a formerly all-white neighborhood in Kansas City. His home was bombed.

One of the bloodiest confrontations in the country occurred in East St. Louis, just across the river from Missouri's largest city. Ten thousand black migrants had come to that city, many searching for jobs in factories holding government contracts. In at least one instance rural blacks were actually imported into the city by white businessmen to break a strike. Clashes between white and black workers ended in a bloody race riot in July 1917. Before it was over, nine whites and thirty-nine blacks had been killed. Across the river tension also ran high, but St. Louis managed to avoid a similar racial explosion. Many of the East St. Louis blacks, frightened by the violence of the riot, fled to the Missouri side of the river, and a large number of them settled in the Kinloch area.

White hostility toward blacks called forth incredible examples of black resiliency and commitment to cultural integrity. Perhaps the most notable example of this was in a neighborhood called "the Ville" in north St. Louis. Ville residents prided themselves on their middle-class values and on the strength of their sustaining institutions, particularly the Sumner High School and the Antioch Baptist Church.

Meanwhile, opposition to black laborers led many workers to try to form labor unions and bargain collectively. Unions such as the Negro Brotherhood of Sleeping Car Porters and Maids, under the Socialist labor leader A. Phillip Randolph, tried to organize black workers. In 1914 there were nine hundred black Pullman porters in St. Louis, the largest block of black railroad workers in the city. But the Pullman Company threatened to fire workers who joined the union, a threat that was carried out on more than one occasion in St. Louis and Kansas City. Black workers still had too little influence to make black labor unions a powerful force. As late as 1929, there were only eighty-one St. Louis blacks in Randolph's union.

The 1920s also saw a renewed interest in black culture and black consciousness in large part due to continuing overt discrimination. A number of black writers, such as W. E. B. Du Bois, James Weldon Johnson, Claude McKay, Jean Toomer, Countee Cullen, Langston Hughes, and Zora Neale Hurston, wrote of both racial pride and oppression. Hughes, a native of Joplin, Missouri, became one of the most prolific and famous. His books *The Weary Blues* and *Fine Clothes to the Jew* assured him lasting literary recognition.

This movement, centered in New York City and known as the Harlem Renaissance, extended to Missouri primarily in the form of a musical revolution. As ragtime music gave way to Jazz, Missouri blacks helped lead the way. Jazz came to Missouri, according to historian Richard Kirkendall, on riverboats bound from New Orleans to St. Louis. Soon St. Louis blacks developed their own jazz groups, such as the Missourians, which featured Cab Calloway. The Missourians were considered one of the best jazz bands from the South when they traveled to New York and performed in the Savoy Ballroom.

Perhaps Missouri's most famous jazz musician of the Roaring Twenties was Will "Count" Basie, who came to Kansas City as a penniless piano player in the mid–1920s. Basie played with Walter Page's Blue Devils until Page dissolved the band and joined Bennie Moten. The Count went along and sent jazz music to new heights. Basie described his own style of music as follows: "I don't dig the two-beat jive the New Orleans cats play, because my boys and I got to have four heavy beats to a bar and no cheating." When Moten died in 1928, Count Basie took the band and carried it to international acclaim.

Another African-American whose childhood roots were in Missouri attained international fame only after leaving the racist United States. Josephine Baker's first show business break came in 1924 when she won a part in the New York musical "Chocolate Dandies" in which she achieved recognition for her comedy role as a member of the chorus line. In 1925 Baker left the United States to tour with Caroline Dudley's Revue Negre in Europe, and there she became an overnight sensation and was celebrated as the toast of Paris. By the late 1920s she was headlining at the Folies-Bergère and other European jazz clubs and drawing huge audiences and rave reviews.

The riverport city of St. Louis was a rich center for urban blues from the period of the 1920s to the 1940s. Mary Johnson and Alice Moore were among many female blues singers who performed in the classic blues style during the late 1920s. And a number of innovative blues pianists also performed in local riverfront saloons, brothels, and gambling houses in the St. Louis and East St. Louis red-light districts, including Lee Green, Roosevelt Sykes, Walter Davis, and Peetie Wheetstraw, who billed himself as "The Devel's Son-In-Law."

By far, the area's premier bluesman of the period was Lonnie Johnson, whom historian William Barlow has called "the most influential musician in St. Louis blues circles during the 1920s." Johnson began performing on a St. Louis riverboat in 1920 and later played in honky tonks across the river in East St. Louis. A gifted composer and an accomplished and versatile musician on the guitar, piano, and banjo, he was a central figure in the development of urban blues and recorded more than one hundred records between the mid–1920s and the early 1930s. He also accompanied the jazz legends Louis Armstrong and Duke Ellington on recordings. Johnson left St. Louis in the late 1920s and eventually settled in Chicago. Other blues guitarists and musicians, such as J. D. Short, Robert Nighthawk, Big Joe Williams, Henry "Mule" Townsend, and Charley Jordan, maintained the city's rich blues tradition during the 1930s despite the hard times of the Great Depression. Of the 1930s Townsend recalled, "St. Louis was a hot town for blues in those days, just like Chicago."

Throughout the 1920s most Missouri blacks still hoped that education would be the key to winning first-class citizenship. But nowhere was discrimination more firmly entrenched than in education. Black teachers were often paid 25 percent less than white teachers in comparable schools.

Inadequate facilities were also the rule. Missouri blacks attended some schools that were so bad that black paint was applied to wooden walls as a substitute for blackboards. Schools were often overcrowded, some seating as many as three students to a desk. Others could afford no desks and seated students on benches of rough hewn wood. One school had no water supply within 200 yards.

State Superintendent Charles A. Lee resolved to improve the educational opportunities of blacks when he assumed his position in 1923. Legislation in 1921 had already begun to point the way. A Negro Inspector of Schools was authorized and provisions were made for the establishment of black high schools in Missouri counties that had a population of one hundred thousand or more. White support for these measures was somewhat self-interested. Lee's predecessor had pleaded with county superintendents to support black education because, in his words, "illiteracy . . . breeds contempt for law and order and lays the foundations for anarchy and bolshevism."

Lee was no more successful in improving black schools than his predecessors had been, however. About all that the Inspector of Negro Schools could do was to document the terrible inadequacy of Missouri's black schools. The single most important problem was the expense of trying to maintain a separate but equal educational system; Missouri simply could not afford it. Inspector Nathaniel C. Bruce summed up the situation in his 1924 report:

> Six Missouri counties have no Negro persons at all, sixteen other counties have less than ten, forty counties have only seven-hundred Negro population, with 243 children in groups from 1 to 8, 12 and 14, not enough for the legal 15 for starting a colored school. Neither, in many counties, do the boards of education feel financially able to run two public schools. Missouri's poor school districts cannot maintain separate race schools except at great disparity and inequality.

The only solution was a single integrated system, although all the signs indicated that Missouri's intention was to move in exactly the opposite direction. In 1921 the Missouri General Assembly transformed the all-black Lincoln Institute into Lincoln University, thereby designating it *the* institution of higher learning for Missouri's blacks. The General Assembly would later transfer control of the Dalton School from the University of Missouri to Lincoln University. But Missouri could no more afford a dual university system for blacks and whites than it could a dual system at the secondary and elementary levels.

The increasing urbanization of Missouri's blacks tied them more closely than ever before to the urban political machines. The Republican party dominated in St. Louis, and blacks tended to stay with that party, although there was continued dissatisfaction with the lack of responsiveness from the old party of Lincoln. Democrats under the leadership of Tom Pendergast controlled Kansas City, and blacks there generally sided with them. Statewide, blacks still tended to support the Republican party, although that was changing, too. The Republicans failed to resolve problems for blacks during the years they controlled the governor's office (from 1921 to 1933), thus adding to the number of alienated and frustrated blacks.

Blacks in St. Louis were becoming better organized by 1920. The nucleus of their group was an alliance known as the Citizens Liberty League. The league, aided by the statewide Missouri Negro Republican League, was able to gain the nomination and election of Walthall Moore in 1920. Moore was the first black person to serve in the Missouri legislature. He lost his bid for reelection in 1922, but St. Louis blacks did see Crittenden Clark become the first black justice of the peace in the city. Charles Turpin and Langston Harrison were elected constables.

Lynching continued to be practiced among hostile and lawless whites; indeed, Missouri has an infamous tradition of lynching. Between 1900 and 1931 mobs in the state lynched twenty-two men, seventeen of whom were black. On April 29, 1923, a mob in Columbia, Missouri, lynched James T. Scott, a thirty-five-year-old black janitor employed by the University of Missouri, from Stewart Bridge, an automobile overpass located a quarter of a mile from the school's campus. Scott was being held in the Boone County jail, charged with assaulting the fourteen-year-old daughter of a university foreign language professor. The day before the lynching, a local newspaper reported that the victim had "positively identified" Scott as her assailant. The paper also published an editorial demanding "swift justice." Perhaps stirred by the newspaper's inflammatory remarks, a mob of fifty men stormed the jail at 11:00 P.M. that night. Around midnight, prominent St. Louis attorney George L. Vaughn, who was in Columbia to assist in Scott's legal defense, telephoned Governor Arthur M. Hyde, urging him to mobilize the 128th Field Artillery of the Missouri National Guard, which was headquartered in Columbia, to disperse the mob.

The national guard never arrived to prevent the lynching. Two thousand spectators witnessed the mob hang Scott around 1:40 A.M. The lynching attracted front-page headlines from newspapers across the country because of the University of Missouri's presence in the community. Subsequently, a grand jury indicted five white men, including a national guard sergeant, for their participation in the lynching, but only one man ever came to trial. Charged with first degree murder, he was acquitted after only eleven minutes of deliberation.

One of the most brutal lynchings in the state occurred at Charleston in southeast Missouri in 1924. A black man named Roosevelt Grigsley was lynched by a mob of two hundred men, who took him from law enforcement officials. He was hanged in front of a grocery store; shots were fired through his body, and later he was tied behind a car and dragged through the streets of the black section of town.

Another brutal lynching occurred in Maryville in northwest Missouri in 1931. Raymond Gunn, a twenty-seven-year-old ex-convict, confessed to the murder of Velma Colter, a twenty-year-old white schoolteacher. At 9:30 A.M. on January 12, 1931, a mob overpowered the Nodaway County sheriff and his deputies and took Gunn. Three miles south of Maryville, the mob chained the prisoner to the roof of the schoolhouse where the murder had been committed, doused the structure with gasoline, and set it on fire. A crowd of three thousand watched Gunn burn alive.

The sheriff refused to call the 128th Field Artillery of the Missouri National Guard, which had already been mobilized in the Maryville armory to protect the prisoner. In contrast to the Scott lynching in Columbia, the *Maryville Daily Forum* had advised against a lynching in its editorial, "Time for Cool Heads," published two days before the incident.

Of major concern to blacks during the 1920s was the rising influence of the Ku Klux Klan. The Klan enjoyed a general revival in America during this decade, tapping the reservoir of resentment against the change that was building in the country and attacking everything that was not "one hundred percent American." The Ku Klux Klan generally drew its membership largely from the rural areas of Missouri, but one urban hotbed of Klan activity in the state was St. Joseph where the weekly *Missouri Valley Independent,* a pro-Klan newspaper, was published. In addition to that paper, the *Missouri Klan Kourier* promoted the organization weekly in the mid–1920s.

In 1923 William S. Campbell of St. Joseph, the "Exalted Cyclops," promised that the Klan would control some four hundred thousand votes in Missouri in the 1924 election, including those of the women's Ku Klux Klan auxiliary. Although Campbell's prediction fell short, the Klan reached the height of its influence in the state in the 1924 election. Arthur Davis, Democratic gubernatorial candidate, refused to sign an affidavit denying membership in the Klan and admitted that he had attended a Klan rally near his home. Republican candidate Sam Baker, on the other hand, willingly signed such a statement and spoke out against the Klan. Baker was elected and received the majority of Missouri's black votes. St. Louis voters also returned Walthall Moore to the General Assembly in 1924 and chose Robert T. Scott as the first black ward committeeman. Moore served in the Missouri legislature until 1930 and was chosen as one of Missouri's delegates-at-large to the 1928 Republican National Convention.

Despite this apparent merger of black and Republican interests, however, all was not well between the traditional allies. Blacks expected more control of their own affairs; instead, they were getting less. They became particularly upset when Governor Baker tried to interfere with the administration of Lincoln University, which had only recently been transformed into a university as a result of legislation sponsored by Representative Moore. After repeated efforts, Baker succeeded in ousting the popular president of Lincoln University, Nathan B. Young. That action, Baker's inability to curtail lynchings, and the party's unwillingness to support a black congressional candidate further frustrated blacks.

As the election of 1928 approached, the Kansas City Pendergast organization used its influence on the Democratic party to tap this frustration. Among other things, the Democrats nominated black St. Louisan Joseph L. McLemore for Congress. Despite McLemore's loss, his nomination and support by Democrats impressed blacks and foreshadowed the 1930s when the black Missouri vote would become solidly Democratic. Jordan Chambers, referred to as the "Negro Mayor of St. Louis" by the *St. Louis Post-Dispatch,* was the dominant force in Missouri's largest city urging blacks to abandon the Republican party.

The stock market crash of 1929 sent the American economy into a downward plunge from which it would not recover for more than a decade. Millions of Americans faced unemployment, handouts, and even soup lines. The Great Depression hit blacks hardest of all. They were the last to be hired and the first to be fired. Whites now openly competed for jobs that were once regarded as "nigger" work. The trend was reflected even in the state capitol where white elevator operators replaced blacks. In his autobiography, *The Big Sea,* the Missouri-born poet Langston Hughes wrote: "The depression brought everybody down a peg or two. And the Negroes had but few pegs to fall." Indeed, some scholars have asserted that black workers began feeling the effects of the depression as early as 1925. In St. Louis, 43 percent of the city's black workers were unemployed by 1930, and in the mid–1930s when 16 percent of all St. Louis families were on relief assistance from the federal government, nearly half of all black families were receiving some form of governmental assistance.

White labor unions, traditionally hostile to black workers, became even more so during the 1930s. Black organizations attempted to create jobs. The Kansas City Urban League, for example, opened a training school for janitors and graduated its first class in 1934. The hardest hit were the sharecroppers of the Bootheel in southeast Missouri. Both white and black tenants of this region were forced to live in crude shacks that were unpainted and lacked plastering and insulation. In 1936 white sharecroppers in the Bootheel could expect to make a little over $400 for the year, while blacks had to settle for approximately $150 less.

In 1939 nearly three hundred men, women, and children were facing death by exposure and starvation in a shack colony near Poplar Bluff after being evicted by their landlords. They were denied federal relief by local officials who were controlled by the white planters of the area. Many in the colony were the remnants of fifteen hundred black and white cotton pickers who had earlier resisted eviction by the planters. The cotton pickers had been led by Owen R. Whitfield, a black preacher and labor organizer.

President Franklin D. Roosevelt's New Deal programs offered some respite from the economic woes. To begin with, Roosevelt's appointment of several blacks to responsible positions created a degree of optimism. In 1934 he named Dr. William J. Thompkins, well-known Kansas City physician and politician, as recorder of deeds for the District of Columbia. The appointment was Thompkins's reward for helping to swing black votes to the Roosevelt camp in the 1932 election. The president also appointed newspaperman Lester A. Walton, a native of St. Louis, to the position of minister to Liberia. At the time of his appointment in 1935, Walton was associate editor of the *New York Age*.

The formation of a "black cabinet" in the Roosevelt administration further encouraged blacks. It consisted of such brilliant individuals as William Hastie, Robert Weaver, Ralph Bunche, Booker T. McGraw, and Mary Bethune, among others. Public works projects using federal funds to perform socially beneficial tasks, such as the building of hospitals, schools, and playgrounds, offered employment to blacks. In 1938, a $3,160,000 black hospital, built with the aid of a New Deal program, was dedicated in St. Louis and named for the late black attorney Homer G. Phillips, who had worked to ensure its existence before his assassination. Phillips was murdered on June 18, 1931, by two black teenagers near his home while he waited for a street car. The murder was apparently motivated by a disagreement over the fee Phillips had charged for handling the case of the wife of one of the alleged murderers. Phillips was fifty-one years old at the time of his death. He had studied law at Howard University and was past president of the National Negro Bar Association. The *St. Louis Argus* eulogized Phillips as "a fighter for the rights of his people, and an untiring worker for the cause he believed to be right." Ironically, in spite of the fact that the Homer G. Phillips Hospital was to be a facility for blacks, white unions kept black laborers from helping to build this structure.

One New Deal program was especially useful to blacks, both nationally and locally: the Civilian Conservation Corps took thousands of young people off the streets and set them to work reforesting stripped lands. The National Youth Administration, under the leadership of Mary Bethune, enabled students and others, particularly at Lincoln University, to earn a college education or to learn trades. Another New Deal program that was a boon to blacks was the Social Security Act of 1935, which provided for old-age pensions and unemployment insurance.

But if relief measures were offering some hope to blacks, competition for the nation's limited economic resources added to the existing tensions between blacks and whites. In 1930 state troopers were twice called into the little town of Ste. Genevieve to prevent a triple lynching. The entire black population, with the exception of two families, left town after the threatened lynchings. In 1933 a mob in St. Joseph murdered and then burned a nineteen-year-old black prisoner, Lloyd Warner, after the sheriff gave him up. Reportedly, women and children cheered as the victim's eyes were gouged out.

A reign of terror swept Missouri during the election of 1934. In March the municipal election was marked by the slaying of a black Democratic precinct captain, William Finley. Eleven others were injured in the bloodiest and most fiercely contested balloting in the city's history. Within a week, gunmen trying to prevent blacks from voting terrorized the southwest Missouri community of Holland, climaxing in a series of antiblack demonstrations that had recently occurred elsewhere in that part of the state.

In 1939 racial friction broke out between blacks and whites in the small town of Oran. The trouble developed around a dispute over the right-of-way on a sidewalk. Then a mob decided to run all blacks out of town. State troopers were called in when the mob nearly destroyed a black family's house.

Segregation was still the rule in Missouri in the thirties. On the positive side, this allowed a number of black entrepreneurs, particularly those in service industries catering primarily to the black population, to enjoy financial success. Annie E. Turnbo Malone, like her more famous contemporary Madame C. J. Walker, was the founder and owner of a hair and cosmetics manufacturing company. Born in Metropolis, Illinois, she was raised by her older brothers and sisters after her father was killed in the Civil War. In 1900 she began producing a hair-growing preparation in Lovejoy, Illinois, and in 1902 she moved her expanding business to 2223 Market Street in St. Louis, Missouri. She was the founder and owner of the Poro Beauty College, which manufactured hair and cosmetic products and also trained beauticians, and in 1918 she relocated to her newly constructed Poro College Building, which cost one million dollars to build. Besides housing her business, the Poro College complex was an important site in the black community. It was home to the National Negro Business League offices as well as other religious, fraternal, and social organizations. In 1930, she relocated her business to Chicago.

Malone was a significant philanthropist, reinvesting her time, money, and efforts back into the community that had made her wealthy and successful. During her lifetime, she donated $8,000 to the building fund of the Pine Street YMCA of St. Louis; $10,000 to the Howard University Medical Fund; $25,000 to the citywide YMCA of St. Louis; a $10,000 building site; and a cash contribution of several thousand dollars to the St. Louis Colored Orphans Home, which still stands and now bears her name.

A number of black insurance companies also thrived. The Douglass Life Insurance Company, started in 1919 with home offices in St. Louis had over twenty thousand policy owners in Missouri by 1923. In addition to St. Louis and Kansas City, it did business in twenty cities and towns across Missouri. The company developed an annual premium income of $38,000 in four years and had the distinction of being the first insurance company in the state financed and managed exclusively by blacks. Jefferson City got its first black law firm in 1933 when Robert J. Cobb, W. Franklin Clark, and Sidney Redmond opened an office.

But the disadvantages of segregation far outweighed any financial advantages gained by a few black businesses. Everywhere in the state blacks were treated as second-class citizens. In 1930, J. G. Ish, Jr., was refused a seat on the Pickwick-Greyhound night coach. Prospective black jurors were systematically barred from jury duty during the 1930s. St. Louis had twenty-one higher educational facilities in 1934, and only two of them—one a normal school and the other a nurses' training school— would admit blacks. Of the city's eighty-four recreational centers, only ten were open to blacks, and four of those were segregated. Only seven out of seventy swimming pools and playgrounds were open to black St. Louisans. Segregation even invaded the world of sports. In April 1939, the University of Missouri was forced to cancel plans for a track meet with the University of Wisconsin and Notre Dame. Wisconsin withdrew when Missouri banned its black hurdler, Ed Smith. Notre Dame then pulled out of the meet in protest.

Inroads against segregation did occur. In January 1938, black professor E. O. Borne won a five-hundred-dollar lawsuit against the segregation policies of the Pickwick-Greyhound Bus Line. And in that same month, white and black citizens worshiped jointly at an interracial religious program in Moberly. But the most exciting challenges to segregation came in the field of education. It was becoming increasingly obvious that the state could not provide "separate but equal" educational facilities for less than 10 percent of the its population. The issue came to a head in the 1930s with demands for black graduate education in Missouri. The famous *Lloyd Gaines* case started with a Lincoln University student and ended with a U.S. Supreme Court decision that struck at the foundation of the state and nation's segregated schools.

Lloyd Gaines graduated from Lincoln University in 1936. He applied for admission to the University of Missouri Law School but was turned down because he was black. Gaines, with the aid of NAACP attorneys, sued the school, but Missouri's courts upheld the university's position. Gaines then appealed his case to the Supreme Court. That body, which had become more liberal with the advent of President Roosevelt's appointees, ruled in favor of Gaines by a six-to-two vote. Chief Justice Hughes, writing for the majority, declared that the state of Missouri had either to admit Lloyd Gaines to the all-white Missouri Law School or provide truly equal facilities for Gaines and other blacks to pursue legal careers. This spelled the beginning of the end of shuttling blacks off to separate and inferior educational facilities. Ironically, Gaines disappeared not long after the Supreme Court handed down its mandate; he has not been heard from since.

Although the *Gaines* case would facilitate future developments in black-white relations, the state of Missouri was not yet ready to give up its segregationist policies. Consequently, rather than allow blacks to enroll at the University of Missouri, it decided to set up a law school for blacks at Lincoln University. Thus, Lincoln University Law School, which was poorly funded, understaffed, and ill-equipped, came into existence in St. Louis during the summer of 1940.

The Gaines challenge to segregated education in Missouri was followed by a similar effort on the part of Lucille Bluford in 1939. Bluford, the managing editor of the *Kansas City Call,* sought admission to the University of Missouri's School of Journalism. Again, the university and the state declined to admit a black person to its campus. Instead, it created in 1941 the Lincoln University School of Journalism. The lengths the state was willing to go to avoid integrating the University of Missouri can be seen in the legislature's first-year appropriation for the Lincoln University School of Journalism: $65,000 for three students.

The *Gaines* and *Bluford* cases did not, of course, cause an immediate groundswell for integration in the state. They did, however, lay the groundwork for the overturn of the 1890s doctrine of the "separate but equal" discriminatory doctrine of *Plessy v. Ferguson*. Henceforth, Missouri's response to its black community would be increasingly open to challenge. Black-white relations could never again be the same.

Suggested Readings

The best work on this period remains a doctoral dissertation completed at the University of Missouri–Columbia in 1970 by Larry H. Grothaus entitled "The Negro in Missouri Politics, 1890–1914."

The urban migration of blacks during the war years is covered in Emmet J. Scott, *Negro Migration during the War* (New York: Oxford University Press, 1920). The economic status of black St. Louis is the subject of William A. Crossland, *Industrial Conditions among Negroes in St. Louis* (St. Louis: Press of Mendle Printing Co., 1914). Also helpful are Katharine T. Corbett and Mary E. Seematter, "No Crystal Stair: Black St. Louis, 1920–1940," *Gateway Heritage* 8 (Fall 1987): 8–15; and Gary R. Kremer and Donald H. Ewalt, Jr., "The Historian as Preservationist: A Missouri Case Study," *The Public Historian* 3 (Fall 1981): 5–22. The latter essay is about the distinctive St. Louis neighborhood known as the Ville.

The role of the Ku Klux Klan in Missouri is dealt with briefly in Kenneth Jackson, *The Ku Klux Klan in the City, 1915–1930* (New York: Oxford University Press, 1976). Also helpful is John J. Large, Jr., "The 'Invisible Empire' and Missouri Politics: The Influence of the Revived Ku Klux Klan in the Election Campaign of 1924 as Reported in Missouri Newspapers," (Master's thesis, University of Missouri–Columbia, 1957). Larry Grothaus reveals much about the shift of Missouri blacks to the Democratic machine in "Kansas City Blacks: Harry S. Truman and the Pendergast Machine," *Missouri Historical Review* 68 (October 1974): 65–82.

Lynching in the nation between the world wars, with some references to Missouri, is discussed in Arthur F. Raper, *The Tragedy of Lynching* (Chapel Hill: University of North Carolina Press, 1933). The tragic 1923 Scott lynching in Columbia is chronicled in Patrick J. Huber, "The Lynching of James T. Scott: The Underside of a College Town," *Gateway Heritage* 12 (Summer

1991): 18–37. Also useful is Proctor N. Carter, Jr., "Lynch-Law and the Press of Missouri" (Master's thesis, University of Missouri–Columbia, 1933).

General information about blacks and the depression, with some references to Missouri, is available in Raymond Wolters, *Negroes and the Great Depression* (Westport, Conn.: Greenwood Publishing Co., 1970). Louis Cantor, "A Prologue to the Protest Movement: The Missouri Sharecroppers Roadside Demonstration of 1939," *Journal of American History* 55 (March 1969): 804–22, is also helpful, as are Arvarh E. Strickland, "The Plight of the People in the Sharecroppers' Demonstration in Southeast Missouri," *Missouri Historical Review* 81 (July 1987): 24–50; and Lorenzo J. Greene, "Lincoln University's Involvement with the Sharecropper Demonstration in Southeast Missouri, 1939–1940," *Missouri Historical Review* 82 (October 1987): 24–50. See also Elizabeth C. Grant, "Some Colored Working Mothers in Columbia" (Master's thesis, University of Missouri–Columbia, 1935); Audrey Nell Kittell, "The Negro Community of Columbia, Missouri" (Master's thesis, University of Missouri–Columbia, 1938); Mary Welek, "Jordan Chambers: Black Politician and Boss," *The Journal of Negro History* 57 (October 1972): 352–69; and Gary R. Kremer and Linda R. Gibbens, "The Missouri Industrial Home for Negro Girls: The 1930s," *American Studies* (Fall 1983): 77–94. The Missouri career of prominent educator Nathan B. Young is chronicled in Antonio F. Holland, "Nathan B. Young: The Development of Black Higher Education" (Ph.D. dissertation, University of Missouri–Columbia, 1984).

The rise of the Jazz Age in Missouri is dealt with in William H. Young and Nathan B. Young, *Your Kansas and Mine* (Kansas City: Published by the Authors, 1950). More recently, Richard B. Kirkendall has written of the same topic in *A History of Missouri, 1919 to 1953*, Vol. 5 of the Missouri Sesquicentennial Series (Columbia: University of Missouri Press, 1986). The blues in Kansas City and St. Louis is covered in William Barlow, *Looking Up at Down: The Emergence of Blues Culture* (Philadelphia: Temple University Press, 1989). The Josephine Baker story is told in her autobiography, written with Jo Bouillon, *Josephine* (New York: Dodd, Mead and Co., 1981). George Lipsitz's *The Sidewalks of St. Louis: Places, People, and Politics in an American City* (Columbia: University of Missouri Press, 1991) contains chapters on Josephine Baker, W. C. Handy, and Scott Joplin.

9

Appeal for Justice
Segregation Challenged

As the decade of the 1940s began, American citizens anxiously watched Adolf Hitler's challenge to Europe. In December 1941, the United States became involved in what had ballooned into World War II. Ultimately, the war had a dramatic effect on black life in America. It opened new job possibilities and provided blacks with an opportunity to demonstrate again the importance of their role in American society. In addition, the war provided Americans, black and white, with an opportunity to see clearly what could happen when racism was carried to its logical extreme by a hostile government. The lynching of a black man in Sikeston, Missouri, in 1942 when other black men were fighting and dying as American soldiers in the European and Pacific theaters of war seemed particularly paradoxical to many Americans.

The Sikeston lynching spurred the U.S. Department of Justice to intervene directly. Shortly after 1:30 A.M. on January 12, 1942, Sikeston law officers arrested Cleo Wright, a twenty-six-year-old black mill worker and ex-convict, for attacking Grace Sturgeon, a local white woman. When he pulled a knife and resisted arrest, Wright was shot four times and severely beaten with a flashlight by police. Near death, Wright was bandaged and sutured at the local hospital, which provided only emergency treatment to black patients, and then transferred to the local jail. At 11:30 A.M., a Scott County mob stormed the jail, overpowered the state troopers on guard, and removed the unconscious prisoner. The vigilantes tied Wright to a car, dragged him through the streets of Sunset Addition, Sikeston's black district, and finally set the battered corpse on fire.

Wright's brutal murder, the first lynching in the country since Pearl Harbor, dramatically linked American racism to the barbarities perpetrated by the totalitarian regimes of Nazi Germany, Fascist Italy, and Japan. While black soldiers were fighting and dying in a war for democracy in Europe and the Pacific, the brutal lynching reinforced the notion that black Americans were only second-class citizens on the home front. As one black editor bitterly commented, "Remember Pearl Harbor . . . and Sikeston, Missouri."

The public outrage over Wright's murder prompted the U.S. Department of Justice to conduct a federal investigation of the lynching, but its efforts proved futile. On July 30, 1942, a federal grand jury refused to return any indictments against the Sikeston lynchers despite a strong legal case. It concluded that the lynchers had denied Wright due process, but they had committed no federal offense since Wright was either already dead or dying. Nevertheless, the United States government's prosecution of the Wright lynchers set a precedent for federal intervention into civil rights cases, and the federal government would urgently renew its investigation of such cases in postwar America in its attempt to protect black Americans' inalienable rights.

World War II created a series of circumstances that led many blacks to believe their long struggle for equality was nearly over. More than three million black Americans registered for the draft during World War II and nearly a million actually served in the various branches of the armed forces. Lincoln University sent so many young men to the war that some people jokingly called the school a women's seminary during those years.

Black leaders fought segregation on several fronts during the war. The *Pittsburgh Courier* conducted a vigorous "Double-V" campaign, calling for a victory at home and abroad. In 1940, Brotherhood of Sleeping Car Porters President A. Phillip Randolph, NAACP Executive Secretary Walter White, and other black leaders succeeded in pressuring the War Department to accept blacks in all branches of the armed services. As in all previous American wars, black soldiers acquitted themselves well. Five American blacks received the Distinguished Service Cross and eighty-two black pilots received the Distinguished Flying Cross. Perhaps Missouri's most famous black fighter was former Lincoln student Captain Wendell Pruitt, a member of the Ninety-ninth Fighter Squadron, who won many medals for his valor in Europe. Pruitt flew seventy missions in Italy and was credited with destroying eleven Nazi planes and sinking one destroyer. He was awarded the Distinguished Flying Cross and the

Air Medal with seven oak leaf clusters. Ironically, although Pruitt survived numerous dangerous missions in the European theater of war, he died in a crash during a training flight soon after his return to the United States.

Racial prejudice was an obstacle even for those who wanted to serve their country. An attempt by the air force to set up black military programs at Jefferson Barracks in St. Louis was successfully opposed by whites in the city. The program had to be moved to Tuskegee Institute in Alabama instead. While the war raged in Europe and the Far East, blacks found new job opportunities at home. A process similar to the one that had accompanied World War I occurred: with immigration from overseas cut off and manpower shortages resulting from the draft, laborers were in great demand. Once again, blacks flooded the urban industrial centers to meet the need. The process was accelerated in June 1941 when President Franklin D. Roosevelt issued an executive order that prohibited racial discrimination in the hiring of workers in defense industries and in the federal government. By 1943 white St. Louisans complained that the demand for black laborers had made it almost impossible to find domestic workers.

It was the flood of black workers to northern cities that stimulated racial tensions. A serious race riot broke out in Detroit in June 1943. Many people in St. Louis braced for what they thought would be an equally serious outbreak in their own city. Bishop William Scarlett, head of the Episcopal Church of Missouri and president of the St. Louis Urban League, formed a committee to defuse racial tensions before they exploded. The Scarlett committee was a voluntary group of approximately twenty members of both races, including business and professional people, labor leaders, sociologists, elected officials, and public-spirited citizens. The committee worked with Governor Forrest Donnell, Mayor William D. Becker, and police and army officials to prevent a major riot, although numerous minor racial conflicts did occur. Racial problems were only magnified when the war ended, and American men returned home, flooding the job and housing markets.

The census of 1950 reflected the changes that occurred during the war years. Missouri's population in 1950 was 3,954,653: 2,954,653 were white, and 297,000 were black. Although blacks constituted roughly 7.4 percent of the population, more than three-fourths (76.9 percent) of the blacks resided in the state's two metropolitan areas. Jackson County, which included Kansas City, had 57,043 blacks out of a total population of 541,032 (10.5 percent), while St. Louis and St. Louis County had 171,461 (13.6 percent) blacks out of a total population of 1,263,145. Within St. Louis, the 154,448 blacks comprised 18 percent of the city's residents. The remainder of the black population was found chiefly in the southeastern counties of the Bootheel and along the Mississippi and Missouri rivers. In Mississippi and New Madrid counties, blacks constituted 21.8 percent and 16 percent of the inhabitants, respectively. The poverty of many of these rural blacks was graphically illustrated in the extremely poor black community of Cropperville, located about fifteen miles southwest of Poplar Bluff. Cropperville was home for about sixty-five black families who were the remnants of the fifteen hundred sharecroppers who had been evicted in 1939. Many residents still lived in tents the year round. Most of the wage earners in this colony worked as seasonal farmhands, some going as far north as Michigan to pick fruit. Family income among Cropperville residents was extremely low, ranging from $35 to $195 per year. The average was only $50.

Once the war was over, former soldiers rejoined the labor force and thus increased the competition for jobs. The blacks who found employment tended to occupy unskilled positions and perform domestic or menial tasks. Of the 109,024 blacks in the Missouri labor force in 1950, 59,081 were in service employments, while another 18,000 were common laborers. Only 23,305 were connected with industry, and most of them were hired as unskilled laborers. Black workers found promotions difficult to obtain, and white collar jobs extremely rare; they were also the first to be fired during slack times. The unemployment rate for blacks in St. Louis was estimated to be 15 percent in 1954, more than two-and-one-half times the rate for white workers. Not surprisingly, blacks who did find jobs made less money than whites. In 1950 the gross average yearly income for black St. Louis workers was only 58 percent of their white counterparts' income. Because of low income, prejudice, or unemployment, housing was almost as critical a problem for blacks as employment. Black neighborhoods were usually overcrowded and lacked adequate police protection, sanitation facilities, and other necessary services. They became fertile breeding places for crime, vice, and delinquency. Virtually every town in the state with a black population had its "niggertown."

Housing restrictions and overcrowding were particularly evident in St. Louis. A subcommittee of the state's Advisory Committee on Civil Rights estimated in 1958 that blacks comprised approximately 30 percent of the city's total population, but only about 16 to 20 percent of the residential housing was available to them. New housing was particularly difficult for blacks to obtain. An estimated ninety-five thousand blacks moved to St. Louis between 1950 and 1957. Despite that huge number, less than one hundred new homes were built for them. A similar situation existed in Kansas City between 1940 and 1958: only 106 building permits were issued for new single-family black housing.

The explanation offered for the unfavorable housing condition in Missouri was the supposedly greater risk posed by the prospective black home buyer; therefore, it was harder for blacks to get credit because of their unemployment and income status. When blacks could get loans, informal agreements among real estate agents not to sell property to blacks in certain areas often made it difficult for willing white owners to sell to them in white neighborhoods. When prominent black sociologist Oliver C. Cox, a graduate of the University of Chicago, came to Jefferson City to teach at Lincoln University in the late 1940s, he found it impossible to obtain suitable housing because of the city's segregationist practices. Ultimately, Cox ended up living in a Lincoln University dormitory where he lived for twenty years.

Discrimination against blacks in places of public accommodation was general throughout Missouri during the period of the 1940s and into the 1950s. Public facilities that whites took for granted were closed to blacks. It was difficult for blacks to find lodging in hotels, motels, or boarding houses. They could not eat in restaurants, cafeterias, snack bars, or roadside stands. Soda fountains, drug counters, ice cream parlors, and similar facilities refused them service. Even black businessmen, legislators, and professionals reported difficulty finding restroom facilities while traveling across the state. Blacks wishing to get a drink of water had to go through the humiliating experience of approaching the fountain marked "colored," and if they could find a white doctor or dentist to treat them, they had to wait in a separate waiting room.

Discrimination was also practiced in recreational facilities, such as theaters, drive-ins, bowling alleys, skating rinks, swimming pools, and golf courses. Jefferson City maintained two public pools—one for whites and one for blacks—throughout the 1940s and 1950s.

In October 1947, Lincoln University paid the Jefferson City school board $50 to rent the city's public high school stadium for its homecoming game against Tennessee State. The school board accepted the arrangement, but after receiving the money the board notified the university that the black players would not be allowed to use the stadium's showers and dressing rooms. When Lincoln officials protested and petitioned the school board about the prohibition, school board president Thorpe Gordon refused to reconsider the matter or to return the $50.

But if the 1940s and early 1950s saw persistent segregation in the state of Missouri, they also witnessed successful challenges to the system. The liberal atmosphere propagated by the New Deal era and the judicial successes against discrimination of the 1930s, combined with the movement of blacks into new higher-paying jobs that resulted from World War II, spurred blacks to step up their challenges against the status quo. Progress came in a variety of areas, including housing.

For many years in St. Louis, blacks were denied housing by the extensive use of restrictive covenants—written agreements among property owners with the expressed purpose of restricting property ownership to whites. The 1940s case of J. D. and Ethel Shelley in St. Louis offered a significant challenge to this practice. The Shelleys had moved to St. Louis from Starksville, Mississippi, in 1930 in search of a better place to raise their children. They first lived with relatives and then rented substandard housing in an overcrowded, segregated area. In August 1945, the Shelleys bought a home at 4600 Labadie and thought they had finally found a decent home for their family. In October the Shelleys moved into the modest, two-story brick dwelling. A day later, two of their neighbors, Louis and Fern Kraemer sued to evict the Shelleys from their new home, citing a restrictive covenant attached to the house's deed. The restriction, dating back to 1911, barred any owners of the property, their heirs, legal representatives, or subsequent owners from selling or renting the property to people who were not of the "Caucasian Race." This restrictive agreement was binding for fifty years and specifically prohibited the transferring in anyway of the property to "persons of the Negro and Mongolian Race."

The restrictive covenant was encouraged by the St. Louis Real Estate Association, which excluded blacks from membership. Blacks, according to the association's rules, could only be sold property in certain areas. In order to challenge this practice, James T. Bush, Sr., a black real estate broker, organized other black real estate agents into the Real Estate Brokers Association of St. Louis in 1946. The Shelleys were Bush's clients. He had arranged for Josephine Fitzgerald, a white woman, to buy the house at 4600 Labadie in order to sell it to the Shelleys. The Kraemers sued in St. Louis Circuit Court to force compliance with the covenant. They alleged that they would "suffer irreparable injury and irremediable damage to their property" if the Shelleys were permitted to retain the title to the property. The Marcus Avenue Improvement Association had urged the Kraemers to file the suit and supported their effort financially throughout the three-year battle.

While the lower court refused to evict the Shelleys, the Missouri Supreme Court overturned their ruling and called for the enforcement of the covenant. George L. Vaughn, the Shelley's attorney from the very beginning of the lawsuit, appealed the case to the U.S. Supreme Court. The high court accepted Vaughn's argument that the enforcement of restrictive covenants by the courts was a state action in violation of the equal protection clause of the Fourteenth Amendment. The May 3, 1948, ruling of the court in *Shelley v. Kraemer* struck down the enforcement of restrictive covenants in nineteen states and the District of Columbia. Thurgood Marshall, NAACP attorney and future Supreme Court justice, remarked that the *Shelley* case gave "thousands of prospective buyers throughout the United States new courage and hope in the American form of government."

According to Richard Kirkendall, while the Shelley decision was a blow to housing discrimination, the case did not end segregated housing in St. Louis. In 1949 the Missouri Supreme Court ruled that damage suits for violation of covenants were still legal. This ruling encouraged the continued use of restrictive covenants in Missouri until the U.S. Supreme Court outlawed this practice in a California case in 1953. Still, housing discrimination continued by informal arrangements. The white St. Louis realtors organization maintained a policy of expelling any member who sold a house to blacks in a predominately white area. This private action could not be challenged in the courts. Despite the success of the Shelley decision, a decade later the 95,000 blacks moving to St. Louis would find only 100 new homes available for them.

One of the most important federal challenges to segregation in the 1940s came at the hands of Harry S. Truman, who succeeded to the presidency in 1945 following the sudden death of Franklin D. Roosevelt. It was President Truman who led the way in abolishing segregation in the armed forces. On July 26, 1948, Truman issued the following order: "It is hereby declared to be the policy of the President that there shall be equality of treatment and opportunity for all persons in the armed services without regard to race, color, religion or national origin. This policy shall be put into effect as rapidly as possible, having due regard to the time required to effectuate any necessary changes without impairing efficiency or morale."

Truman also created a Committee on Equality of Treatment and Opportunity in the Armed Services to implement this order. Although the armed services dragged their feet in complying with Truman's order, by 1949 the army had at least officially opened all jobs to servicemen regardless of race and had abolished racial quotas. The navy and air force later followed suit. Thereafter, the military became one of the most important sources of vocational training and career employment for blacks, although some discrimination continued. As late as 1967, blacks made up only 5 percent of the army's eleven thousand officers.

Challenges to segregation also came in the area of public accommodations. A number of social organizations were active in promoting racial goodwill: among them were the NAACP, the Urban League, the Missouri Association for Social Welfare, the League of Women Voters, the Catholic Interracial Conference, and the National Conference of Christians and Jews. Often these groups sponsored lawsuits against discriminatory agencies and institutions. Private individuals of both races and all faiths also joined the struggle for human rights. Indeed, it was only through legal challenges to segregation that changes were made. It was, for example, court pressure that opened the public swimming pools to blacks in St. Louis and Kansas City in 1950 and 1953, respectively. These legal successes encouraged voluntary desegregation. After long negotiations with civil rights organizations, the Jefferson Hotel of St. Louis opened its doors to blacks for the first time in 1952, which in turn prompted several others to do the same around the state. Restaurants were next in accepting black patrons, with railroad and airport dining facilities leading the way.

The establishment of official groups signaled the greater concern of communities to improve race relations. Two municipal bodies of this nature were the St. Louis Council on Human Relations, of which Chester Stovall was executive director, and the Kansas City Commission on Human Relations with William Gremley as its director. Jefferson City had, for a short time, a Mayor's Committee on Human Relations.

White churches generally continued to deny membership to blacks in the forties, although there were notable exceptions. The Catholic church, in particular, took a strong stand in favor of integration. The movement toward integration was the result of a decade or more of prodding by St. Louis priests. Archbishop John J. Glennon of St. Louis refused to follow the priests' lead, however, largely because he feared alienating wealthy church supporters. It was left for his successor, Joseph Cardinal Ritter, to end segregation in 1947. Cardinal Ritter directed all pastors under his jurisdiction that "there should be no discrimination. . . . This is in keeping with our Catholic teaching and the best principles of our American form of democratic government." Churches of other denominations began slowly to open their doors to black membership.

Perhaps the greatest challenge to segregation came in the area of education. Access to education had long been seen as the major vehicle for social progress. In the 1940s most black schools were still physically inferior to white facilities, often located in undesirable places near taverns or houses of prostitution. The textbooks that were used, especially in rural districts, were often old, outdated castoffs from the white schools. The subjects taught and the facilities provided in white schools were frequently not offered in, or furnished for, black schools. Black teachers were poorly paid as compared to their white counterparts. In large urban communities the training of black teachers compared favorably with that of white teachers, but in small urban and rural centers frequently the reverse was true. Many black and white rural teachers had only a high school diploma or, at best, a two-year normal school certificate.

Black children, lacking schools in their own districts, were often transported long distances to schools in other towns. Fifty high school children from Fulton traveled twenty-five miles to the Lincoln University Laboratory High School in Jefferson City. In 1952 Jack McBride refused to be bussed to Jefferson City and integrated the Fulton public high school simply by showing up for classes. Madison's eight black children who were transported to Moberly had to leave home an hour and a half before the other children. Moreover, supervision in most black schools was not as strict as in white schools. Even more disastrous was the effect segregation had upon the black child. It automatically branded him as inferior within the sanction of the law. It affected his aspirations and his motivation to learn, filled him with frustration, and made him regard himself as an outsider. In short, separate schools for blacks usually meant inferiority all around.

Continual efforts were made after 1945 to open the University of Missouri to qualified black students. Leading the vanguard were the metropolitan newspapers of St. Louis and Kansas City, as well as the black newspapers of those cities whose editorials advocated integrating the university. Student support at the University of Missouri also helped. Campus polls showed overwhelming support for immediate integration. Liberal faculty members at the university, in concert with colleagues from Lincoln University, lent their support. Likewise, individuals and organizations throughout the state—lay, professional, and religious— swelled the ranks of those working for greater educational opportunities for blacks. Integration-minded groups sponsored legislation to eliminate segregation in education; however, the bills introduced by these organizations were lost either in the House or the Senate.

In 1949 a bill to admit blacks to the University of Missouri when similar courses were not offered at Lincoln University was amended in the House to apply to all the state colleges. The House passed the bill by an overwhelming vote, but the Senate defeated it. Disillusioned by the failure of the legislature to open the university to all qualified students, three seniors at Lincoln University applied for admission to the graduate school at Columbia and to the School of Mines and Metallurgy at Rolla in the spring of 1950. Elmer Bell, George Everett Horne, and Gus T. Ridgel believed that they would be admitted should a court case become necessary, but the Board of Curators of the University of Missouri sought a ruling from the Circuit Court of Cole County. In a crowded courtroom on June 27, 1950, Judge Sam Blair ordered the students admitted forthwith to the University of Missouri. They were duly enrolled in September 1950 along with several other blacks, including Hazel McDaniel Teabeau, an

English instructor at Lincoln University. Thus, after more than a century of segregation, the University of Missouri finally opened its doors to black students. In 1959, at the age of 66, Teabeau became the first African-American to earn a doctorate degree from the University of Missouri.

With the walls of the university breached, efforts between 1950 and 1954 centered upon opening other public educational facilities. Between 1950 and 1954, four attempts were made by blacks in St. Louis, St. Louis County, and Kansas City to enroll in white schools. In *State ex rel Toliver v. Board of Education of the City of St. Louis,* a black student at Stowe Teachers College applied for admission to the white Harris Teachers College. His application was denied. The student then sought a court order to compel Harris Teachers College to admit him. The applicant contended that substantial inequalities existed between Stowe and Harris colleges in the accreditation granted to the two schools, the inequality of the faculty, the libraries, and the laboratories. The plea was denied on the ground that substantially equal privileges and facilities existed.

More successful was a black student at the Washington Technical High School for Negroes in St. Louis, who in the same year applied for permission to enroll at Hadley Technical High School. Hadley Tech was for white students only. When his application was rejected, the black student tried unsuccessfully to get the St. Louis Board of Education to overturn the school's decision. The board refused the request, stating that such a course could not be offered unless ten students were enrolled. The student then filed suit against the board of education. The court of appeals ruled in favor of the student and ordered his enrollment in the course. Hadley Tech dropped the course, however, rather than admit a black student. Often white and black students suffered deprivation of instruction so segregation could be maintained.

With the *Hadley* case as a precedent, 150 black students in Kansas City attempted to integrate a school for whites that had an auditorium and a gymnasium. These facilities, the defendants argued, were essential to education in the modern era. The court denied the appeal on the grounds that sufficient evidence had not been produced to substantiate the appellant's plea. The record cited by the court showed nineteen schools without auditoriums and ten without gymnasiums. Although the court held it did not discount the importance of gymnasiums and auditoriums in the total educational program, the law required *substantial* equality.

Such equality was not denied when facilities were not identical. The guarantee was for substantially equal educational opportunities; differences in the physical plant, therefore, were not inequality.

Obviously, because of the peculiar interpretation of the courts, the separate but equal doctrine was difficult and expensive to challenge successfully. Nevertheless, a changing attitude in the federal appellate courts toward segregation cases paved the way for *Arnold v. Kirkwood School District R–7* when a black student tried to attend a white school in his district, contending only the illegality of separateness, conceding equality of opportunity and faculties. Denied in the federal district court, the plaintiff appealed to the U.S. Court of Appeals. After hearing arguments, the latter tribunal decided to withhold judgment because the Supreme Court was expected shortly to decide five education cases, and the lower court elected to wait for the Court's decision.

On May 17, 1954, in its long-awaited decision in *Brown v. Board of Education of Topeka, Kansas,* the Supreme Court held that racial segregation in public education was unconstitutional. Thus, fifty-eight years after the Supreme Court had put its stamp of approval upon segregation in *Plessy v. Ferguson,* an enlightened judiciary struck down the constitutional and legal basis for racial discrimination in education in seventeen states and the District of Columbia. Missouri was one of those states.

Perhaps just as important to racial progress during these years was the fact that numerous blacks from all walks of life were rising to positions of achievement and success despite discrimination. They were therefore able to offer black youths positive role models while illustrating to whites the absurdity of racial stereotypes.

Oscar S. Ficklin was the first black chemist to work for the Union Electric Company in St. Louis. He had gone to work as a porter for the company in 1905. After completing correspondence courses in chemistry through a school in Scranton, Pennsylvania, in 1920 he was promoted to chemist in charge of the testing laboratory, a position he held for nearly a quarter of a century. In 1945 he became the first black person in Missouri to be named foreman of a court jury, having been elected by his eleven white counterparts.

Elmer Simms Campbell, a native St. Louisan, had become an internationally acclaimed illustrator and commercial artist by the 1940s. *Esquire* magazine featured his work from its beginning in 1933. James D. Parks of Jefferson City began a career in art that also led to international recognition. James W. Spaulding of Kansas City went to work as a porter for the City National Bank in 1919. He stayed with the bank for more than thirty years, later rising to the position of superintendent of records and supplies.

In the 1940s Chauncy Downs replaced Count Basie as the leading jazz figure in Kansas City. Running a close second to Downs was the legendary alto saxophonist Charlie "Yardbird" Parker, who died in 1955 at the young age of thirty-five. Etta Moton gained fame as a singer.

The 1940s also saw the passing of one of Missouri's most famous black scientists, George Washington Carver. Carver was born a slave near Diamond Grove, Missouri, during the Civil War. He later gained fame at Tuskegee Institute, Alabama, for his research with sweet potatoes, peanuts, cotton, soybeans, and wood. His discoveries revolutionized southern agriculture. On July 14, 1943, the 210-acre farm on which he was born was dedicated as a national monument under the supervision of the National Park Service, the first such honor paid in the United States to an African-American.

In 1945 Dr. J. C. Castron became the first black member of St. Louis's Board of Aldermen. William A. Massingale of St. Louis was elected to the General Assembly in 1946. He was joined in 1948 by the prominent Kansas City pharmacologist J. McKinley Neal, who was only the second Kansas City black to serve in the legislature. He followed L. A. Knox, dean of Kansas City's black lawyers, who was elected in the late 1920s. Newspaper reporter Lester Walton of St. Louis served as United States minister to Liberia from 1935 to 1945. In 1954 President Dwight D. Eisenhower named Jess Ernest Wilkins of Farmington as an assistant secretary of labor.

Missouri's most accomplished black writer, Langston Hughes, had reached the apex of his career by the 1940s. He gained fame during the Harlem Renaissance of the 1920s, and in 1930 he wrote a widely acclaimed novel entitled *Not without Laughter* and in 1934 a volume of short stories, *The Ways of White Folks*. Later, he produced a number of plays, the most famous of which was *Mulatto*. In 1943 black Missourian Lorenzo J. Greene published a book that was destined to become a classic in its field: *The Negro in Colonial New England*. Near the decade's end, Greene began editing at Lincoln University the *Midwest Journal*, a magazine of research and creative writing that published many seminal essays on black life and culture in America. Numerous scholars, who later gained national fame during the 1960s and 1970s, had their early works published in the journal during the 1940s and 1950s. The first volume set the tone with pieces by Herbert Aptheker, T. Thomas Fletcher, John Hope Franklin, Lorenzo J. Greene, Rayford W. Logan, Booker T. McGraw, Benjamin Quarles, and Melvin B. Tolson. In the late 1940s, Oliver Cromwell Cox, professor of sociology at Lincoln University, published a book also destined to become a classic: the sociological treatise *Caste, Class and Race*. Over the next decade and a half, Cox produced his famous trilogy on capitalism: *The Foundations of Capitalism* (1959), *Capitalism and American Leadership* (1962), and *Capitalism as a System* (1964).

Three black Missouri newspapers were also thriving in the 1940s: the *Kansas City Call*, founded by Chester A. Franklin in 1919; the *St. Louis Argus*, founded in 1912 by Joseph E. Mitchell, Sr.; and the *St. Louis American*, founded in 1928 by Nathaniel Sweets. These newspapers provided a forum for discussion of issues of particular importance to blacks, as well as a source of racial identity and accomplishment. They were supplemented by the work of the YMCAs and YWCAs of Kansas City and St. Louis. Mrs. Elsie Mountain of Kansas City was particularly effective in preparing girls for jobs that they ordinarily could not have obtained. Ms. Anna Lee Hill Scott performed the same service in St. Louis.

By 1954 segregation was being challenged successfully in both the state and the nation. Optimism began to crop up among blacks in the state. Hope—as real and intense as the hope born during the Civil War—was again the watchword for black life in Missouri.

Suggested Readings

The best general account of the black soldier in World War II is Ulysses Lee, *The Employment of Negro Troops* (Washington: U.S. Government Printing Office, 1967). Richard M. Dalfiume's *Desegregation of the U.S. Armed Forces: Fighting on Two Fronts, 1939–1953* (Columbia: University of Missouri Press, 1969) is an authoritative study of the efforts to integrate the military. Richard S. Kirkendall's *A History of Missouri, 1919 to 1953,* Vol. 5 of the Missouri Sesquicentennial Series (Columbia: University of Missouri Press, 1986) offers useful insights into race relations in the state during the 1940s and early 1950s. The relationship between Harry S. Truman and black Americans is discussed by Philip H. Vaughan in "The Truman Administrations's Fair Deal for Black Americans," *Missouri Historical Review* 70 (April 1976): 291–305.

The early efforts of the Catholic church to desegregate in St. Louis are covered by Donald J. Kempker in "Catholic Integration in St. Louis, 1935–1947," *Missouri Historical Review* 73 (October 1978): 1–22. The best overall treatment of the status of Negro education and general social conditions before the 1954 *Brown v. Board of Education of Topeka, Kansas* decision is Lorenzo J. Greene, *Desegregation of Schools in Missouri* (Jefferson City: Missouri Advisory Committee on Civil Rights, 1959). An excellent examination of black civil rights in Missouri before and after 1954 is Thomas E. Baker, "Human Rights in Missouri" (Ph.D. dissertation, University of Missouri–Columbia, 1975). The story of Missouri's most famous black scientist is told by Gary R. Kremer, ed., in *George Washington Carver: In His Own Words* (Columbia: University of Missouri Press, 1987).

Struggles in St. Louis are recounted by Patricia L. Adams in her essay, "Fighting for Democracy in St. Louis: Civil Rights during World War II," *Missouri Historical Review* 80 (October 1985): 58–75. The tragic case of Cleo Wright is the subject of Dominic J. Capeci, "The Lynching of Cleo Wright: Federal Protection of Constitutional Rights during World War II," *Journal of American History* 72 (March 1986): 959–87. Oliver Cromwell Cox's significance as a writer and thinker is chronicled in Herbert M. Hunter and Sameer Y. Abraham, eds., *Race, Class, and the World System: The Sociology of Oliver C. Cox* (New York: Monthly Review Press, 1987). The *Shelley v. Kraemer* case is the subject of A. Leon Higginbotham, Jr., "Race, Sex, Education and Missouri Jurisprudence: *Shelley v. Kraemer* in a Historical Perspective," *Washington University Law Quarterly* 67 (Fall 1989): 674–708.

10

Free at Last?

From Civil Rights to Black Power, 1954–1968

May 17, 1954, was a day of rejoicing for black Americans and their liberal white allies. On that day the U.S. Supreme Court unanimously decreed that segregation in public schools was a violation of the equal protection clause of the Fourteenth Amendment and therefore unconstitutional. Speaking for the full Court, Chief Justice Earl Warren said in part that to separate black children "from others of similar age and qualifications solely because of their race generates a feeling of inferiority as to their status in the community that may affect their hearts and minds in a way unlikely to be undone. . . . We conclude that in the field of public education the doctrine of 'separate but equal' has no place. Separate educational facilities are inherently unequal."

This famous case of *Brown v. Board of Education of Topeka, Kansas* took its name from Linda Carol Brown, whose father tired of seeing his daughter denied access to a nearby white school and challenged the constitutionality of the Kansas law that separated white and black students. The result was perhaps the most important decision handed down by the Supreme Court in the twentieth century. Most black Americans hailed the decision as the dawn of a new era. At last, they believed, they had the key to full citizenship. Black Americans would apply this new doctrine to all phases of American life. Once segregation in education had been declared in violation of the Constitution, they reasoned, they could no longer be denied all other benefits of American society solely on the basis of their skin color.

The decision caused mixed reactions throughout the nation. It brought forth angry responses in the deep South. Elsewhere, there was less resistance initially. In the northern and border states, many whites joined with blacks in praising the decision. In Missouri, the State Commission of Education asked the attorney general what effect the *Brown* case would have on the state's racially segregated schools. In June 1954, he responded that Missouri's school segregation laws were null and void. Integration, as the Supreme Court ordered the next year, must proceed "with all deliberate speed."

Although Missouri generally escaped the determined and violent opposition to integration that later occurred in the South, the process in Missouri was not without its difficulties. Most school districts in the state agreed to submit desegregation plans. There were notable exceptions, however, particularly in the southeastern section of the state. Charleston, for example, made determined efforts to avoid any form of school desegregation until the mid–1960s. In other parts of the Bootheel as late as the mid–1960s, black children still went to school in the summer to make up for the two-month cotton-picking recess in the fall. In addition, despite the Supreme Court ruling, many black pupils still traveled as far as thirty-five miles, past all-white schools, to attend black schools in dilapidated sections of small agricultural towns. Many libraries, parks, theaters, and other recreational facilities also remained closed to blacks. In some southeastern and mid-Missouri communities, blacks were still required to sit behind ropes in the all-black sections of movie houses.

Black teachers often became expendable because of desegregation. In Malden, Potosi, Lexington, Jefferson City, Clinton, Henrietta, and other communities, 125 to 150 black teachers lost their jobs. Eleven teachers lost their jobs in Moberly when desegregation took place in 1955, so they sued the school board but lost their case. There were other unanticipated effects of desegregation as well. For some black Americans, the *Brown* decision and the changes it portended were frightening. In a 1989 interview with historian Lori Bogle, Betty Robinson of Joplin recalled how she felt in the mid–1950s when she was suddenly transferred from an all-black school to a predominantly white school. She remembered that she was "anxious, scared, not happy. . . . There might have been some people happy. At Lincoln School we were not happy . . . because when you live in a racist society you learn your place. . . . We didn't know what to expect and we did not expect acceptance, in fact we expected rejection."

Desegregation got off to a slow start in St. Louis and Kansas City where 90 percent of the state's black school-age children lived. The major problem with implementing the *Brown* decision there was that blacks were segregated into all-black neighborhoods. Integration of the school district meant little if the district itself was virtually all black. Consequently, even though most Missouri school districts were legally desegregated by the 1960s, most black students were still attending all-black schools.

One way to address this form of segregation was to bus students from one district into another, but difficulties only multiplied when school districts began busing students to achieve racial integration. The process that occurred in St. Louis illustrates the point. During the school year 1961 through 1962, the St. Louis school board decided to bus pupils from predominately or all-black schools. The twenty schools receiving the bused students were all-white, and 95 percent of the bused pupils were black. The students were bused as entire classes rather than as individuals, so classrooms remained segregated, even though a school building might be integrated. Indeed, many of the transported students had little contact with pupils who lived in the receiving districts. In some schools blacks and whites ate at different times. They were also restricted to separate parts of the playgrounds.

In 1961 and 1962, some forty-six hundred black students were transported from the overcrowded schools of St. Louis's West End. The following school year approximately six thousand black students were bused. However, the segregated housing situation nullified any real efforts at successful integration. By 1965, 91 percent of the black elementary schoolchildren in St. Louis attended all-black or predominately black schools. In 1966 nearly 40 percent of Missouri's black schoolchildren were in schools that were at least 95 percent black, and 35 percent of the black pupils were in all-black schools.

The more basic problem, of course, was housing, and the fact that black people were not free to choose where they lived. Housing, in turn, was at least partly dependent upon income and jobs; black people who were occupationally discriminated against on the basis of race found it difficult to move out of the ghetto. Therefore, it became increasingly apparent that the fight against segregation was a complicated, many-pronged affair. A more organized effort was needed.

Many Missourians looked for the state to lead the way in fighting discrimination. Social welfare groups and interested individuals reasoned that if segregation and discrimination were to be combated successfully, the majesty of the state's laws had to be invoked. In 1954 liberal organizations such as the NAACP, the Missouri Association for Social Welfare, the National Conference of Christians and Jews, the Urban League, and the National Catholic Conference persuaded a bipartisan group of senators and representatives to back a bill that called for a state human rights commission. Furthermore, they secured a promise from the governor-elect, James T. Blair, that he would support such a bill. Although opposition to the bill delayed its passage, it finally became law in mid–1957. At last the state of Missouri officially recognized that the deprivation of rights on the basis of race was the government's concern.

The new Human Rights Commission did not change race relations in Missouri overnight. With a limited budget and little power, all it could do was document the reality of discrimination in Missouri and encourage individuals who were discriminated against to file charges. But this alone proved to be helpful. The Human Rights Commission attacked racial discrimination on a broad front during the late 1950s and 1960s. Much of the housing market was still closed to blacks because a majority of St. Louis realtors were still in favor of blacks being permitted to buy housing only in restricted "Negro districts." The Human Rights Commission conducted a survey in 1960 and found residential segregation widespread in nearly every part of the state. Some areas of the state excluded blacks altogether. They maintained "sundown laws," that is, no blacks were permitted to stay in town after sunset. One northwest Missouri township advertised that it had a "nigger free" work force for any new industries.

The federal government tried to solve at least some of the housing problems by erecting public housing projects in inner cities. One of the earliest efforts was the Pruitt-Igoe Housing Project, which was built during the early 1950s near downtown St. Louis. Designed by architects George F. Hellmoth and Minoru Yamasaki, Pruitt-Igoe was envisioned as a place where low-income residents could live cheaply while accumulating the wherewithal to buy their own homes. Early on, Hellmoth proclaimed, "St. Louis is showing the way in modern public housing construction with emphasis on consideration for the health and comfort of the occupants without sacrifice in economy in building." Unfortunately, this well-intentioned project never achieved the dreams of its planners.

First occupied in 1954, Pruitt-Igoe was an all-black project containing thirty-three eleven-story buildings with 2,762 apartments and 10,000 residents. The buildings were poorly planned—their elevators stopped only on the fourth, seventh, and tenth floors—and they quickly became centers of crime and vice. By the 1970s, the government admitted its failure and destroyed all of the buildings in the complex.

In June 1963, the Missouri Advisory Committee to the United States Commission on Civil Rights reported discriminatory practices in housing in several Missouri communities, including Charleston, Kansas City, Mexico, Poplar Bluff, St. Joseph, and St. Louis, and the counties of Cape Girardeau, Clay, Mississippi, New Madrid, and Pemiscot. In the late 1960s, 18 percent of all black housing in St. Louis was overcrowded, compared with 10 percent for the rest of the city. In Kansas City the figures were similar: nearly 10 percent of the housing in the nonwhite area was overcrowded, compared with 5 percent for the rest of the city. Unfortunately, however, Missourians would have to wait until the 1970s for a statewide fair housing law.

Things were little better in the area of public accommodations. In 1949 the Missouri Association for Social Welfare had conducted a survey on discrimination in public facilities in the state. The investigators discovered "few places in Missouri where a Negro can get overnight accommodations at a respectable hotel or eat in a first class restaurant." Ten years later, the Human Rights Commission found that there had been little or no improvement. The commission drew the following conclusion:

> Negroes are prohibited from using the eating and sleeping accommodations in the majority of Missouri's hotels, motels, resorts, restaurants, dining rooms, cafes, soda fountains, drugstores and department store eating facilities. . . . In most cases in Missouri a Negro may order food to "take out," but he is refused permission to eat on the premises. In a number of counties, a Negro can be served food in the kitchen, a back room, or in a screened-off area. . . . A Negro can actually travel the width or breadth of the state and not find one cafe, restaurant, hotel, motel or resort that will accommodate him. Even when traveling on an interstate bus in the uniform of his country, the Negro is often refused service at the bus station rest stops.

Missouri blacks suffered humiliation and indignity for many more years before discrimination in public accommodations was finally made illegal. It took several years of lobbying by groups such as the NAACP, Missouri Association for Social Welfare, the Urban League, and the Human Rights Commission before a reluctant legislature passed into law the Missouri Public Accommodation Act of 1965. Indeed, that act was passed in large part because the state was being threatened by federal intervention if it failed to end discrimination in public facilities.

In 1960 a study by the Human Rights Commission found that even in the large metropolitan areas, like St. Louis and Kansas City, "the great mass of Negro workers remains on the lowest levels of employment." In St. Louis more than 10 percent of all nonwhite males in the labor force were unemployed compared with 2.8 percent of white males. Blacks were also confined mainly to the lowest-paying jobs. An examination of all industries revealed that 22 percent of white male laborers were craftsmen, foremen, or kindred workers; only 8 percent of the black males were so employed. While only 5 percent of the whites were employed as common laborers, 21 percent of the blacks fell into that category. Only 3 percent of the black males in the labor force were classified as professionals, as opposed to 11 percent of the white males. In other parts of the state the situation was often worse. The Missouri Advisory Committee to the United States Commission on Civil Rights reported in 1963 that employment discrimination existed throughout the state. Referring to the employment situation in Mexico (Audrain County) the report stated:

> The economy of the Negro community is kept at a substandard level as a consequence of Negroes being restricted to menial and low salaried jobs. Their range of occupations is narrowed down to custodial or janitorial workers in stores, factories, and offices; domestic and janitorial workers in the City Hall and Court House; cooks and waiters at the Missouri Military Academy, and small businesses in the Negro ghetto. . . . Negroes are not employed in the construction of urban renewal projects because they must belong to unions.

The report found similar conditions existing throughout southeast Missouri and in Clay, Jackson, Platte, and Buchanan counties in northwest Missouri. In these areas employment was largely agricultural, and discrimination was perhaps the worst in the state. Even the menial jobs traditionally reserved for blacks were held by whites. The economic situation of the black population of Charleston was such that approximately 50 percent of the black people there could not afford housing with running water or modern bathroom facilities. In St. Joseph the attitude of many members of the business community was expressed by one businessman who publicly complained to a fellow businessman who had recently hired a black clerical worker: "Well, you're starting a precedent now. All the white businessmen in St. Joe are going to have to put nigger gals in their offices."

In Poplar Bluff there was equally widespread discrimination in employment. Two blacks were employed as janitors at the courthouse. Some blacks were employed at car lots and garages as "flunkies." At the three local hospitals blacks were employed primarily as maids and dishwashers, although there were a few black nurses. One black was employed at the local box factory, but neither the Missouri Highway Maintenance Department nor the shoe and garment factories employed blacks.

On the bright side of the employment picture, professional sports were finally being integrated. As early as the late nineteenth century, Tom Bass from Mexico distinguished himself as a jockey and horse trainer. Bass's participation in a "white" sport was the exception, however, not the rule. Major league baseball was especially resistant to integration. As a consequence, all-Negro baseball teams flourished in the first half of the twentieth century. The St. Louis Giants was the first black professional baseball team that played at Athletic Park on Garrison and North Market. The team moved to Kuebler Park in 1914 and became the St. Louis Stars in 1922 after being purchased by Dick Kent and Dr. Sam Shephard.

The St. Louis Stars played in the Negro National Baseball League and featured such key players as Oscar Charleton, Dick Wallace, Frank Wickware, and "Steelarm" Taylor. The most famous of the St. Louis Stars was a talented center fielder named James "Cool Papa" Bell. Tweed Webb, historian of the Negro leagues, reported that Bell, who joined the Stars in 1922, played baseball for twenty-nine summers and twenty-one winters.

The Stars' cross-state rivals, the Kansas City Monarchs, were also members of the Negro National Baseball League. The Monarchs dominated the league during the 1920s, winning the league championship in 1923, 1924, 1925, and 1929. In 1924 the team won the first Negro World Series by defeating a Philadelphia team of the Eastern Colored League. The most famous of the Monarchs, Satchel Paige, played in the Negro leagues during the 1940s, as did the legendary Jackie Robinson, who finally broke the color line that banned black baseball players in the major leagues during the twentieth century. Robinson was brought up to the Brooklyn Dodgers in 1947 and paved the way for future Missouri African-American all-stars, such as Bob Gibson and Lou Brock, although the St. Louis Cardinals did not hire black players until Tom Alston joined the team in 1954. Not until 1964, when Bill White and Curt Flood joined Gibson and Brock on the field, did St. Louis have as many as four blacks in their starting lineup.

There was as much discrimination in employment in the public sector as in private business during the generation following *Brown v. Board of Education*. In 1963 the Human Rights Commission conducted a survey on black employment in state agencies. Although the percentage of black state employees nearly equalled their percentage of the general population, blacks were mostly employed in janitorial, maintenance, and other menial jobs; they were still barred from professional, technical, and even clerical jobs. Even by 1963, then, blacks constituted a little less than 8 percent of the state employees, but only about 2 percent earned over four thousand dollars a year. Many of the largest state agencies had few black employees. This was particularly true of the Highway Patrol, the Highway Department, the Conservation Department, the Department of Corrections, the Division of Health, and all state colleges except Lincoln University.

There was little improvement in the situation by 1968 when the commission conducted another survey. Blacks represented a little over 9 percent of the state workers. Yet widespread discrimination in employment opportunities kept them disproportionately confined to the lowest-paying jobs. While more than 70 percent of black state employees earned less than four hundred dollars a month, only 35 percent of the white state employees earned so little. The percentage of blacks employed varied from agency to agency. The Missouri Highway Patrol employed only thirteen blacks out of a work force of nearly thirteen hundred employees. Similarly, the State Highway Department had only thirty-three black workers out of a total of 5,768 employees. Both agencies made greater efforts in minority employment after 1968.

The slow progress in the face of the great promise of *Brown v. Board of Education* emboldened blacks to push more forcefully for an equal share of the rights of citizenship. The 1960s witnessed organized black protests such as the state and nation had never seen before. In both Kansas City and St. Louis, banks and stores that had refused to hire blacks in other than menial positions were boycotted. Since blacks comprised nearly two-thirds of the unemployed in the St. Louis area in 1963, they felt that the boycotts were justified.

Ivory Perry became one of the most prominent black community activists in Missouri during the 1950s and 1960s, as a crusader for public school, restaurant, and theater desegregation and fair employment legislation. He was also active in the civil rights movement in the South, particularly in Selma, Alabama, and Bogalusa, Louisiana. Born in 1930 to a poor sharecropper family in rural Arkansas, Perry moved to St. Louis in 1954 after being discharged from the U.S. Army. He had fought in the Korean War in one of the last all-black units. Perry participated in the 1963 Jefferson Bank boycotts, which his biographer, George Lipsitz, calls "St. Louis's most important civil rights campaign."

In the summer of 1963, the St. Louis chapter of the Congress of Racial Equality (CORE) demanded that the Jefferson Bank hire black tellers, or CORE would stage a public boycott and protest. Jefferson Bank responded by obtaining a state circuit court restraining order that prohibited any protests outside its building. When the CORE-appointed deadline of August 31 arrived and no blacks had been hired, approximately 150 demonstrators picketed in front of the bank, while a smaller group staged a nonviolent sit-in. The police quickly arrested many of the protesters. Judge Michael Scott, who had issued the restraining order, meted out extremely severe punishment to the demonstrators by ordering jail sentences as long as one year and fines as high as $1,000. Robert Curtis of CORE asserted that the defendants, as Lipsitz reported, "received sentences more appropriate for bank robbers than for bank demonstrators."

Undaunted, CORE increased the pressure on Jefferson Bank through daily demonstrations outside its buildings to protest its discriminatory hiring practices. In addition, the chapter staged marches on city hall and held public rallies to raise money to pay jailed protesters' bails and fines. Ivory Perry and his wife, Anna Cox, were instrumental in all phases of the campaign, from planning fund-raising events to participating in the demonstrations and marches. Several times, Perry was arrested during demonstrations. On one occasion, Perry and another CORE leader disrupted traffic on a busy downtown street by lying down in front of the wheels of a city bus. Gene Tournour, the local field representative to the national CORE office, described Ivory as "one of the more active leaders in the chapter. He had no official leadership position at the time, but he played a big role in planning and executing strategy. He struck me as completely dedicated. People at the time were jeopardizing their jobs and their livelihoods by demonstrating. Ivory was one of the people you could always count on being there."

Finally, in March 1964, the stalemate between CORE and Jefferson Bank ended when the bank agreed to hire its first black tellers. In the following months local banks hired more than eighty other black employees. CORE's six-and-a-half-month campaign against Jefferson Bank not only gained African-Americans equal employment opportunities in St. Louis's banking institutions, but it also politicized the city's black community and inspired its members to challenge other racial and class injustices that they encountered in their daily lives.

Organized demonstrations had positive results elsewhere, too. As early as 1960, Jefferson City, St. Louis, and Kansas City opened their restaurants to all segments of the public. That happened, however, only after demonstrations against a number of restaurants practicing discrimination, particularly in the two larger cities. In 1963 one Kansas City cafe owner who had operated at the same location for forty-three years still refused to serve blacks. A sit-in forced him to close the establishment. It never reopened. In Jefferson City, sit-ins and threatened boycotts by Lincoln University students forced city entrepreneurs to open their restaurants. At one time, Jefferson City's undefeated high school football team, after winning a hard fought contest, stopped with its component of victorious whites and blacks at a restaurant on Madison Street to buy hamburgers. The black students were denied service, but the white students ordered anyway. After the food was prepared, however, the white students refused to eat it or pay, telling the proprietor that they wanted no part of an eating establishment that would not serve blacks. They then went out and sat in silent protest on a curb in front of the restaurant.

Statewide boycotts and sit-ins were inspired by national black leader Martin Luther King, Jr., chairman of the Southern Christian Leadership Conference. Advocating a nonviolent but persistent demand for black equality, King organized protests throughout the South. His strategy called worldwide attention to the plight of black people and prompted the nations's leaders to outlaw segregation.

The most effective response to organized black protests was at the federal level. In 1964, under President Lyndon B. Johnson's leadership, Congress enacted a Public Accommodations Act, which prohibited discrimination in all restaurants, theaters, stores, parks, and other places generally open to the public. Getting a law passed was only the first step; enforcing it was quite another. In Kansas City, for example, a local judge temporarily restrained the implementation of the law on the grounds that it would cause too many social problems. Nevertheless, the action on the federal level meant that battles for these rights would not have to be fought by blacks in all the individual states.

The Public Accommodations Act of 1964 was followed by the Voting Rights Act in 1965. It opened the way for hundreds of thousands of blacks to use the franchise more freely than they had ever done before. Although blacks had possessed the right to vote since the adoption of the Fifteenth Amendment in 1870, the South had denied them the ballot through such ruses as grandfather clauses, white primaries, and the threat of violence. The civil rights acts of 1964 and 1965 inspired a new confidence nationwide, prompting blacks to turn out in greater numbers for candidates who promised to support their struggle for equality. Specifically in Missouri, the effects of this national legislation determined the 1964 election when black voters defied ward leaders in Kansas City to support the reelection of Congressman Richard Bolling. Freedom, Inc., a black political organization, led the pro-Bolling fight, arguing that the congressman's strong civil rights record and support for medical care for the aged entitled him to renomination.

Despite these gains, however, the status of the black masses had not improved very much. The opening up of white colleges and universities and the right to frequent hotels and restaurants were relatively unimportant to blacks who could not afford to take advantage of their new liberties. Black unemployment remained high, housing poor, and the general quality of life low. Many blacks argued that not enough was being done to end discrimination. The nonviolent and patient protesting of leaders such as King came under fire as a new contingent of black leaders began to emerge.

Gradually black militants exercised more and more influence in the civil rights movement. Malcolm X, Stokely Carmichael, H. Rap Brown, and others began to advocate a violent response to white racism and talked openly about black power. This slogan was difficult to define; it could mean black nationalism, black political power, a separate black economy, or a third world made up of like-minded people of all races, creeds, and nationalities.

To most people involved in the movement, however, it meant a new sense of pride in the black past. Africa, rather than America, was defined as the homeland of blacks. The word *Negro* was replaced by *black* and *African-American*. Often these blacks shunned Christianity as the "white man's religion" and turned instead to the Nation of Islam, a religion founded in the 1930s by Elijah Muhammad. Many black Americans changed their names to African or Arabic ones and donned African dress. Black men and women changed their hairstyles and read about their heritage both in the United States and in Africa. The more they learned, the more they identified themselves as an oppressed people whose liberty could be gained only by revolutionary struggle.

The black power movement had both its advocates and critics. Both sides had to admit, however, that it caused blacks to become more active in the civil rights movement than they had ever been before. Black militants refused to associate with moderate blacks, decided that they could do without the monetary assistance of whites, and clamored for black control of the ghetto and its institutions. They scoffed at Martin Luther King's direct nonviolent action; instead, they called for black unity as a separate group and direct confrontation with the white man.

This hard-line approach met with an equally hard response; perhaps violence and bloodshed were inevitable. The years 1967 and 1968 saw riots all over the country. Beginning with the Watts district of Los Angeles in 1965, blacks pillaged and burned businesses in ghettos. Missouri remained relatively quiet until the death of Martin Luther King in 1968. To most blacks, King's death signaled the killing of a dream. Frustration and anger turned to violence all over the country. When a local newspaper in Jefferson City ran a syndicated column the day before King was assassinated branding him a communist, Lincoln students staged what was to have been a peaceful march on the newspaper office. After being told by the editor that the column could not be rescinded and that no apology would be forthcoming, the students responded by breaking windows in the building. Students then marched back to campus, breaking more windows in buildings along their route.

The Jefferson City incident seems minor when compared to what occurred in Kansas City in 1968. The protest started because city officials refused to close schools in honor of the death of Martin Luther King. This angered Kansas City's black students, particularly since schools across the river in Kansas City, Kansas, had been closed. Approximately three hundred black students marched to city hall to demand the closing of the schools. The gathering was dispersed by police with tear gas. Later the same day, five all-black schools were closed temporarily after the police used tear gas against students milling about outside Lincoln High School. The students were forced into the school and then driven out again when police fired more tear gas into the building.

At dusk the first outbreaks began. Carloads of blacks were reported throwing Molotov cocktails at police. Police Chief Clarence M. Kelley immediately authorized his force to shoot any firebombers. Authorities called out the entire 900-man police force, 1,700 National Guardsmen, and 168 state troopers to quell the disturbance. On the first day of rioting two persons were killed, forty-four injured, and 175 arrested. The next day the violence escalated, and five black civilians were killed. At least ten persons were wounded as police and National Guardsmen exchanged fire with snipers.

The National Guard force was increased to 2,200 and an additional 700 troopers were rushed by Governor Warren E. Hearnes from central and eastern Missouri to Kansas City. During the evening sixty persons were arrested and fifty-seven were injured—seven by gunfire. Windows were broken in over two hundred businesses and seventy-five fires were started. The evening ended with more than 275 people arrested. Most of the damage was in the black sector. Later, some public officials admitted that law enforcement personnel overreacted to the situation.

In St. Louis there were protests but few incidences of violence, although there were advocates of violence in St. Louis. Fortunately, the more moderate voices won out; partly because many blacks in the Gateway City already felt that they had a greater part to play in local decision making than their fellows across the state. Blacks were being elected to citywide positions during the late 1950s and early 1960s. In 1959, the Reverend John J. Hicks became the first black to win a citywide election in St. Louis when he was chosen to serve on the school board. Of his election, Hicks noted, "There had been apathy, a lethargy on their [blacks'] part for some time concerning things political, especially relating to the total life of the city." Likewise, in 1961 Chester E. Stovall became St. Louis's director of welfare, the city's first black person in that position and the first black to hold a cabinet-level job there.

It also helped that St. Louis was the home of Missouri's first black state senator, Theodore McNeal. Elected to the senate from Missouri's Seventh Congressional District, McNeal was born on November 5, 1905, in Helena, Arkansas, and educated in the Arkansas public schools. McNeal was active in union politics, having served on the national staff of the Brotherhood of Sleeping Car Porters and Maids Union since 1937. McNeal was elected as an international vice-president of the union in 1950. Long active in north St. Louis ward politics, McNeal belonged to the Antioch Baptist Church, which was an important social anchor of the northside's Ville.

McNeal was joined in the Senate in 1968 by Raymond Howard, a thirty-three-year-old native of St. Louis. Educated at Banneker Elementary School and Vashon High School in St. Louis, Howard attended the University of Wisconsin at Madison and St. Louis University School of Law. After law school, Howard engaged in general practice in St. Louis while also serving as legal counsel for the NAACP and CORE. Prior to his election to the state senate, Howard served two terms in the Missouri House of Representatives.

In the violence-ridden year of 1968, Missouri also elected its first black Congressman, William L. Clay, Sr., who was elected from the First Congressional District. Born in St. Louis in 1931, Clay earned degrees in history and political science from St. Louis University. Prior to his election to Congress, Clay was active in St. Louis politics and served for a number of years as alderman from the Twenty-sixth Ward. As an alderman, Clay sponsored numerous bills promoting improved opportunities for blacks.

The violence of 1968 had mixed results. On the one hand, it called attention to the grievances of blacks in the ghettos. Demands for better jobs, better housing, better health services, better police protection, and an end to police brutality opened up new opportunities. On the other hand, since most of the violence occurred in black neighborhoods, it left even more blacks homeless and jobless. But violence is not a logical response to problems; rather, it is an emotional rejoinder to frustration and disappointment. The 1950s had started on such a positive note. The *Brown* decision in 1954 seemed to be the answer to the collective prayer of millions of black Americans. The successes of Martin Luther King and the verbal commitments to racial equality by Presidents Kennedy and Johnson further nurtured the dream. Black people's expectations were raised so high; in return, they got so little. Many wondered whether the dream could be revived in spite of the violence, and in spite of King's assassination.

Suggested Readings

Two works mentioned earlier are also useful in explaining the efforts of Missouri blacks to secure equality of education and first-class citizenship after 1954. For the successes and failures of school desegregation in Missouri until 1959, Lorenzo J. Greene, *Desegregation of Schools in Missouri* (Jefferson City: Missouri Advisory Committee on Civil Rights, 1959), is an authoritative study. It should be supplemented with Monroe Billington, "Public School Integration in Missouri, 1954–1964," *Journal of Negro Education* 35 (1966): 252–62.

Thomas E. Baker's doctoral dissertation, "Human Rights in Missouri" (University of Missouri–Columbia, 1975), provides an excellent overview of the African-American struggle for first-class citizenship in Missouri and an inside view of the advances and shortcomings of the Missouri Commission on Human Rights during its first fifteen years.

The Missouri Commission on Human Rights' *Study of Human Rights in Missouri* (Jefferson City: Missouri Commission on Human Rights, 1960) shows the lack of progress in the area of human rights in Missouri up through 1960. The Missouri Advisory Committee to the United States Commission on Civil Rights, "Report on Employment," an unpublished report, Jefferson City, 1963, provides much evidence of the continued discrimination in outstate Missouri and the two major urban areas—Kansas City and St. Louis.

The problems of Pruitt-Igoe are emphasized in Lee Rainwater, *Behind Ghetto Walls: Black Family Life in a Federal Slum* (Chicago: Aldine Publishing Co., 1970). Also very useful is a compilation of newspaper articles that appeared in the *St. Louis Post-Dispatch* between 1951 and 1975: *Pruitt-Igoe: The Story of a Public Housing Development: A National Prototype as Seen in the St.*

Louis Post-Dispatch, 1951–1975 (St. Louis: St. Louis Post-Dispatch, 1975). Rex Campbell and Peter C. Robertson, *The Negro in Missouri, 1960* (Jefferson City: Missouri Commission on Human Rights, 1967), compiled useful statistical data from the U.S. Census of 1960. Lori Bogle provides an interesting case study of desegregation in the Joplin public schools in "Desegregation in a Border State: The Example of Joplin, Missouri," *Missouri Historical Review* 85 (July 1991): 422–40. George Lipsitz tells the admirable story of Ivory Perry in his *A Life in the Struggle: Ivory Perry and the Culture of Opposition* (Philadelphia: Temple University Press, 1988).

James Frank, president of Lincoln University, 1973–1982 and, subsequently, president of the NCAA. (Inman E. Page Library of Lincoln University, Jefferson City).

Leona Rice talking with customers in her restaurant inside the Booker T. Hotel, 1950. (Courtesy Leona Rice.)

Booker T. Hotel (1964), a prominent black business at 600 Lafayette in Jefferson City before it fell victim to urban renewal. (Courtesy Leona Rice.)

Gerald Early, author
and director of
African and African-
American Studies,
Washington Univer-
sity (Courtesy Gerald
Early).

Oliver Cromwell Cox, pioneer black sociologist during the McCarthy years, taught at Lincoln University for twenty years. (Inman E. Page Library of Lincoln University, Jefferson City.)

William L. Clay, Jr., Missouri state senator (Courtesy William L. Clay, Jr.)

Emmanuel Cleaver II,
first black mayor of a
major city, Kansas City
(Courtesy Emmanuel
Cleaver, II).

194

Philip B. Curls, Sr.,
Missouri senator
(Courtesy of Missouri
State Archives).

Wendall G. Rayburn, president of Lincoln University, 1988–. (Inman E. Page Library of Lincoln University, Jefferson City)

Marguerite Ross
Barnett, chancellor
of the University of
Missouri–St. Louis,
1986–1990 (Courtesy
University Archives,
UMSL).

Marie Wilburn
Williams, Springfield,
Missouri, Red Cross,
World War II (Cour-
tesy Katherine
Lederer).

Alan D. Wheat, U.S. senator (Courtesy Missouri State Archives).

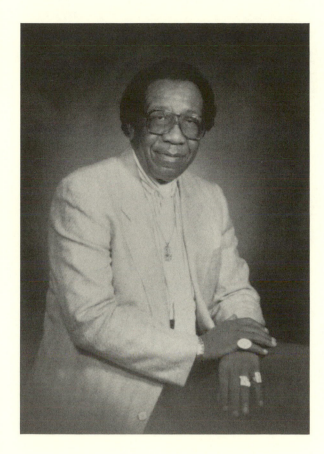

J. B. "Jet" Banks,
Missouri senator
(Courtesy Missouri
State Archives).

Mary Groves Bland,
Missouri state repre-
sentative (Courtesy
Missouri State
Archives).

Carson Ross, Missouri
state representative
(Courtesy Missouri
State Archives).

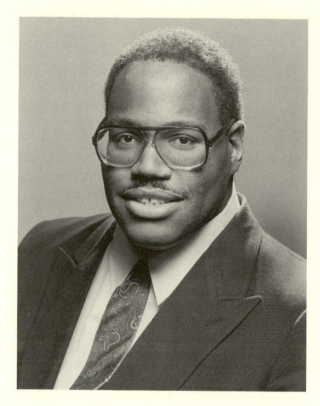

Gregory Freeman,
St. Louis Post-Dispatch
columnist (Courtesy
Gregory Freeman).

Lincoln University campus disturbance in 1969. Mayor John Christy of Jefferson City talks with student leaders. (*St. Louis American.*)

Redd Foxx of "Sanford and Son" TV fame (*St. Louis American*).

Felicia Weathers, soprano opera singer (*St. Louis American*).

Grace Bumbry, opera star (*St. Louis American*).

Dick Gregory returns to native St. Louis for rally. (Courtesy *St. Louis American*.)

Black demonstrators marching in Kansas City, 1968 (*Kansas City Star*).

Leon Jordan,
cofounder and
president of Kansas
City's Freedom,
Inc., a black politi-
cal action group
(Courtesy of *Kansas
City Star*).

Senator Gwen Giles, first black woman elected state senator in Missouri. (Courtesy of *St. Louis American*.)

State Representative DeVerne Calloway and former President Jimmy Carter (Courtesy of *St. Louis American*).

William L. Clay, Sr.,
U.S. congressman
(Courtesy William L.
Clay, Sr.).

11

Shall We Overcome?
The Struggle Continues

The assassination of Martin Luther King, Jr., occurred in a year filled with momentous events. For many young black Americans, King's assassination was the last straw. They had seen their leaders—Medgar Evers, Malcolm X, and King—killed off, and their disillusionment and frustration turned to anger and violence. Social justice, which had seemingly been the goal of the 1960s, gave way to a white backlash. When Robert F. Kennedy was murdered in June 1968, American idealism and the hope of social justice seemed shattered. Many Americans were fearful of the future.

Conservative whites turned to Richard M. Nixon in the 1968 presidential election. Nixon did not create a new mood in the country so much as he tapped and nurtured a sentiment that already existed. Americans, and among them Missourians, were tired of the rapid social changes of the 1960s, tired of violence, tired of fighting a losing war in Vietnam, and tired of the general confusion and anxiety. They blamed most of the problems on an idealism that they thought was unworkable. Therefore, many white Americans began to concern themselves more with their individual problems than with the social aspirations of less-fortunate members of society.

Richard Nixon interpreted his election as a mandate to reverse the liberal trends of the 1950s and 1960s. He believed that Americans had become less willing to pour money into a war on poverty whose end was nowhere in sight. Predictably, federal funds for the poor, a disproportionate number of whom were black, began to dry up. It became increasingly difficult to pass programs allocating funds for health, education, and welfare, and once again the nation's deprived citizens were forced to fend for themselves.

As if things were not bad enough, the 1970s saw Americans confronted by economic problems that puzzled even the experts. Runaway inflation of 10 percent or more a year threatened to lower the living standards of middle-class citizens; to the poor and aged, many of whom were on fixed incomes, it was disastrous. The long-held American dream that each generation of American citizens would live better than its parents was jeopardized. The poor and many blacks in the nation's cities gave up hope of moving ahead; they struggled merely to survive.

In January 1980, Vernon Jordan, president of the National Urban League, issued a report entitled "The State of Black America." According to the report, the mid–1970 recession—the worst recession in forty years—hit blacks the hardest: "Blacks lost their jobs at almost double the rate experienced by whites" during the mid–1970s. Moreover, blacks were slower to be rehired than whites once businesses began to call people back to work. One unemployed African-American in Kansas City summed up the situation to *New York Times* reporter Jon Nordheimer: "The truth is that black people ain't no closer to catching up with whites than they were before. A black man can work hard, if he can find work, but there's no catching up with what the whites got already."

This depressing atmosphere nurtured frustrations. Affirmative action, the policy that was seen by many as an opportunity for blacks to receive preferential treatment in jobs and educational opportunities, became, ironically, a source of discontent rather than a solution to the problem. Middle-class whites, whose own aspirations for success were threatened by an unpredictable and unstable economy, raised questions that no one was ready to answer: in a tight job market, should a more-qualified white be forced to give up a job to a less-qualified black, even if the less-qualified black was the victim of racially inspired inferior training? Blacks countered with the equally legitimate claim that they could not be held responsible for their own oppression, and that something had to be done in reparation for past wrongs to them as a people. No American institution, not even the U.S. Supreme Court, seemed either able or even willing to resolve that dilemma.

The 1970s witnessed a revival of white racism and antiblack violence. In 1973, for example, a black couple's home in the Little Dixie town of Auxvasse was firebombed. The Ganaway family alleged that their house was bombed because they were the first blacks to live in a previously all-white neighborhood. Likewise, Ku Klux Klan activity enjoyed a resurgence. Mary E. Carr, the KKK's Grand Genie (head of the women's wing of the Klan) ran for mayor of Black Jack, Missouri, in 1979 and for city marshal in 1976 on an openly racist platform. In 1979 she received nearly 15 percent of the votes cast in the community.

The Reverend James L. Betts, Grand Dragon of the Ku Klux Klan in Missouri, claimed a membership total of two thousand in 1978, although other membership estimates were much lower. Betts claimed that the Missouri Klan had dwindled to approximately twenty-five members when he took over the top leadership position in 1974. In the late 1960s, Betts had been an ardent supporter of segregationist Alabama governor, George Wallace. But he became disenchanted with Wallace, as he told a *St. Louis Post-Dispatch* reporter in a 1978 interview: "Wallace began sounding more like a Republican or a Democrat. He started having Negroes working in his campaign. And he failed to come out and name Jews as the cause of the trouble this country is in, when he talked against the 'financial interests.'" Betts claimed that Kansas City was the most fertile area in the state for Klan recruitment. He described a Klansman as "a person who believes his country should be totally against Communism and is militant enough to fight for it. He's a person who loves his own race enough not to marry with colored races." In Centralia, St. Peters, and other cities the Klan openly appeared and sought permission to parade and hold rallies.

In Missouri's capital city the prestigious Jefferson City Country Club continued to accept only whites. In April 1971, State Representative J. B. "Jet" Banks filed a complaint with the Missouri Human Rights Commission charging the club with discrimination against blacks. The next month, the chairman of the commission, Richard Chamier, ruled that while the commission disapproved of the all-white clause in the club's charter, it could take no action since the club was private. Nevertheless, the Jefferson City Country Club voluntarily removed its all-white membership provision several months later, although few blacks could afford its annual membership fee.

In 1975 the Missouri Human Rights Commission completed a study entitled "Integration in Missouri Public Schools: Faculty and Students Twenty Years after Brown." The report showed that throughout the state, faculties and students remained segregated, especially in southeast Missouri. There were complaints that desegregation only meant the shutting down of black schools and the dismissal of black teachers. Within the school buildings, the report charged, segregation was maintained by class assignments, and black pupils faced unfair and unequal disciplinary policies, which seemed aimed at forcing them to drop out of school. The report went on to state that 72 percent of the schools in St. Louis and 63 percent of those in Kansas City had student bodies with 95 percent or more of one race.

By 1978 things were not much better. In that year, the Missouri Department of Elementary and Secondary Education completed a survey of urban-metropolitan education in the state. More than 90 percent of the minority students still attended schools in minority school districts, and the staff composition of the school districts generally reflected the districts' racial makeup. In short, nearly all the black students and staff were located in largely black school districts. In addition, the dropout rate was highest in the two largest minority school districts, St. Louis and Kansas City. Minority school districts generally received the least amount of money per pupil, although the amount varied from district to district. Perhaps most frustrating was the Department of Education's prediction that Missouri urban schools would become increasingly segregated in the 1980s.

As with the elementary and secondary schools, desegregation of Missouri's higher education facilities was very slow. In 1979 a survey was conducted of the desegregation of several mid-Missouri colleges and universities, and the only institution to achieve any real degree of desegregation was the formerly all-black Lincoln University. Out of a total of 2,085 undergraduates, white students comprised 1,094 of them. On a faculty of 189 instructors, 101 were white. By contrast, at the University of Missouri–Columbia less than 4 percent of the student population were black undergraduates. Likewise, out of a total faculty of 2,062, barely more than one percent was black.

The greatest problem facing black Missourians in the 1970s was unemployment. In 1970 the black population of Missouri stood at 480,172, or 10.3 percent of the total population of 4,676,501. Eighty-six percent of these blacks lived in the St. Louis and Kansas City areas. The income of the average black family was still 25 percent lower than that of the average white family, and approximately three times as many blacks as whites were unemployed. The poorest Missourians in the 1970s, black or white, lived in Missouri's Bootheel. Residents of Hayti Heights, the nearly all-black city adjacent to the nearly all-white Hayti in Pemiscot County, had an average annual income of $751 in the late 1970s. This appallingly low sum compared unfavorably to $2,253 for the rest of the county, which, in turn, was way below the state and national averages.

Kevin Horrigan of the *St. Louis Post-Dispatch,* who wrote three articles on the Bootheel for his paper in 1978, described Hayti Heights as follows: "Hayti Heights has the kind of poverty you'd like to think didn't exist in the United States any more. Southern, rural, tin-roof-tarpaper-shotgun-shack poverty with a crumbling privy in the back. Children in rags throwing stones at emaciated dogs. Old people hoeing gardens, hoping for a better day tomorrow, but really kind of doubting it."

Blacks in St. Louis likewise found themselves in dire economic straits. There were approximately fifty-four thousand people in the city unemployed in 1970—90 percent of whom were black. This situation was created in part by the fact that several large companies, such as the Chrysler Corporation, relocated their plants in suburban communities. With restrictive codes making housing more difficult for blacks to obtain in St. Louis County, the percentage of blacks working in such large plants was greatly reduced.

Housing was also a serious problem for blacks who remained in the city. Urban renewal programs often displaced many blacks. Between 1960 and 1965, for example, about six thousand new housing units were built in St. Louis. At the same time more than twelve thousand units were destroyed by urban renewal and highway construction projects. Moreover, the quality of much of the housing available to blacks declined dramatically in the 1960s and 1970s. Once neat and prosperous neighborhoods occupied by the black middle class turned into desolate ghettos. A particularly dramatic case was the Ville in north central St. Louis. From the 1920s through the 1960s, the Ville was home to African-American doctors, lawyers, teachers, and other professionals. But as those persons moved out of the city, their previously well-kept homes became rental property that attracted a less-stable and often unemployed population. The neighborhood quickly declined.

Public housing offered no better alternative for blacks. The federal government's urban renewal programs of the 1950s and 1960s displaced tens of thousands of blacks from inner-city housing across America. In St. Louis, thirty-three thousand dwellings targeted for urban renewal were destroyed between 1950 and 1969. Racial discrimination and poverty limited affordable housing for blacks, forcing many into dilapidated, poorly managed public housing projects. Inflation and rising utility costs also compounded the tenants' problems. After a series of rent hikes in St. Louis's public housing projects forced many tenants to pay more than half of their income for rent, residents at the Carr Square Village housing project began a rent strike in February 1969. The Reverend Buck Jones, a community activist, was the key organizer of the strike, while Jean King, Loretta Hall, and other activists drew upon their community organizing experiences in the civil rights movement to also become important leaders in the strike. By refusing to pay the rent, the strikers sought to mobilize tenants to demand concessions, including lower, more affordable rents, and tenant management boards to supervise the projects. Tenants from six other housing projects joined those of Carr Square Village in their strike, which dragged on for nine months.

Ivory Perry, who had played a major role in the 1963 Jefferson Bank demonstrations, persuaded CORE, the Black Liberators, ACTION, and other black organizations to endorse the tenants' strike. He also led a series of sit-ins and demonstrations to bring the housing problem to public attention. Perhaps Perry's most important contribution was securing St. Louis as the site of the annual convention of the National Tenants Organization, which focused national media attention on the tenants' plight.

Finally, in October 1969, the leader of the St. Louis Teamster's Union, Harold Gibbons, organized a coalition of business, labor, and community leaders into the Civic Alliance for Housing. The coalition was instrumental in locating more funding for local public housing and for negotiating a settlement to the rent strike. The Civic Alliance for Housing settlement was supported in large part because St. Louis politicians and businessmen feared and wanted to avoid the inner-city strife that had recently devastated Detroit and other American cities.

As a field housing specialist for the Human Development Corporation, an antipoverty organization, Ivory Perry began an intensive campaign in the late 1960s to eliminate the threat of lead poisoning to St. Louis inner-city tenants. He hoped to get legislation passed that would force landlords to remove lead-based paint from their buildings. Missouri had outlawed the use of lead-based paints in buildings in 1950, but some of the paint still remained on the walls of many older, dilapidated buildings, and its effects caused skin rashes and other minor health problems for those who came in daily contact with it. More severe cases of lead poisoning, however, could result in permanent brain damage and mental retardation. Perry was especially concerned with the problem because the victims of lead poisoning were usually small children. One study conducted in 1971 showed that of a group of 2,752 children tested, 40 percent had abnormally high levels of lead in their bloodstreams. Compounding the problem was the fact that as late as 1969 St. Louis hospitals and clinics had no facilities to test for or treat lead poisoning.

In April 1970, largely due to Perry's and Alderman Henry Stolar's efforts, St. Louis passed an ordinance forcing landlords to remove lead-based paint from their properties. But judges and municipal authorities failed to actively enforce the law. Frustrated by the political indifference, Perry turned to mass community organization to solve the problem by forming the People's Coalition against Lead Poisoning. The organization started public educational programs on the dangers of lead-based paints, established lead-poisoning testing and treatment centers at local hospitals and clinics, and organized fund-raising benefits to support the campaign. The organization's task, however, was a difficult one. Dr. Ursula Rolfe of Cardinal Glennon Hospital estimated that as many as thirty thousand St. Louis children were exposed to lead poisoning, and health officials estimated that it might cost as much as $100 million to remove lead paint from city apartment buildings. For his work in educating the public and helping to eliminate the dangers of lead poisoning, Perry received praise from Mayor A. J. Cervantes, the St. Louis Urban League, and others.

Despite these problems, the black business community in St. Louis remained active, and at least some black businesses prospered. C. W. Gates and I. O. Funderburg provided leadership as president and executive vice-president, respectively, of the Gateway National Bank. The bank opened in June 1965, and before the year's end had deposits of nearly $1.5 million. By 1971 the bank had assets of $13 million. In 1975 Gates became a Miller beer distributor and established the Lismark Distributing Co., which by the early 1980s had annual sales of nearly $8 million.

Gates was also interested in community affairs. In 1966 he became the first black member of the St. Louis Board of Police Commissioners. He also held a major interest in a local radio station and was a copublisher of the black-owned *St. Louis American* newspaper.

Perhaps one of the strongest traditions in black business was represented by the city's three black-owned weekly newspapers. The *St. Louis American* and the *St. Louis Argus* each represented more than fifty years of service by two newspaper families, the Sweets and the Mitchells. The third weekly, the *St. Louis Sentinel,* is of more recent origin, having been established in 1968 by Howard B. Woods.

One of the most creative black businesses in St. Louis was a corporation called Jeff-Vander-Lou, chartered in 1966. The organization made great progress in the rehabilitation of dwellings for area residents in the city's poorest neighborhoods. Besides rehabilitating several hundred homes, Jeff-Vander-Lou, under the leadership of founder Macler Shepard, operated day-care and senior citizens centers. The corporation also broke down a good deal of union discrimination in the construction business. Shepard, a native of Arkansas, moved to St. Louis in the 1920s at the age of six after his mother's death.

Three McDonald franchises were owned during the 1970s by Dr. Benjamin Davis. Other businesses included mortuaries, real estate firms, a casket factory, construction companies, repair shops, taverns, grocery stores, and barbering and hairdressing salons. Some black Missourians held high managerial positions with large international and national corporations. Among these were Archie Price at Laclede Steel Company and James Webb, marketing manager of all forms of transportation for AT&T.

The employment problems of blacks in Kansas City were just as bad, if not worse, than those in St. Louis. The Federal Bureau of Labor Statistics estimated that the unemployment rate for nonwhites (most of whom were black) in Kansas City for 1976 was 17.4 percent, even greater than St. Louis' 14.2 percent.

Most of Kansas City's black businesses remained service-oriented in the 1970s. There were no black-owned banks or insurance companies as there were in St. Louis. McKinley Edmunds owned one of the largest car dealerships in the country. Two successful black-owned businesses served barbecue to Kansas Citians: Ollie Gates & Sons and Arthur Bryant's. Everett P. O'Neal owned a tire company, a security-guard service, and was involved in real estate. A public relations, advertising, and marketing research firm was owned by Inez Y. Kaiser. B. Lawrence Blankinship operated a wholesale drug and hair care products company.

One of the most influential black-owned businesses was the newspaper, the *Kansas City Call*. The Black Economic Union, formed in 1967 by Curtis McClinton, Jr., a former player with the Kansas City Chiefs, was successful. The union created a Community Development Corporation in 1972 and encouraged the development of the Downtown East Industrial Park. Drug stores, mortuaries, grocery stores, filling stations, real estate firms, house and window cleaning firms, contracting companies, barbering and hairdressing salons, and a building and loan company were among the other businesses owned by blacks in Kansas City.

The black population was more successful in politics than in economics. In 1969 Missouri ranked second in the nation in the number of blacks serving in state and national legislative bodies. In that year there was one black U.S. congressman, two state senators, and thirteen state representatives; only Illinois with eighteen had more. One practical result of the increased strength of blacks in the General Assembly was that in 1969 a law was finally passed repealing a statute that banned interracial marriages. One of the important sources of Kansas City's black political power was an organization called Freedom, Inc. This organization was established in 1962 by Leon Jordan and Bruce Watkins, two black businessmen. In that year the organization helped elect Leon Jordan to the Jackson County Democratic Committee. Shortly thereafter, Bruce Watkins was elected to the city council. Freedom, Inc., had eight candidates running in 1964, seven of whom won elective positions. By 1978 Freedom-endorsed officials included four state representatives, two city councilmen, three county legislators, one city judge, three school board members, many members of municipal boards, and several committeemen and committeewomen. In 1970 the organization suffered a blow when its president, Leon Jordan, was assassinated; however, the organization continued with Bruce Watkins as its president. Jordan's widow, Orchid, won his seat in the General Assembly. In 1976 the organization suffered another setback when Harold Holliday, Sr., was defeated in the Democratic primary in a bid for a state senate seat. Likewise, Bruce Watkins lost his bid to become mayor of Kansas City in 1979.

Missouri did not elect its first black woman to the state senate until

1977 when Gwen B. Giles was chosen to fill an unexpired term from the state's Fourth District. Subsequently, Giles was reelected to a full senate term in November of 1978. An urban affairs consultant prior to being elected to the senate, Giles was educated in St. Louis Catholic schools and at St. Louis University. Giles joined Senator J. B. "Jet" Banks, who had left his house seat in 1976 to run successfully for the senate.

There were more African-Americans working in state government during the 1970s than ever before. According to a report prepared by black lawyer Calvin Johnson for Governor Christopher S. Bond, blacks held almost 12 percent of the 33,875 state jobs available in 1974, although Johnson charged that blacks "have little responsibility and the lowest salaries."

Johnson's allegation notwithstanding, fifty-five blacks held key appointments in thirty-two agencies. Among them were Johnetta R. Haley, president of the Lincoln University Board of Curators; Kelsey R. Beshears, a member of the Missouri Housing Development Commission; Leah Brock McCartney, vice-chairman of the Public Service Commission; Sherill Hunt, director of Office of Economic Opportunity; Vernell E. Fuller, director of the State Affirmative Action Office and adviser to the governor; and Alvin Brooks, chairman of the Missouri Commission on Human Rights.

During the 1970s, Betty Adams became not only the first black but the first woman to head a state department in Missouri's government. Adams came to state government in 1974 after spending a number of years as a dean at Lincoln University. Initially, Adams was a management specialist in the office of Administration's Division of Budget and Planning. Later, Governor Bond picked her to head the Labor and Management Relations Department. She also served as chairman of the Missouri Commission on the Status of Women from 1974 to 1976.

Among the state agencies that were least successful in hiring and promoting blacks in the 1970s were the Missouri State Highway Patrol, the Conservation Department, the Department of Natural Resources, and the Highway Department. The patrol did not hire its first black trooper until 1965. Although Colonel Al R. Lubker, patrol superintendent, claimed in 1980 that "there's no discrimination in the Highway Patrol," only forty-five blacks among the 847 uniformed personnel were employed by the patrol in that year. One of the last bastions of racial segregation in Missouri, the Missouri State Penitentiary, was finally integrated in December 1973. Prior to that time, the prison's black population was crowded into a single segregated building—the oldest cellblock in the prison complex. Ironically, peaceful integration of the prison came about in large part through the efforts of the black Muslims. Feared in the 1960s as radicals and violent revolutionaries, Muslims gradually came to be seen as model inmates by prison officials because of their opposition to drugs, homosexuality, and violence. By enlisting the aid of Muslims, prison officials were able to avert the bloodshed that had followed in the wake of an unsuccessful 1969 effort at desegregation of the prison.

Blacks did increase steadily in the legal profession in the 1970s. Most of Missouri's black lawyers practiced in St. Louis and Kansas City. Frankie Freeman, a member of the United States Civil Rights Commission, was nominated in June 1979 by President Jimmy Carter to be the first inspector-general of Health, Education, and Welfare. Inspector-General positions were created in 1978 as "watchdog" positions over thirteen separate federal agencies. At the time of her appointment, Freeman was a senior partner in the St. Louis law firm of Freeman, Whitfield, Montgomery, and Walton.

Theodore McMillian became the most prominent African-American jurist in Missouri. Born in St. Louis in 1919, McMillian graduated from Vashon High School before attending Stowe Teachers College and Lincoln University. McMillian aspired to be a physicist before World War II, but the draft interrupted his studies. After the war he inquired at St. Louis University about entering medical school. After being told he would have to wait at least four to five years before he could get in, if at all, McMillian turned his attention to law. He graduated at the top of his class from St. Louis University in 1949. McMillian served a number of years as an assistant St. Louis circuit attorney, a position in which he earned a reputation as a brilliant trial lawyer. In 1956 Governor Phil M. Donnelly appointed McMillian to a circuit judgeship, making him the first black in Missouri history to be a judge. In 1972 he was appointed to the Missouri Court of Appeals by Governor Warren E. Hearnes, and in 1978 President Carter appointed him to the United States Eighth Circuit Court of Appeals. Recommended to the president by Missouri Senator Thomas Eagleton, Judge McMillian replaced William H. Webster, who had stepped down from the bench to become the director of the Federal Bureau of Investigation.

But success for people like McMillian did not mean advancement for all blacks. Indeed, the success of people like him only accentuated the reality of the emergence of three distinct classes in Missouri and the nation: whites, middle-class blacks, and the poor blacks of the inner city whose lives were often more desperate than ever before. Census figures for 1980 revealed that two-thirds of Missouri's 514,276 blacks lived inside central cities of major metropolitan areas. The largest concentration of Missouri blacks continued to reside in St. Louis City on the city's north side.

But in St. Louis during the 1970s, one measure of success for middle-class blacks was their ability to join whites in escaping the inner city for the county. In 1970 there had been 45,495 blacks living in St. Louis County; by 1980 that figure more than doubled to 109,684. The blacks leaving the city for the county tended to be better educated and either employed or more easily employable than the blacks they left behind. According to the 1980 census figures, 52.7 percent of African-Americans in the state age twenty-five or older had a high school diploma. This was 1.7 percent higher than the national average for blacks. By contrast, the figure was 44.8 percent for blacks in St. Louis. St. Louis County blacks were well above the state average with 67 percent of its population having a high school diploma. Likewise, national black median income, after adjustments for inflation, increased by 5 percent to $12,600. St. Louis City blacks fell below this figure at $11,442, while St. Louis County blacks greatly exceeded it with $19,171.

In part, these figures reveal that things were getting both better and worse. A substantial number of St. Louis blacks achieved upward and spatial mobility between 1970 and 1980 by improving their education and their income and, subsequently, by escaping the inner city for the suburbs—much like their white counterparts. But they left behind blacks whose lives were more desperate than ever before. Ernest Calloway, professor emeritus of Urban Studies at St. Louis University, said that those left behind were "a poorer group of blacks, a less-educated group of blacks" who no longer had "the old social anchors," such as the stable middle-class churches of the inner city to turn to. For a majority of black Americans living in Missouri's inner cities, the important question was whether a new decade with a new president and a new governor would bring new opportunity and hope to their lives.

Suggested Readings

As yet very little published material exists for the period 1968 through 1979. The Missouri Commission on Human Rights' *Annual Reports* and the commission's newsletter, *Progress,* should be examined. In addition, Rex Campbell and Thomas E. Baker, *The Negro in Missouri—1970* (Jefferson City: Missouri Commission on Human Rights, 1972), analyze the racial characteristics of the Missouri population based on the U.S. Census of 1970. Thomas E. Baker and Rex Campbell, *Race and Residence in Missouri Cities* (Jefferson City: Missouri Commission on Human Rights, 1971), also provide an analysis of continued housing discrimination in ten Missouri cities based on the 1970 U.S. Census. Two reports in 1979 by the Missouri Advisory Committee to the United States Commission on Civil Rights are quite helpful. They are *Race Relations in the "Kingdom of Callaway"* and *Race Relations in Cooper County, Missouri—1978.*

The problems of bringing true integration to Missouri schools are examined by David Henderson in *Integration in Missouri Public Schools* (Jefferson City: Missouri Commission on Human Rights, 1974); and in *A Study of Urban-Metropolitan Education in Missouri* (Jefferson City: Missouri Department of Elementary and Secondary Education, 1978).

Useful information on the economic life of black St. Louisans can be found in "St. Louis," *Black Enterprise* 2 (August 1971): 30–33. The economic and political situation of blacks in Kansas City is covered by Jeanne Allyson Fox, "In Kansas City, Missouri, Economic Development Plays Catch Up to Political Clout," *Black Enterprise* 8 (March 1978): 43–46. The 1980 federal census provides a wealth of information about black life in Missouri during the 1970s. The 317-page Missouri report, *General Population Characteristics* (Washington, D.C.: GPO, 1983), contains age, sex, marital status, and household relationship statistics for the total population, which includes Spanish, Caucasian, African-American, Native American, and Asian and Pacific Islander populations. Data are shown for all Missouri counties, county subdivisions, standard metropolitan statistical areas, urbanized areas, and places of one thousand or more inhabitants.

In addition to the above sources, the major metropolitan newspapers should be consulted: the *St. Louis Post-Dispatch* and the *Kansas City Star.* Likewise, the state's African-American weekly papers are indispensable: the *Kansas City Call,* the *St. Louis Argus,* the *St. Louis American,* and the *St. Louis Sentinel.* Ed Wilks's article on the Ku Klux Klan, "A Peek beneath the Sheets," *St. Louis Post-Dispatch,* July 30, 1978, is especially helpful, as is an essay by Jon Nordheimer entitled "Three Societies Emerging in U.S.," *St. Louis Post-*

Dispatch, February 27, 1978. Keven Horrigan wrote a three-part series on the Bootheel in the *St. Louis Post-Dispatch* during June 11 through 13, 1978, that is very revealing. Judge Theodore McMillian is the subject of a useful article by William J. Shaw, "Why Judge McMillian Worries," *St. Louis Post-Dispatch Magazine,* August 11, 1991.

12

The 1980s and Beyond

The 1980s began with the "Reagan Revolution," a period in which America's fortieth president tried to restore fiscal and philosophical conservatism to the country. Advocating tax reductions for the wealthy over relief programs for the poor, Reagan hoped that his plan would result in a reinvigorated economy based upon expansion in the private sector.

Traditional tactics of the civil rights movement—particularly busing and the establishment of racial quotas—were also attacked by the president. Under Reagan the federal government all but ceased to use its power to force compliance with civil rights mandates in lieu of allowing the states jurisdiction over such matters. Indeed, in 1989 the U.S. Supreme Court, dominated by Nixon-Reagan appointees, reversed many of the affirmative action principles previously accepted as inviolate.

The 1980s did witness the largest peacetime prosperity in modern America. Unfortunately, for black Americans their share of this prosperity was minimal. Moreover, prosperity was achieved in large part by mortgaging the country's future. Toward the decade's end, the national deficit reached unprecedented proportions. Efforts to reduce the deficit once again victimized black Americans. In the name of balancing the budget, officials at the federal, state, and local levels cut social welfare programs, the beneficiaries of which were disproportionately black.

The decade of the 1980s was a period of both optimism and pessimism for black Missourians. On the positive side, more blacks moved into the middle-class mainstream of American society than ever before, sometimes in rather dramatic ways. But on the negative side, the hopelessness and despair engendered by poverty and inner-city ghetto life reached all-time highs. Life itself remained especially precarious for the masses of African-Americans.

The largest concentration of Missouri blacks continued to reside in the St. Louis area in the 1980s, although the black population of north St. Louis declined by approximately twenty-seven thousand people, according to 1990 census figures. This total, as *St. Louis Post-Dispatch* reporters Bill Smith and George Landau pointed out, was equivalent to the entire population of the St. Louis suburb of Kirkwood. Some north St. Louis black neighborhoods lost nearly one-third of their population over the decade. Blacks who moved told Smith and Landau that they were "fleeing drugs, crime and deteriorating housing." Many moved to the north county area, like a father of three who grew up on the city's north side but wanted to escape: "There was a lot of gang activity in the city. This is better here; I don't feel threatened here. I wanted my children to have better than what I had."

In addition to the north county migration, blacks moved in unprecedented numbers into south St. Louis, an area that had previously been overwhelmingly white. Indeed, so intense was the black movement into south St. Louis that one demographer, John G. Blodgett, manager of the Urban Information Center at the University of Missouri–St. Louis, predicted that south St. Louis would be predominantly black within twenty years.

While middle-class blacks were moving in large numbers from St. Louis to the county, whites were moving even farther into St. Charles and Jefferson counties, which left St. Louis increasingly blacker and poorer. By 1990 St. Louis had become America's second most-segregated large urban area in the country, only slightly less segregated than Chicago. By contrast, Kansas City became slightly less segregated in the 1980s, although it ranked tenth on the census bureau's list of most segregated urban areas.

In St. Louis, especially on the north side, the quality of black life reached depressingly low levels during the 1980s. Black-on-black crime, for example, reached an all-time high. On February 16, 1989, Ivory Perry, the black St. Louis civil rights activist whose name had so often been in the news during the 1960s and 1970s, was stabbed to death by his son during a domestic quarrel. Perry's death, tragic as it was, became something of a metaphor for the 1980s, as black-on-black violence reached alarming new heights.

By the mid–1980s, the homicide rate for black St. Louis males between the ages of fifteen and forty-four exceeded that of any other major city in the United States. At the mid–1980s rate, one out of every thirteen black males aged fifteen could expect to be murdered before they turned forty-five. In 1986 there were 196 recorded homicides in St. Louis; 169 of the victims were black. Male victims outnumbered female victims nearly four to one. Over 83 percent of the black male murder victims in St. Louis were between fifteen and forty years of age, with the largest concentration (27.5 percent) twenty-five to twenty-nine years old. A majority of the murder victims (more than two-thirds) were killed by gunfire near their homes.

Missouri blacks were dying prematurely in other ways as well. In April 1990, the Missouri Health Department reported on a study of cancer mortality covering the period from 1980 to 1988. According to the study, there was an average of 210 white men out of every hundred thousand who died from cancer each year of the study, compared to the 49 percent higher death rate of 313 out of every hundred thousand black men. Similarly, an average of 178 out of hundred thousand black women died each year, compared to the smaller average of 132 white women.

The cancer death rate from prostrate cancer was more than twice as high for blacks as for whites. The Department of Health study attributed much of the cause of the higher incidence of cancer deaths among blacks to their "lower socio-economic status." The study concluded that "lower socio-economic status is an important predictor of the high cancer mortality among blacks. Lower socio-economic status affects other factors that influence cancer survival, such as knowledge of primary prevention, knowledge and availability of early detection practices, and state-of-the-art treatment."

Another serious threat to urban blacks in the state in the 1980s and 1990s was the virulent AIDS epidemic. In St. Louis more than half the number of people found to have AIDS at city health clinics were black. State Representative Charles "Quincy" Troupe was among the black leaders who tried to raise both black and white consciousness about the AIDS epidemic. One black St. Louisan, Ardella Johnson, responded to Troupe's plea and started an organization called African-American Women for Wellness. After incorporating as a not-for-profit organization with Johnson as its president, the group raised $10,000 with a benefit performance of a play written by a member of the organization, Shirley LeFlore. The play, "Deliverance," explored the issue of AIDS and its effect on blacks.

On a more promising note, Missouri blacks made considerable progress in the political arena during the 1980s. In Kansas City, black candidates defeated several incumbents for General Assembly seats. Backed by Freedom, Inc., People in Politics, and the Brotherhood Democratic Club-United for Victory, three black candidates defeated white incumbents in primaries and then went on to victories in the fall election. The Reverend James Tindall, pastor of the Metropolitan Spiritual Church of Christ, defeated Representative Paul Rojas, who had previously represented Missouri's Twenty-third District; Mary Groves Bland defeated Representative Phillip Scaglia, who had represented the Thirtieth District for sixteen years; and Earl A. Pitts, Sr., a Kansas City businessman, defeated Thirty-second District Representative Joseph S. Kenton.

In a senate race, black Kansas City lawyer Lee Vertis Swinton defeated Senator Mary L. Gant by less than fifty votes in the Democratic primary. Swinton defeated his black Republican opponent, Robert L. Collins, to become Kansas City's first black senator. Tindall, Bland, and Collins joined four black Kansas City incumbents to give Missouri's second largest city seven members in the statehouse. The black incumbents were Orchid Jordan, of the Twenty-fifth District; Alan Wheat, of the Twenty-sixth District; Phil B. Curls, of the Twenty-eighth District; and, Leo McKamey of the Thirty-sixth District.

Perhaps no African-American political leader gained more power and prestige in the General Assembly in the 1980s than Senator J. B. "Jet" Banks. A Lincoln University graduate and a St. Louis businessman, the flamboyant Banks served four terms in the Missouri House before being elected to the Senate in 1976. Banks emerged as the state's first black Senate Majority Floor Leader in the late 1980s. The St. Louis Democrat earned praise from both Democrats and Republicans for his legislative skills.

On the national level, the Honorable William L. Clay, Sr., Missouri's United States Congressman from the First Congressional District, soared to new heights of influence and power. In late 1990 Clay was elected to a committee chairmanship for the first time. He replaced Congressman William D. Ford, a Democrat from Michigan, as the head of the influential House Post Office and Civil Service Committee.

The new rising star among black political figures in Missouri during the 1980s was William L. Clay, Jr. Born in St. Louis, Clay was educated in Maryland and worked for six years as an assistant doorkeeper in the House of Representatives. Clay was elected to a seat in the Missouri General Assembly in a special election in 1983 after a close political associate of his father's resigned, and he was chosen by the Democratic party as the party's nominee. In 1991 the younger Clay was again the beneficiary of his father's political influence when state Senator John Bass, longtime friend of the Clay family, stepped down from his senatorial seat to pave the way for another special election. In that election Clay was easily elected to replace Bass.

Major Clarence Harmon became in 1990 the first black secretary to the St. Louis Police Board in the 129-year history of the police department. St. Louis black leaders applauded the selection and expressed the hope that Harmon's appointment would signal the movement of more African-Americans into decision-making positions within the police department. Zaki Reed, a University City teacher, said, "It's a step in the right direction, and we hope a step that will continue in an ongoing direction." Harmon, a veteran of more than twenty years with the St. Louis Police Department, had joined the department in 1969, was promoted to sergeant in 1976, lieutenant in 1980, captain in 1984, and major in 1988. Of his appointment to the secretary's position, Major Harmon remarked: "I think it's significant that an Afro-American has been appointed to a position of such responsibility and visibility within the department. I think it relates to the department's changing image and the desire of the board to be representative in its appointments of the community at large." On August 21, 1991, fifty-one-year-old Harmon was appointed the first black chief of police of the St. Louis Police Department. Harmon was widely respected and drew praise from whites and blacks alike. Civil rights leaders in St. Louis applauded the decision to appoint him. Norman Seay, often a critic of the police department, commented that Harmon's appointment gave blacks hope: "It's giving a message to all African-Americans that if they work hard and have the qualifications, they can succeed. The police recruit can now be told, 'You may someday be chief.' That person now has a dream."

Also in 1990, Judge Fernando J. Gaitan, Jr., of the Missouri Court of Appeals, became the first African-American to serve as a United States

District judge for the Western District of Missouri. Gaitan, a native of Kansas City, Kansas, served as a Jackson County Circuit Court judge from 1980 to 1986, the year he was appointed to the appeals court.

The movement of increasing numbers of blacks into St. Louis County brought with it efforts to gain greater political power in the county. In 1990 a group known as Black Elected County Officials (BECO) organized to effect greater black political participation in the county government. One of the group's goals was to increase the percentage of minority contracts awarded by the county. (The *St. Louis Post-Dispatch* had reported that minority contracts awarded by the county represented only 1 percent of the total value of the top ten St. Louis County contracts.) In general, BECO also sought to facilitate the appointment of black police commissioners, assistant county prosecutors, public defenders, and black county officials.

Perhaps the greatest political setback for Missouri blacks during the 1980s was the imbroglio surrounding Billie Boykins, St. Louis license collector. A St. Louis native, who was elected to the Missouri General Assembly from the Eighty-second District in 1978, Boykins became the city license collector in 1982, thereby becoming the first African-American woman to be elected to a citywide office in St. Louis. Boykins's position put her in charge of more than fifty patronage jobs in the city. Unfortunately, she inherited an office that was notorious for its corruption. One of Boykins's predecessors, Benjamin Goins, had left a trail of malfeasance that resulted in a prison term.

However noble or well intentioned her motives, Boykins was unable to improve the office's operation. Charges of corruption and negligence reached a crescendo in March 1989 when State Auditor Margaret Kelly issued an audit and called Boykins's office "the most poorly run" public office that she had ever examined. Among Kelly's criticisms were: Boykins was lax in collecting business-license taxes, she kept inadequate records, she maintained poor controls on cash and bank accounts, and she engaged in illegal investment and banking practices. Boykins responded to the charges with allegations of her own. She accused the Republican Kelly of political and racial harassment.

The *Boykins* case divided St. Louis politicians along racial lines. In June 1989 in a move strongly supported by St. Louis Mayor Vincent Schoemel, the City Board of Aldermen voted sixteen to thirteen to strip Boykins of most of her powers and the fifty-odd patronage jobs she controlled. All eleven black aldermen supported Boykins; all but two of the eighteen white aldermen opposed her. The city comptroller, Virvus Jones, another black officeholder, was given most of Boykins's duties. Thirty-two black elected officials joined together to urge Jones not to assume the duties. In a letter to Jones, the officials told him: "One of the main reasons we supported you for comptroller was because you convinced us that you would stand up for the interests of citizens of St. Louis in general and the interests of African-Americans in particular. Now is the time!"

In spite of this groundswell of support, Kelly's allegations formed the foundation for an ouster suit filed by the St. Louis circuit attorney. The *Boykins* case was heard by Boone County Circuit Judge Frank Conley, who acted on behalf of the Missouri Supreme Court. On July 27, 1989, Conley issued a fifteen-page report in which he stated: "The authority to oust an elected office holder must be used sparingly and only when a compelling need occurs. The facts of this case speak clearly. If the authority to oust an officer exists at all, it exists in this case." Boykins was subsequently removed from office.

Racial hatred remained an important part of Missouri's social and cultural landscape in the 1980s. Forty-four incidences of racial harassment in Missouri were reported to the United States Justice Department in 1988, making Missouri the leading state in the nation for such violations. The state of Washington ranked second to Missouri with thirty-four such incidences; in 1989 the two states switched rankings. The FBI investigated incidents of racial harassment in northeast Kansas City. A street gang known as "Lykins Dawgs," or "Ninth Street Dogs," had allegedly tried to intimidate two black families who lived in the area by destroying their property.

One harbinger of hatred, the Ku Klux Klan, remained alive and active in Missouri throughout the decade. In April of 1982, James L. Betts, Grand Dragon of what he called the New Order Party, Knights of the Ku Klux Klan, and Mary Carr, Grand Genie, organized a Klan rally in Hannibal, Missouri. Although Carr predicted that two thousand members and supporters would show up, only about thirty arrived on the appointed day. The gathering had been widely publicized, and at least two St. Louis-based groups traveled to Hannibal to protest the rally. Law enforcement officials, fearing a fight between Klansmen and their opponents, ordered the rally to be held in Clemens Field, an area surrounded by an eight-foot-high wall, which was used during World War II to detain German prisoners of war.

Despite tight security, a violent clash occurred. Led by Paul Gomberg, the anti-Klan International Committee against Racism engaged in a short-lived battle with Klansmen before the melee was broken up by police. On June 17, 1990, about a dozen KKK members clad in hoods and robes marched two miles through Lebanon in south central Laclede County. Led by Jimmy Russell of Camdenton, Missouri Grand Dragon of the Christian Knights of the Ku Klux Klan, the small band of Klan members were heckled by two hundred onlookers. The poor response the Klan received in Lebanon apparently caused Klan members to cancel a proposed march in nearby Marshfield. That decision greatly relieved Bobbie Reed of Marshfield, the black owner of a barbecue restaurant in town. Reed's restaurant was the only black business in the Webster County town and had reportedly been targeted for protest.

During the 1980s, African-Americans in Missouri, like blacks elsewhere in the country, continued to believe in education as a key to upward social and economic mobility. Their hopes were nurtured during those years by the federal courts. In the city of St. Louis, the courts' involvement in local public education really began in the early 1970s. In 1972 a group of black north side parents sued the St. Louis City Board of Education, alleging that the city's school system was racially segregated and in violation of the U.S. Constitution. In October 1973, Senior U.S. District Judge James H. Meredith ruled that the suit could proceed as a class action case.

Several years of maneuvering on each side followed. In 1977 the U.S. Department of Justice entered the case on the side of the plaintiffs, and two parent groups, mostly whites, joined the defendants. Subsequently, the State Board of Education and the State Commissioner of Education were added as defendants. The case finally went to trial in October 1977. Over the course of the next seven months thirty-nine witnesses testified, resulting in a transcript of more than seven thousand pages.

On February 2, 1979, Judge Meredith heard final arguments in the case. On April 12, he ruled in favor of the defendants and against the black parents, the NAACP, and the Justice Department. Undaunted, the NAACP appealed the case to the U.S. Court of Appeals of the Eighth

Circuit. In January 1980, the court of appeals heard the arguments, and by March the seven-member court of appeals ruled in a unanimous opinion that "voluntary techniques will not effectively desegregate the St. Louis school system." The city school board would no longer be allowed to continue integrating city schools on a voluntary basis.

Later that same year, Judge Meredith named a desegregation planning committee chaired by Dean Edward T. Foote of Washington University's Law School. Meetings, discussions, and modifications to the plan followed until Meredith approved it in May. Meredith laid the bulk of the blame for segregated schools in Missouri on the state and its officials, thereby laying the groundwork for using state funds to remedy the situation. Subsequently, Judge William Hungate replaced the physically ailing Meredith and proceeded to order the state to pay more than $3 million for desegregation programs in St. Louis. In 1986 court-ordered desegregation payments were extended to Kansas City. By the decade's end, Missourians found out just how expensive historic racism could be. By 1990 the state of Missouri reached the billion dollar mark in payments to St. Louis and Kansas City school districts for court-ordered desegregation. As Kansas City school board member Paul Ballard said, "I guess that's the cause of years of repressive laws."

Looking toward the last decade of the twentieth century, an interracial task force sought to decrease racial polarity in Missouri's "hypersegregated" city of St. Louis. Reacting to a November 1989 report by the Confluence St. Louis Task Force on Racial Polarization, approximately fifty area leaders gathered for a weekend retreat in June "to deal with the problem of racial polarization." The group met at St. Louis University's Fordyce House, the same site used by another group for a similar purpose twenty years earlier.

In 1969 the St. Louis Fordyce Conference reported "a problem in attitude . . . results in the failure of citizens of one race or economic class to show true economic opportunity, education and availability of housing and health care. All of this contributes to an ever-widening gulf between individuals and groups in the St. Louis community." Two decades later, the Confluence St. Louis Task Force on Racial Polarization documented the lack of improvement: "The St. Louis region is highly segregated by race. People live, vote, go to work, entertain themselves and worship in environments which are predominantly of one race. Personal relationships with people of another race do not occur, and blacks and whites are therefore cut off from real opportunities to benefit from one another."

Kansas City also sought to identify areas in need of improvement with regard to race relations. The Kansas City Consensus Task Force on Race Relations worked for more than two years to produce a ninety-four-page report whose purpose was to improve both racial attitudes and the opportunities for African-American entrepreneurs. But, as journalist Al Ansare pointed out in the *Kansas City Call,* the report "did not say much that Kansas City blacks didn't already know." It revealed that minority-owned businesses in the city were actually worse off by the mid–1980s than they had been in the 1960s. The report summarized the status of black businesses as follows: "As a result of a lack of business heritage, adequate capital and training, minority-owned businesses are concentrated in labor-intensive areas . . . that are economically and geographically unfavorable. For instance, most minority-owned businesses are sole proprietorships and are concentrated in personal services and mom-and-pop retail trade."

Among the organizations seeking to reverse this trend, the most active was the Black Chamber of Commerce of Greater Kansas City. In 1992 the Black Chamber hired Marcellus N. Hughes, a former general manager of the National American Insurance Company in Overland Park, Kansas, as its full-time executive director. It was the first time that the 317-member organization had a full-time director in its seven-year history.

In contrast to the depletion of the black-owned businesses in the 1980s, there emerged in Kansas City during the early 1990s what the *Kansas City Star* called "a rare cadre of high-level black executives in the Kansas City area." Among them are Frank L. Douglas, executive vice-president of Marion Merrell Down, Inc.; Louis W. Smith, president of the Kansas City division of Allied-Signal Aerospace Co.; John Walker, executive vice-president of Blue Cross and Blue Shield of Kansas City; and Reginald Smith, president of United Missouri Mortgage Company.

Lincoln University experienced considerable difficulty during the 1980s. Public attention focused on the school during the middecade as a combination of historical underfunding and fiscal mismanagement brought the school to the brink of financial disaster. Student enrollment plummeted in the wake of adverse publicity surrounding the school, which added further to the crisis. President Thomas Miller Jenkins, whose failing many thought lay in his desire to effect too many changes too quickly, was forced to resign as the university's governing body declared a state of financial exigency. Stability was restored under the interim administration of William E. Givens, a Lincoln University alumnus who took time away from his duties as president of predominantly black Harris-Stowe College in St. Louis to return to his alma mater. In January 1988, Wendell G. Rayburn, former president of Savannah State College in Savannah, Georgia, became Lincoln's new leader and presided over a period of unprecedented growth. Record enrollments were reached in the early 1990s, although by that time the student population had become more than 70 percent white.

Lincoln's proportional decline in black enrollment reflected in part the fact that blacks could go to college elsewhere in the state. The University of Missouri system was particularly effective at attracting black students to its Kansas City and St. Louis campuses. In particular, the St. Louis campus was perceived by many as a storehouse of opportunity when Marguerite Ross Barnett was appointed to the chancellorship.

Barnett came to the University of Missouri–St. Louis in June 1986 after serving as vice-chancellor for academic affairs at the City University of New York. A widely published political scientist, Barnett was the first black chancellor in the University of Missouri system. Joseph Palmer, publisher of *Proud Magazine,* noted: "Before Chancellor Barnett arrived at the university, there were a lot of black students who wouldn't even consider going there. There was a feeling—an undertone—that black students weren't all that welcome there. She made the campus more welcome." During Barnett's tenure, an unprecedented number of African-Americans and other minority members were appointed to positions of authority and responsibility.

Barnett was not the only new African-American celebrity to emerge in Missouri in the 1980s. Perhaps the most widely publicized new celebrity of the decade was Debbye Turner, who became Miss America in 1990. Turner had been Miss Missouri in 1989 after competing against forty other women. After her reign as Miss America, she returned to her studies and graduated from the University of Missouri School of Veterinary Medicine in 1991. In St. Louis Ozzie Smith, the perennial National

League Gold Glove winner as shortstop, became one of major league baseball's highest paid players and a major fan attraction.

"Old" celebrities reached new heights in the 1980s and early 1990s. Tina Turner, whose rise to stardom began in the 1960s, attained superstar status in 1984 when she earned a Grammy Award for the best song of the year, "What's Love Got to Do with It?" Tina Turner and her onetime singing partner and former husband, Ike Turner, were inducted into the Rock 'n' Roll Hall of Fame in 1991. Another Rock 'n' Roll Hall of Fame member who remained active throughout the 1980s was Chuck Berry, an innovative blues guitarist and gifted lyricist who had been one of the central figures in the development of rock 'n' roll during the 1950s. By the 1980s, his songs "Maybelline," "Roll Over Beethoven," and "Johnny B. Goode" had become classics. Still another African-American long familiar to Missourians was Hal McRae, a former Kansas City Royals outfielder, who made history in 1991 when he was named manager of his old team, thus becoming the first black American to head a professional sports team in Missouri.

Other African-Americans gained attention in the state, if on a somewhat less grand scale. James Frank, who had been president of Lincoln University through much of the 1970s, became the first black president of the National Collegiate Athletic Association (NCAA) in the early 1980s. Henry "Mule" Townsend, a blues musician who began playing in St. Louis and Kansas City in the 1940s, gained new attention and respect in the 1980s. Even as an octogenarian, Townsend maintained a rigorous performance schedule and continued recording with Nighthawk Records. In 1991 LeRoy Pierson, one of the Nighthawk's founders, reported that Townsend was playing better than he ever had.

A gifted writer named Gerald Early came to Missouri in the 1980s. Early served as the director of African and African American studies at Washington University. His book *Tuxedo Junction* established him as an essayist of great eloquence and insight. In March 1991, Early was the driving force behind Washington University's Black Heartland Conference, which brought together a wide array of scholars from a variety of disciplines to discuss African-American history, life, and culture in the Midwest. Sadly, in 1991 Early was the victim of an incident that spoke volumes about the persistence of racism in Missouri. While waiting for his wife, who was attending an evening meeting in the Frontenac Mall complex in St. Louis County, Early was stopped and questioned by police as he wandered through the mall, looking in the display windows of the closed shops. Later his wife reported that the police chief had told her "in so many words that I would have to understand that there were few blacks in Frontenac."

Other African-American writers who achieved notoriety during the 1980s included Ntosake Shange and Quincy Troupe. Although not a native of Missouri, Shange spent part of her childhood in St. Louis, where she attended an integrated school. She is best known for her novels, *Sassafras, Cypress and Indigo* (1982) and the autobiographical *Betsy Brown* (1987) and her play *for colored girls who have considered suicide / when the rainbow is enuf* (1976). Quincy Troupe, a native of St. Louis, is a poet, author, and professor of American and Third World literature at the College of Staten Island of the City University of New York. He is the coauthor of Miles Davis's critically acclaimed 1989 autobiography, the editor of *James Baldwin: The Legacy* (1989), and the author of several books of poetry.

The decade of the 1980s also saw the passing of one of Missouri's most intense opponents of racial bigotry and injustice, Ernest Calloway. Born in West Virginia in 1909, the son of a political activist and union organizer, Calloway followed in his father's footsteps. In 1950 he came to St. Louis where he joined Teamster's Local 888, headed by Harold Gibbons. He was research director for the teamsters for twenty-three years. During the 1950s and 1960s, he was active in CORE and was president of the St. Louis chapter of the NAACP from 1955 to 1969. He also managed several successful campaigns, most notably those of the Reverend John J. Hicks in 1959, Theodore McNeal in 1960, and his wife, DeVerne, in 1962. DeVerne Calloway's election to a General Assembly seat in 1962 made her the first black woman to serve in the Missouri state legislature.

Ernest Calloway sought the Democrat nomination to the First Congressional District in 1968 but was defeated by William Clay, Sr. In 1973 Calloway retired from his teamster position to become a professor of urban studies at St. Louis University. In a laudatory reminiscence after Calloway's death, *St. Louis Post-Dispatch* columnist William Woo paid him this tribute: "On matters of jobs and wages, particularly as they applied to black men and women, he was the unquestioned authority."

Of himself, Calloway once wrote: "I grew up hating white people. Later I found hatred a waste of time. What you have to deal with are institutions, laws, customs. I have spent 50 years working hatred out of my system."

The 1980s and early 1990s brought signs of at least some political change. For one thing, a growing minority of black politicians began to turn to the Republican party as the party of hope for the future. In 1988, for example, Carson Ross of Blue Springs, Missouri, a Kansas City suburb, became the first African-American in more than forty years to be elected to the Missouri General Assembly on the Republican ticket. Ross, a buyer for Hallmark Cards, and other black Republicans, such as James H. Buford, former president of St. Louis Urban League, and Judge David C. Mason of the St. Louis Circuit Court, argued that Democratic policies had stifled black initiative. Said Buford in a 1991 interview with Ellen Utterman: "The black community is in total disarray. What the black conservatives are saying is: 'If welfare and affirmative action are so good, why hasn't this changed?' They are saying that there needs to be more self-help and an end to looking toward government for everything."

The debate between black conservatives and liberals produced more heat than light in 1991 with the nomination of black conservative Clarence Thomas to the U.S. Supreme Court. Thomas, a staunch conservative and outspoken critic of racial quotas, was supported most earnestly in his confirmation hearings by Missouri Senator John C. Danforth, a fellow-Republican whom Thomas worked for when he was Missouri's attorney general in the 1970s. While neither side in the debate between liberal and conservative blacks was willing to concede victory to the other side, the fact that the debate was occurring at all signified a portent of things to come.

Two political events of the early 1990s offered a glimmer of hope, both occurring in the March election in 1991. In Kansas City, three-term Councilman Emmanuel Cleaver II became that city's first black mayor by defeating Bob Lewellen, another city councilman, by the decisive margin of 53 to 46 percent. Perhaps of even more significance was the fact that the issue of race played very little importance in the contest. Cleaver proved popular among many whites, particularly the white business establishment, largely because of his support for the expansion of the city's convention center and the building of a new facility to house the American Royal Livestock and Horse Show. As *Kansas City Star* political correspondent Rich Hood pointed out, "Cleaver's election represented a trend that would have been unheard of in this country a decade ago." Hood also noted that Cleaver became "one of at least 15 black mayors in cities where blacks make up less than 50 percent of the population, following the lead of New York City, Los Angeles, Philadelphia, Cleveland and Seattle." According to 1990 census figures, African-Americans comprised just under 30 percent of Kansas City's population of 435,146 people.

Across the state in St. Louis, an integrated slate of candidates—two whites and two blacks—won a hotly contested school board election. Calling themselves "4 Candidates 4 Kids," they defeated an all-white slate called "Friends and Advocates of Neighborhood Schools of St. Louis." The Friends' group, made up of residents of the city's predominantly white south side, was widely perceived as opposing citywide integration of schools in favor of reestablishing segregated neighborhood schools. The "4 Kids" slate garnered 97 percent of the black vote, a development labeled by political scientist Kenneth Warren of St. Louis University as "nothing short of amazing." The election thus posed the practicality and even efficacy of black and white political cooperation, rather than the politics of confrontation that have been the touchstone of so much of Missouri's racial history.

Suggested Reading

The best sources for events of the 1980s are the major metropolitan newspapers: the *St. Louis Post-Dispatch* and the *Kansas City Star.* Columnist Gregory Freeman's columns in the *Post-Dispatch* are particularly helpful. Ellen Utterman's essay "Black Republicans: A Contradiction, or the Wave of the Future," *St. Louis Post-Dispatch Magazine,* September 22, 1991, is an insightful analysis of the movement of a growing minority of African-Americans into the Republican party.

The following black newspapers are also indispensable: the *St. Louis Argus,* the *St. Louis American,* and the *St. Louis Sentinel.* For the black conservative point of view, see especially Stephen L. Carter, *Reflections of an Affirmative Action Baby* (New York: Basic Books, 1991); and Shelby Steele, *The Content of Our Character: A New Vision of Race in America* (New York: St. Martin's Press, 1990). For the Tina Turner story, see Tina Turner with Kurt Loder, *I, Tina* (New York: Morrow Books, 1986). Finally, a 1991 publication by the Urban League of Greater Kansas City, entitled *The State of Black Kansas City, 1991,* is useful.

Appendix
Missouri's Black Legislators

U. S. Congress
House of Representatives

William L. Clay, Sr. (D)	St. Louis District 1	1968–1992
Alan D. Wheat (D)	Kansas City District 5	1982–1992

Missouri General Assembly
Senate

J. B. "Jet" Banks (D)	St. Louis District 5	1977–1992
John F. Bass (D)	St. Louis District 4	1983–1990
William L. Clay, Jr. (D)	St. Louis District 4	1991–1992
Phillip B. Curls, Jr. (D)	Jackson County District 9	1985–1992
Gwen Giles (D)	St. Louis District 4	1979–1980
Raymond Howard (D)	St. Louis District 5	1971–1976
Theodore D. McNeal (D)	St. Louis District 7	1960–1962
	District 4	1963–1971
Franklin Payne (D)	St. Louis District 4	1971–1978
Lee Vertis Swinton (D)	Jackson County District 9	1981–1984

House of Representatives

Johnnie S. Aikens (D)	St. Louis District 74	1967–1972
	District 66	1973–1982
J. B. "Jet" Banks (D)	St. Louis District 54	1969–1972
	District 80	1973–1976
Mary Groves Bland (D)	Jackson County District 30	1981–1982
	District 43	1983–1992
Billie Boykins (D)	St. Louis District 82	1979–1982
Fred E. Brown (D)	St. Louis District 73	1971–1972
J. Clayborne Bush (R)	St. Louis District 17	1947–1948
DeVerne Lee Calloway (D)	St. Louis District 13	1963–1966
	District 17	1967–1968
	District 70	1969–1972
	District 81	1973–1982
James M. Carrington (D)	St. Louis District 67	1973–1980
William Clay, Jr. (D)	St. Louis District 59	1985–1992
Frank W. Clegg (R)	St. Louis District 3	1931–1932
William A. Cole (D)	St. Louis District 10	1949–1950
John Conley, Jr. (D)	St. Louis District 15	1963–1966
	District 75	1967–1972
Phillip B. Curls, Sr. (D)	Jackson County District 28	1973–1982
	District 39	1983–1984
Fletcher Daniels	Jackson County District 39	1985–1992
John A. Davis (R)	St. Louis District 3	1927–1928
Louis H. Ford (D)	St. Louis District 58	1983–1992
Russell Goward (D)	St. Louis District 76	1967–1972
	District 65	1973–1982
	District 60	1983–1992
John Wilson Greene (D)	St. Louis District 17	1949–1956
Elsa Debra Hill (D)	St. Louis District 71	1967–1968

Harold L. Holliday (D)	Jackson County District 5	1965–1966
	District 4	1967–1968
	District 14	1969–1972
	District 26	1973–1976
Raymond Howard (D)	St. Louis District 10	1965–1966
	District 54	1967–1968
Herman A. Johnson (D)	Jackson CountyDistrict 13	1969–1972
Leon M. Jordan (D)	Jackson County District 4	1965–1966
	District 11	1967–1970
Orchid I. Jordan (D)	Jackson County District 11	1971–1972
	District 25	1973–1978
	District 28	1979–1980
Edwin F. Kenwil (D)	St. Louis District 4	1943–1944
Walter V. Lay (D)	St. Louis District 11	1949–1954
Roscoe L. McCrary (D)	St. Louis District 82	1975–1978
Jacqueline Townes McGee (D)	Kansas City District 38	1987–1992
Leo McKamey (D)	Jackson County District 36	1973–1982
LeRoy Malcolm (D)	St. Louis District 75	1969–1970
Harold Martin (D)	St. Louis District 82	1973–1974
William A. Massingale (D)	St. Louis District 11	1947–1948
Walthall M. Moore (R)	St. Louis District 6	1921–1922
	District 3	1925–1930
James McKinley Neal (D)	Jackson County District 4	1945–1946
		1949–1964
Raymond Quarles (D)	St. Louis District 63	1973–1978
Franklin Payne (D)	St. Louis District 73	1967–1970
Walter R. Peterson, Jr. (D)	Jackson County District 38	1983–1986
Earl A. Pitts, Sr. (D)	Jackson County District 32	1981–1982
Nathaniel J. Rivers (D)	St. Louis District 71	1969–1972
	District 79	1973–1982
	District 59	1983–1984

Carson Ross (D)	Blue Springs District 49	1989–1992
Henry Ross (D)	Jackson County District 2	1965–1966
	District 10	1967–1972
O. L. Shelton (D)	St. Louis District 57	1983–1992
James W. Spencer (D)	Jackson County District 13	1967–1968
Josiah C. Thomas (R)	St. Louis District 10	1947–1948
Vernon Thompson (D)	Jackson County District 36	1987–1992
James Dennis Tindall (D)	Jackson County District 23	1981–1982
Charles "Quincy" Troupe (D)	St. Louis District 63	1979–1980
	District 62	1981–1992
James P. Troupe, Sr. (D)	St. Louis District 11	1955–1960
	District 9	1963–1966
	District 53	1967–1972
LeRoy Tyus (D)	St. Louis District 10	1951–1960
Robert L. Walker (D)	St. Louis District 80	1977–1978
Elbert A. Walton, Jr. (D)	St. Louis District 80	1979–1982
	District 61	1983–1992
Alan D. Wheat (D)	Jackson County District 26	1977–1980
	District 16	1981–1982
Henry W. Wheeler (D)	St. Louis District 17	1957–1962
Hugh J. White (D)	St. Louis District 16	1961–1964
Ronnie L. White (D)	St. Louis District 63	1989–1992
James Whitmore (D)	St. Louis District 67	1981–1982
Fred Williams (D)	St. Louis District 72	1969–1972
Rev. William Wright (D)	St. Louis District 11	1961–1962
	District 78	1973–1982
	District 56	1983–1986

About the Authors

Lorenzo J. Greene (1899–1988) was Professor Emeritus of History at Lincoln University in Jefferson City, Missouri. He was the author of several books, including *The Negro in Colonial New England, 1620–1776* and *Working with Carter G. Woodson, the Father of Black History: A Diary, 1928–1930,* which was edited by Arvarh E. Strickland. Professor Strickland is currently editing a second volume of Greene's memoirs.

Gary R. Kremer is Professor of History at William Woods College in Fulton, Missouri. He is the editor of *George Washington Carver: In His Own Words* and the author of *James Milton Turner and the Promise of America: The Public Life of a Post–Civil War Black Leader,* both available from the University of Missouri Press.

Antonio F. Holland is Professor of History and Chairman of the Department of Social and Behavioral Sciences at Lincoln University in Jefferson City, Missouri. He is the coauthor of *The Soldiers' Dream Continued: A Pictorial History of Lincoln University of Missouri.*

Index